PUBLIC HEALTH COMMUNICATION INTERVENTIONS

To my parents, Ruth and Louis

PUBLIC HEALTH COMMUNICATION INTERVENTIONS

Values
and
Ethical
Dilemmas

Nurit Guttman

Sage Publications, Inc.
International Educational and Professional Publisher
Thousand Oaks ▪ London ▪ New Delhi

For information:

Sage Publications, Inc.
2455 Teller Road
Thousand Oaks, California 91320
E-mail: order@sagepub.com

Sage Publications Ltd.
6 Bonhill Street
London EC2A 4PU
United Kingdom

Sage Publications India Pvt. Ltd.
M-32 Market
Greater Kailash I
New Delhi 110 048 India

Printed in the United States of America

Library of Congress Cataloging-in-Publication Data

Guttman, Nurit.
  Public health communication interventions: Values and ethical dilemmas / by Nurit Guttman.
      p. cm
  Includes bibliographical references (p.   ) and index.
  ISBN 0-7619-0259-7 (c: acid-free paper)—ISBN 0-7619-0260-0 (p: acid-free paper)
  1. Health risk communication. 2. Health behavior. 3. Medical ethics. 4. Social values. I. Title.
  RA423.2.G885 2000
  362.1—dc21   99-050602

This book is printed on acid-free paper.

00   01   02   03   04   05   10   9   8   7   6   5   4   3   2   1

Acquiring Editor: Margaret H. Seawell
Editorial Assistant: Brian Newmann/Sandra Kramholz
Production Editor: Astrid Virding
Editorial Assistant: Nevair Kabakian
Designer/Typesetters: Janelle LeMaster/Marion Warren
Cover Designer: Michelle Lee

Contents

Foreword

Why a book on the ethics of health communication?

After all, even a cursory review of the basic literature of this fledgling field will uncover numerous accounts of how public health, and by extension, health communication, is an inherently noble enterprise, a profession dedicated to promoting the public good, enhancing the human condition, even saving lives. To read many of these accounts is to conjure up the image of the contemporary public health professional as the modern-day crusader: ordained to act, licensed to serve, dedicated to fight the righteous fight.

But as we know from centuries of painful experience, the ideals of all crusades must be distinguished from the pragmatic realities of their implementation and outcome. For example, the religious Crusades of the 11th and 12th Centuries, though sanctioned by divine decree and motivated by virtuous dreams, are remembered rather for the slaughter of innocents, ethnic cleansing, and political machinations. The end was seen as justifying the means, and ideals quickly gave way to rationalizations.

Granted, crusaders of public health rarely resort to slaughter to achieve their goals. But the earliest municipal boards of public health were licensed to engage in physical torture and to arrest and impose fines on actual and presumed carriers of infectious disease (Gottfried, 1983). In time, these boards became hated by the citizenry for the restrictions they imposed, the fines they levied, the power they wielded to restrict individual liberties—all in the name of promoting the public good. If we dismiss these incidents merely as historical anecdotes and discount their relevance to contemporary public health, then we blind ourselves to the likelihood that history will repeat itself. Indeed, discussion in the early 1980s of quarantining persons with AIDS, implementation of Draconian measures to win the "drug war," and dissemination of messages that attempt to marginalize and stigmatize health "offenders" are merely variations on earlier historical themes. It is little wonder, therefore, that some segments of society perceive us as health "vigilantes" rather than mere health promoters, and believe that we are fashioning a "tyranny of health" rather than an environment of empathy and understanding (Levin, 1987; Fitzgerald, 1994).

Indeed, this book is long overdue. It represents the first full-length and in-depth treatment of a topic that is the very essence of our field. Values and politics are every bit as much a part of health communication campaigns as are sources, messages, and channels. We cannot merely assume that using communication to change individuals' behaviors is the most appropriate solution to solving complex health problems that are deeply rooted in the fabric of society, nor can we assume the ideological neutrality of this approach to social change (Tesh, 1988). We cannot merely assume that common outcomes of our persuasive messages—anxiety, cognitive dissonance, guilt, ostracization—are necessarily acceptable ones in the larger context of what constitutes a physically *and* mentally healthy society. And we cannot merely assume that the particular utopian vision of the public interest that motivates us so keenly is shared by anyone else, especially segments of society who consider our efforts as intrusive rather than well-intentioned, as imperialistic rather than benevolent through the imposition of unfamiliar class-based norms and values.

The good news is that in encouraging us to acknowledge the previously unacknowledged assumptions, cultural values, and ideologies that necessarily underlie our health-promotion efforts, this book reduces our naïveté and forces us to confront the inherently political and controversial nature of what we normally take for granted in our daily work. It is a book that is rich in practical application as well as theory, a book that signals the dawn of a more sophisticated and potentially more effective era in the ongoing evolution of our field.

—Charles T. Salmon
Michigan State University

REFERENCES

Fitzgerald, Faith T. (1994). The tyranny of health. *The New England Journal of Medicine, 331*(3), 196-198.

Gottfried, Robert S. (1983). *The Black Death: Natural and human disaster in medieval Europe.* New York: The Free Press.

Levin, Lowell S. (1987). Every silver lining has its cloud: The limits of health promotion. *Social Policy, 18*(1), 57-60.

Tesh, Sylvia N. (1988). *Hidden arguments: Political ideology and disease prevention policy.* New Brunswick, NJ: Rutgers University Press.

Acknowledgments

This book would not have been written without the encouragement of Stanley Deetz, who initiated the idea and patiently challenged my thinking, and the invaluable help of Brent Ruben, Jack Elinson, Lea Stewart, Gary Kreps, and Robert Like. Their contributions may be invisible, but they are substantial. Special thanks also to Vicki Freimuth for her encouragement and for directing me toward research sites and resources. My research fellowship at the Department of Family Medicine at the University of Medicine and Dentistry of New Jersey-The Robert Wood Johnson Medical School (RWJMS), under the supportive directorship of Mary Breckenridge, allowed me to continue the research and development of the ideas presented in this book, which originated in my dissertation work at Rutgers University. The main thrust of this book was completed after moving to the Department of Communication at Tel Aviv University, Israel, while maintaining a part-time position at the Department of Family Medicine at RWJMS. At Tel Aviv University, I am grateful for the support of Akiba Cohen, Chair of the Department of Communication, the administrator, Liora Gabay, and my colleagues. Also, I am grateful to David Swee, Chair of the Department of Family Medicine at RWJMS, and my research and clinical colleagues and the administrative staff at the Department of Family Medicine for their ongoing support. I am truly indebted to Marilyn Aguirre-Molina, whose passion for public health and advocacy had been contagious, for broadening my own perspective on health promotion and for enabling invaluable contacts, some prominently cited in these pages. Paul Speer has since continued to enrich my perspective on community development, power, and empowerment, and Vince Silenzio, my critical perspective on health, medicine, and society.

This book owes many of its ideas to the numerous scholars who shared their wisdom and expertise with me. They include Dan Beauchamp, Lawrence Greene, Kenneth McLeroy, Reinhart Priester, Robert Veatch, Larry Wallack, Dan Wikler, Everett Rogers, and Scott Ratzan. A very special acknowledgment goes to Charles T. Salmon, whose work originally triggered my interest in the topic of this book and whose approach to health communication inspired it. He has graciously proffered his keen insights and critical suggestions. Any misinterpretations and misrepresentations are mine alone. This book could not have been written without the contribution of the numerous practitioners who let me visit program sites and generously shared their insights, time, and materials; especially that of John McGrath at the National Heart, Lung and Blood Institute and Doreen Colatrella, formerly with the Middlesex Healthy Heart Program. Special thanks for the editorial suggestions of Janet Lillie and the Sage editorial staff. Last, a well-deserved acknowledgment to my incredible family, especially to Bob, who read far too many drafts, and my friend Fran Yungher, who helped with editorial comments on earlier versions.

The work on this book has been supported in part by Grant Number 1T32 PE 10011-02 from the Division of Medicine of the Health Resources Services Administration. Early versions of several chapters have appeared in the journals *Health Communication, Communication Theory,* and the *Journal of Health Communication.*

This book is dedicated to my father, Louis Guttman, who taught me—both in words and example—that when it comes to scholarly work, one should do (with passion and conviction) what one thinks is important rather than what may receive more popular acclaim.

Introduction

There is a strong temptation to write about how to make public health communication interventions better, more effective, more successful. Interventions for health or disease prevention are an exciting endeavor. They proffer a promise that scholarship, when applied to practice, can help individuals and groups with particular needs, or better society as a whole.

Historically, interventions for public health promotion have been primarily associated with people with a strong service motivation and willingness to take professional and personal risks. Such efforts were less likely to be associated with a sense of flair and more with lackluster didactic enterprises. Increasingly, however, many public health interventions incorporate communication strategies as a primary or integral part of their planned effort: thus, although they may not be commercially motivated,[1] their activities can carry with them the excitement, trappings, and hyperbole of marketing (Goodman & Goodman, 1986). As such, they often appear to attract some of the intensity, glamour, and allure associated with mass media and advertising.

Making public health communication interventions more strategic—by merging behavior-change theories, practice, and creativity—has had a strong appeal both to practitioners and researchers. This is evident in the growth of prolific literature on this topic across disciplines, including communication, public health, sociology, political science, psychology, and marketing. Having

practiced as a health education coordinator and having worked in the development and implementation of health communication interventions, I also
found this strategic approach intensely appealing. My fascination, though,
after reading Charles T. Salmon's (1989) chapter, "Campaigns for Social
'Improvement': An Overview of Values, Rationales and Impacts," in his book,
Information Campaigns: Balancing Social Values and Social Change, suddenly
shifted to a less glamorous venture: the advancement of conceptual approaches to identify values and ethical concerns embedded in public health
communication interventions. Salmon's chapter, with its succinct articulation
of why we need to consider implicit and taken-for-granted values in public
communication interventions, made it clear to me that I could no longer engage in studying, implementing, and evaluating public health communication
interventions without focusing on values. It jolted me into realizing that, both
as a practitioner and a student of such interventions, I had taken values for
granted, without examining what they were or how they affected the interventions I was involved in.

As I began to examine the literature on this topic, I found that its treatment
of values—although certainly thought provoking—tended to provide analyses
that were either very broad or rather narrow. Authors typically would focus on
ethical implications of persuasion or would describe value clarification techniques. I did not find analytic frameworks that could help develop a systematic
examination of the public health communication intervention phenomenon
from a value-centered perspective. The purpose of this book is to describe the
development of such an analytic enterprise, which draws on Salmon's (1989,
1992) writings on values in information campaigns, Kenneth McLeroy and his
colleagues' writing on ethics in health education (McLeroy, Gottlieb, &
Burdine, 1987) and the ecological approach to health promotion (McLeroy,
Bibeau, Steckler, & Glanz, 1988), John Forester's (1989, 1993) critical perspective applied to the area of planning and adapted here to the context of
health, and Brown and Singhal's (1990) discussion of ethical dilemmas in the
use of television programs to promote social issues. The frameworks also draw
from discussions with bioethicists, public health and community development
scholars and practitioners, public health policy advocates, academic medicine
faculty and administrators, and communication scholars and practitioners.

Whether they are hidden, invisible, or extremely obvious, the role of values in most social phenomena is paramount: "It is difficult for me to conceive
of any problem social scientists might be interested in that would not deeply

implicate human values," says Milton Rokeach (1973, p. ix) in the introduction to his seminal book on values, titled *The Nature of Human Values*. This book picks up a challenge posed by Sylvia Tesh (1988) in her book *Hidden Arguments*—to make values embedded in public health more explicit. It addresses this challenge by specifying values and dilemmas inherent in the public health communication intervention process and provides examples of how to develop conceptual frameworks to analyze the implications of these dilemmas. Application of these frameworks can contribute both to theory and practice as well as to the identification of ethical concerns embedded in the intervention process, as the examples in the book aim to illustrate. By doing so, the book aims to address another challenge, posed by Charles T. Salmon (1992) in his critique of current theoretical approaches: to advance the development of conceptual frameworks *of* rather than only *for* public health communication interventions.

Public health communication interventions are increasingly pervasive social phenomena as they become part of international and national agendas and are launched through national and local initiatives, community groups, and workplace enterprises. They engage numerous individuals and organizations across diverse populations, disciplines, and orientations. Typically, however, the analysis of these interventions or campaigns is done in terms of "did they accomplish what they intended to do?" rather than "why is it they intended to accomplish what they intended to?" or "what did they actually accomplish, beyond official objectives?" Values, although recognized as important in health intervention studies, tend to be treated as independent variables that may serve as barriers to interventions' behavior-change goals or as dependent variables that can be manipulated to achieve these goals. This book broadens this approach, and its value-centered conceptual frameworks can be adopted to identify claims used to justify programs as well as communicative distortions that can occur in health interventions' definitions of problems, the solutions they adopt, and the way their outcomes are evaluated.

The conceptual frameworks developed in this book draw on a series of assumptions that underscore the main purpose of the book. They propose that (a) dilemmas inherent in the intervention process are associated with the value-laden nature of a planned social-change phenomenon, (b) the value-laden nature and moral implications of choices made in the design and implementation of interventions require a theoretical perspective that attends to values and ethical concerns, (c) constructs and systematic frameworks can be used to examine the design and implementation of interventions from a normative perspective, (d) current criteria used for program evaluation and policy making can be broadened by focusing on values, and (e) practitioners, planners, policymakers, researchers, intended populations, and others directly or indirectly involved in the intervention can develop and use practice-oriented questions to identify ethical concerns and values embedded in the intervention process.

The first chapter begins with a rationale of why we need to consider values in the design and analysis of public health communication interventions. A set of 10 propositions are presented that explicate the importance of considering values in all intervention facets from a normative and critical perspective. The chapter concludes by summarizing the main distinctions between a strategic and value-centered approach according to (a) the way values are studied, (b) the main purpose of the analytic or research approach, (c) the way problems are defined, (d) intervention approaches and behavior-change models, (e) assessment and evaluation, and (f) ethical concerns.

Why do we need public health communication interventions? Why should they be supported? What gives interventionists the right to intervene in people's lives? The second chapter furnishes a reminder that public health communications—as publicly sponsored social-change undertakings—need to be justified to policymakers and the public. The chapter provides an overview of major justifications for health interventions, mainly as they are presented in the health promotion and bioethics literature, with several additional ones. The third chapter takes the previous discussions of values a step further in the development of a value-analytic approach by specifying intervention facets and providing a conceptual approach for examining values embedded in each. Drawing from the assumption that each facet of the intervention is value laden and that the intervention phenomenon creates value conflicts, each component is described as associated with often-conflicting social values and raising a multitude of ethical concerns.

The fourth and fifth chapters present a framework of models or prototypes as a conceptual approach to help draw differences between interventions, even when they seem to emphasize the same prominent values. By distinguishing whether the intervention emphasizes a certain value as a goal or a strategy, distinct and important differences between specific approaches can be made, despite apparent similarities. This conceptual approach helps to point out how intervention programs, even when they seem to be emphasizing the same justification or values, can represent very different intervention approaches. Intervention types described in these chapters are not presented as fixed phenomena. Instead, they can be seen as potentially dynamic undertakings that can evolve from one type of model to another.

The sixth chapter describes a series of questions that raise ethical dilemmas inherently associated with the public health communication intervention enterprise. Many of the ethical issues—although they have important implications to individuals and society—tend to be invisible to health promoters, researchers, and the public. We cannot, as the dilemmas remind us, take for granted or presume that potential effects of health interventions are utterly beneficial. The intervention context is complex, involving diverse stakeholders and competing interests. What, then, do public health communication interventions actually do and what do they not do? What should we expect from interventions? What should raise our concerns? Because as public health communication interventions increasingly adopt sophisticated social marketing techniques, they have an enhanced potential to influence targeted audiences. Through a series of 13 ethical dilemmas and examples to illustrate them, this chapter underscores the need for both conceptual approaches to identify these type of concerns and the need to address them. The chapter concludes with practice-oriented questions that can be used to identify ethical concerns in the design and implementation of interventions or in their analysis by scholars or evaluators.

The seventh chapter concludes the book with a reminder that whatever frame of analysis is developed, like any other structure, it has enabling and constraining aspects (Ball & Smith, 1992). But, like the interventions it aims to analyze, the frame of analysis is also based on value-laden assumptions. Two approaches to the development of a normative approach are presented: One focuses on issues of social development in the context of health promotion (Minkler, 1989) and the second, on the communicative nature of the public health communication intervention phenomenon (adapting Forester's 1989, 1993 approach), which by implication notes the moral commitment of the analyst, who—without an ethical framework to shape her or his analysis—may find these commitments precarious.[2]

Values in public health communication interventions may be disguised or hidden, as Sylvia Tesh (1988) eloquently explains, yet they are deep-seated in the way public health communication interventions' goals are defined, as well as their theoretical approaches and their designs. Values are inherent in what the interventionists emphasize, overlook, or ignore. The contribution of theories and conceptual approaches in the analysis of social phenomena can serve to draw attention to social values when they are not apparent or remain invisible (Deetz, 1992). The ability to see what *cannot* be seen, as Lewis Carroll's king lamented, is not a skill that is easily acquired:

> "I see nobody on the road," said Alice.
> "I only wish I had such eyes," the King remarked in a fretful tone.
> "To be able to see Nobody! And at that distance too! Why, it's as much as I can do to see real people, by this light!"

My hope is that this book will contribute to an ongoing scrutiny of and discourse on the often invisible assumptions and priorities that underlie public health communication interventions. My hope is that readers may also find, as I have, that attending to the value-laden nature of interventions inescapably raises questions about one's own and others' beliefs regarding human nature, planned attempts to change people's behavior, and how to advance just social institutions.

NOTES

1. Though increasingly, public relations and other professionals have been making considerable profit from contracting work in health communication interventions from not-for-profit sponsors.

2. This is an adaptation of Bellah, Madsen, Sullivan, Swidler, and Tipton's (1986) discussion cited in Chapter 7.

1

Values in Public Health Communication Interventions

Beyond Strategic Analytic Approaches

> It can be tempting to think that work for health is value-free, that some endeavors are simply good and desired by all, and have no effects that can be described as bad or undesirable. . . . It is an inescapable truth that all work for health, every last bit of it, is at some point inspired by a human value that has been chosen from alternatives.
>
> —*David Seedhouse (1988, p. 57)*

The enterprise of public health communication interventions is inherently value laden. By their very nature, public health communication interventions are a purposeful attempt to bring about desired health-related changes. They aim to help people lead healthier lives in healthier environments. As such, they are a social-change phenomenon (Salmon, 1989), which "necessarily involves taking value positions, in seeking to influence health policies and, in general terms, collaborating with the Establishment in various ways" (Rogers, 1994, p. 213). Values are embedded in all facets of the intervention process and both influence and serve as justifications for the choice of the intervention goals and objectives. Values also underlie the reasons for choosing what populations should be targeted by the intervention, what strategies and techniques should be used, and how to evaluate the interventio/ (Hornik, 1990). Although values associated with helping, being of service

doing good appear self-evident as part of the public health communication effort (Rogers, 1994), other important values linked to the intervention tend to be implicit. These embedded values can constitute a key to a more profound understanding of the intervention as a social change phenomenon and to its accomplishments (Salmon, 1989; Tesh, 1988). But how do we go about identifying and analyzing such values and ethical or moral issues? The purpose of this book is to present an analytic approach to address this challenge.

INTERVENTIONS AND HEALTH

When a person or an organization aims to intervene—whether in the name of health or for any other reason—the intervention's goal is to change and influence someone, a social institution, or a certain situation. People intervene when they intend to stop something from happening or when they aim to change the course of affairs. The word *intervention* connotes the meaning of *interfering* in the state of another (Mish et al., 1994) and is associated with interrupting, interceding, mediating, and even meddling. In the health promotion context, communication interventions aim to intervene by helping bring about desired changes in people's beliefs and behaviors or in their physical or social environments. Such interventions mainly include two types of intended changes: (a) to reduce, inhibit, or modify behaviors or social and physical environments considered hazardous or disease promoting or (b) to increase behaviors or enhance social and physical environments considered health promoting. Intervention objectives cover a wide array of contexts and topics. Examples of the first type are efforts to influence people to refrain from smoking or to modify behaviors related to excessive alcohol consumption or nonmedical drug use. Some aim to increase people's compliance with prescribed medical regimens, whereas others urge the persistent use of seat belts when traveling in motor vehicles, or, in more intimate circumstances, the consistent use of condoms or other latex barriers when engaging in sexual intercourse, to prevent the spread of infectious diseases. The foregoing also exemplify interventions mainly directed at behavioral changes made at the individual level. Examples of the second kind of interventions are those that aim to increase people's physical activity, make sure their children are immunized, have them practice self-exams to increase the likelihood of the detection

of early signs of disease, or have them adopt dietary practices that conform to recommended guidelines.

Some interventions specifically aim to make changes in social systems or institutions. To accomplish this, they typically aim to change or enforce social policies and regulations. Their strategy to influence people's behavior corresponds to the two main approaches outlined earlier: (a) limiting people's access or exposure to substances or physical environments or inhibiting behaviors considered disease promoting or (b) increasing behaviors or amplifying environments that are considered health promoting by making them more feasible, attractive, or accessible. An example of the use of policies to modify individuals' behavior by inducing them to adopt certain practices is the mandate to use seat belts. Some policies aim to regulate commercially manufactured products. The purpose is to manufacture products that will literally force consumers to adopt particular health-promoting practices. For example, car manufacturers can be mandated to produce cars with air bags, or milk producers may be asked to add certain vitamins or minerals to milk. Promoting health through policies may, in turn, focus on societal institutional arrangements: for example, the legislation of national health insurance coverage to ensure that all members of the population can have access to preventive health services. Other types of policies may identify and enforce corporate responsibility for environmental pollutants and develop guidelines and regulations regarding the protection of the environment through discourse with the public and its representatives.

The topics of public health communication interventions can range from highly intimate and personal matters associated with individual lifestyle and personal choices to societal and macroeconomic issues. Each of the health-related topics mentioned earlier, and many others, has been the subject of numerous public health communication interventions carried out in local, national, and international arenas. Interventions may focus on topics associated with medical care: these include encouraging people to take medications as prescribed by their physicians or to engage in screenings (procedures that identify medical symptoms or conditions that indicate that a person is at risk for certain diseases or actually has a disease). Other types of interventions are devoted to psychosocial topics that may be indirectly linked to a specific health topic. For example, programs may aim to enhance the self-esteem of adolescents considered high risk, to prevent substance abuse. Programs may also aim to promote processes associated with community development and economic issues. For example, they would focus on activities to increase employment opportunities as a means to promote health-related issues.[1] Clearly, this diverse spectrum of intervention objectives reflects a multitude of goals and strategies, as well as distinct underlying assumptions on what makes people do what they do and what is likely to influence the target population to adopt recommended changes.

Planned health-related interventions have a long history. Ancient Hebrew religious authorities called on their people to purify themselves after being in contact with the dead or to wash their hands before eating. In the Middle Ages, when plagues spread in Asia and Europe and masses of people were dying, interventions to protect the public ranged from creating smoke for the purpose of fumigating the air, quarantining individuals, and literally isolating whole towns.[2] Isolation remained an important strategy up to the 19th century (in certain instances, attempts even continue today[3]) and it can be viewed as compatible with the contagion theory of its time. The social, political, and economic circumstances of the 19th century, however, could no longer uphold isolation as a viable disease-prevention approach because modernization and the industrial revolution called for openness of borders, and dominant players enthusiastically embraced values proclaiming individualism and personal freedom. This brought about an era that envisioned the cause of disease and ways to control it differently than previous generations and gave way to interventions that placed more prominence on the role of personal behaviors both as causes of and factors that can affect the course of illness (Tesh, 1988).

In Europe, following the first world war, the notion that the state had the responsibility to be concerned with the health of its citizens gained prominence. Combined with medical science's increasing focus on nearly invisible germs as major causes of diseases, this resulted in a growing emphasis on public educational for infectious disease prevention. One early effort was a British program to prevent the spread of sexually transmitted diseases (STDs). British soldiers were warned to resist temptation and to avoid any physical intimacy with women while overseas. In the meantime, back home in Britain, laws were passed to provide public education for civilians, because it was feared that the soldiers would bring the diseases with them on their return. This public education campaign, concerned almost exclusively with sexual continence, was primarily carried out through public meetings, school biology lessons, pamphlets and films produced by the National Council for Combating Venereal Disease, officially formed "to fight the terrible peril of our imperial race" (Sutcliffe & Duin, 1992, p. 131).

In the United States in the 18th century, public health communication interventions addressed topics that included the promotion of immunization for smallpox and reducing alcohol consumption.[4] The latter, when addressed again in the 19th century, was noted for its use of mass media and characterized as the most sustained organized mass communication initiative on a social issue (Scherer & Juanillo, 1992). The American temperance movement paid its tribute to Benjamin Rush (1746-1813), who was considered the most prominent medical professor of his era. Rush was an advocate for reducing alcohol consumption and launched an educational campaign to warn the public about the hazards of distilled beverages. True to his training as a physician at the University of Edinburgh, where distilled beverages were considered strong nervous stimulants that caused imbalances in the nervous system, and such imbalances were considered the main cause of disease, he was horrified at the increased production and consumption of these beverages in the newly independent nation. Earlier in his career, he had been a strong believer in the force of rational arguments regarding the hazards of alcohol to win over the minds and practices of people to dispel notions about its presumed beneficial effects. Later, however, he moved to advocating taxation policies to inhibit the production of distilled drinks. Rush's justifications for promoting temperance were based on his medical orientation and on what were considered scientific grounds. After his death in the 19th century, however, as the temperance message was taken over by clergy and other groups, it became more of a moral rather than health-focused crusade. The blend of medical science and moralism was not new and was viewed as natural at the time. Rush himself had had an evangelical Christian education before his medical training and his writing reflects an era in which science and rationalism were seen as means to address human and moral problems (Katcher, 1993).

The American Temperance Society, formed in 1826, extended Rush's ideas but moved them to a more prohibitionist approach. This movement has been characterized as one of the biggest and most important social movements in American history. Sections of this movement successfully campaigned for what they called public "scientific temperance" instruction, which eventually became mandated for public education in nearly every state at the time. In addition, the movement's efforts led to the 18th Amendment to the Constitution, prohibition, which went into effect in 1920 and was repealed in 1933 following the economic, social, and political changes of the Depression (Katcher, 1993).

With increasing emphasis on the prevention of chronic illness and with heart disease elevated to the status of the "number one killer" in industrially developed countries, one of the most cited demonstration research projects in public health communication is the Stanford heart disease prevention project (Winkleby, Taylor, Jatulis, & Fortmann, 1996). This project, sponsored by the U.S. National Institutes of Health, began in 1972 and tested the effects of two types of interventions: mass media alone and mass media supplemented with interpersonal contacts. Behavioral objectives of the intervention included reduction in cholesterol levels, high blood pressure, and smoking and increase in physical exercise and weight control. Findings indicated that certain (but not all) risk-reduction behaviors (as defined by the intervention) could be learned through mass media alone. Other modifications of health-related high-risk behavior were found to need the enhancement of social support and skills training (Farquhar et al., 1985).

The Stanford project consequently expanded to a 5-year intervention. Similar demonstration projects in the United States were implemented in Minnesota (Loken, Swim, & Mittelmark, 1990; Carlaw, Mittelmark, Bracht, & Luepker, 1984), and Pawtucket, New England (Flora, Maccoby, & Farquhar, 1989), both supported by the National Institutes of Health. Parallel projects in other countries have been hailed for holding significant promise for the development of models for community-level interventions (Bracht, 1990a) and social marketing-style health promotion campaigns (Lefebvre & Flora, 1992; Andreasen, 1995), the most noted being in North Karelia, Finland (McAlister et al., 1982; Puska, Nissinen, & Tuomilehto, 1985). One of the main components of these interventions has been the emphasis on the development of networks and social-support systems in the community. This approach expanded the social-marketing perspective (e.g., Solomon, 1989), which traditionally did not include such a component (Rogers & Storey, 1987).

A plethora of public health communication interventions, both large and small scale and publicly and privately funded, have become almost ubiquitous. The topics they address are numerous, diverse, and often overlapping. Interventions may focus on a specific medical condition, such as high blood pressure or tooth decay in children; the importance of consumption of particular food substances, such as dietary fiber; or the dangers in the consumption of tobacco and marijuana. Interventions may also address broader topics, such as good nutrition and physical activity. In the United States in the 1990s, relatively wide-scale federally funded interventions were designed to address specific topics, including mental health topics (e.g., depression), high blood pressure, cholesterol, AIDS, substance abuse, smoking, family planning, cancer, asthma, and maternal and infant health. Interventions in other countries abounded and often addressed the same topics, though with different emphases. Topics across countries, though, have differed. For example, a topic highly emphasized in some of the less industrially developed nations, but not in more industrially developed ones, has been the prevention of dehydration in infants (e.g., Hornik, 1989).

In some countries, state-supported major intervention approaches have relied heavily on the use of entertainment media to disseminate and promote health-related messages, for example, through popular music, radio and television soap operas, or telenovellas (Piotrow, Kincaid, Rimon, & Rinehart, 1997; Rogers & Antola, 1985; Rogers, Vaughan, & Shefner-Rogers, 1995; Singhal & Rogers, 1989). Some interventions are formally structured as field experiments or employ "before-and-after" measurements to control for potential effects (e.g., Rogers et al., 1995). Most interventions, however, are not reported in the scholarly literature, and many apply limited evaluation procedures.[5]

A growing body of books and monographs on the analysis, design, and implementation of public health communication interventions is available.[6] This literature presents theories, models, and conceptual approaches on how to design interventions. It draws from communication and mass media theories and sociological, psychological, social-psychological, political science, and community development perspectives, as well as from marketing and public relations strategies. Yet to understand and evaluate interventions, we need to study their embedded values. Although values are referred to as important in much of the public health communication intervention literature, they are typically discussed from a strategic perspective.[7] A rationale for broadening this perspective is the main topic of this chapter.

STRATEGIC AND VALUE-CENTERED ANALYTIC APPROACHES

Values and beliefs are generally treated as critical factors in the design and implementation of public health communication interventions. This is evident in the extensive application of conceptual approaches characterized as value expectancy models or theories that include the health belief model and theory of reasoned action (Carter, 1990; Rosenstock, 1990). The conspicuous role given to values corresponds to the main thesis of this book—that to understand public health communication interventions, we need to consider values. Some significant differences, nonetheless, can be found between the way this book treats values and the way they are treated in much of the literature on public health communication interventions.[8] Although recognized as important, values tend to be treated in much of the literature as independent variables that may serve as barriers or facilitators to certain behavioral goals. Alternately, they are viewed as dependent variables that can be manipulated to achieve these goals. This strategic perspective is consistent with the main purpose of many of the researchers and practitioners who work in the area of public health communication interventions: to design and implement interventions that will accomplish the health-related objective of the interventions' sponsors. By implication, the sponsors' particular goals and objectives are adopted or taken for granted as goals and objectives that *should* be pursued. For example, if the objective of a public health communication intervention is to get people to reduce their personal stress at the workplace, researchers or planners involved in the intervention are likely to take for granted that reducing workers' personal stress is an objective that should be accepted as good and appropriate. Their task—as it relates to values—is primarily to analyze the extent to which workers may hold certain beliefs or values that are relevant to the intervention. The official goal of the intervention tends to be accepted as a given, and the interventionists' challenge is to find ways to harness workers' values or the organization's culture to implement a successful intervention.

The differences between focusing on strategic goals and a value-centered analysis are presented as a series of 10 propositions, which also suggest that the role of values in the intervention enterprise should be broadened. Values have a pivotal role in shaping the intervention process as a whole: Implicit in the intervention phenomenon are value-laden choices and preferences. These may be linked to particular ideologies or support a specific social order.[9] A value-centered analysis can contribute to more effective interventions because a strategic approach that adopts sponsors' goals as a given may not take into account alternative conceptualizations of the problem and may preclude alternative useful courses of action. Broadening the perspective on the role of values—beyond strategic objectives—can deepen our understanding of the intervention process itself as a social-change phenomenon that involves choices and decisions about value priorities and ethical concerns associated with them (Rogers & Storey, 1987; Salmon, 1989, 1992; Warwick & Kelman, 1973).

THE PROPOSITIONS

Locus of Analysis

What are the goals of the intervention, or what are the main reasons for its initiation? Although official goals and objectives may seem easily identified in interventions' formal goals and objectives, the following two propositions suggest there may be other underlying processes that are important in their design and evaluation.

> 1. *Most analyses of public health communication interventions accept their goals as givens. Because such interventions are social phenomena, we need to explore why the particular goals were chosen.*[10]

Communication or educational initiatives are at the heart of many health promotion efforts: The provision of relevant and persuasive health information is a social process that, according to communication scholars, can empower individuals to take charge of their own health and reduce behaviors that may put them at risk (Kreps & Maibach, 1991). Much of the research in this area reflects this assumption and concentrates on the development and application of information-transmission and behavior change models.[11] Studies rarely examine why the interventions are approaching particular issues in certain ways.[12] Yet to gain a fuller understanding of a particular health communication intervention, we need to identify what values are responsible for certain goals and strategies to be chosen (Salmon, 1989, 1992).[13]

A comparative study by Ostaria and Sullivan (1991) of AIDS prevention campaigns illustrates both the method and potential contribution of an analysis that focuses on values. The analysis centers on how interventionists' values and priorities influenced the choice of the interventions' goals and strategies and explained how this had implications for the outcomes of the campaigns. In their analysis, these authors describe how particular values endorsed by the governments in Malaysia and in the Philippines affected the way government-sponsored prevention programs were developed. They suggested that the governments in both countries seemed "to be using AIDS education programs to shore up traditional values and patterns of behavior" (p. 145). One example was a campaign that took place in Malaysia, where the dominant religion is Islam. Muslim doctrine is reflected in the country's legal penal code, and AIDS-relevant codes include the prohibition of intoxicants and punishable sexual conduct that are considered offenses according to the Muslim religion, such as rape, incest, and extramarital relations, as well as the illegal status of the practice of homosexuality. Malaysian law also mandates strict censorship of dissemination of information on undesirable social influences and of criticism of religious beliefs. As a result, the authors (Ostaria & Sullivan, 1991) suggested that it was difficult to target those at risk and to disseminate messages that could provide explicit information about sexual practices that may expose people to HIV infection, because such messages contradict dominant cultural mores. With increasing recognition that AIDS is a growing problem, extensive plans to deal with public education regarding HIV prevention were developed in the late 1980s in Malaysia. Certain practices and behaviors, such as extramarital sexual relations, homosexual and bisexual practices among males, and intravenous drug use, were identified to predispose individuals to the risk of HIV infection. Although Malaysian planners saw the need to disseminate "accurate, and up-to-date facts about AIDS and its transmission" (p. 135) to the public, the actual messages disseminated emphasized abstinence from using drugs or engaging in homosexual or extramarital sex and failed to provide information on specific practices that can put people at risk. The Malaysian messages also did not specify pragmatic recommendations for AIDS prevention that could be adopted by individuals whose behavior puts them at particular risk, including commercial sex workers, men who have sex with men, or users of intravenous drugs, and in general, people who were not likely to adhere to abstinence messages and would need alternative risk-reduction strategies (for a review, see Brown, Waszk, & Childers, 1989)

In the Philippines, according to the authors' (Ostaria & Sullivan, 1991) analysis, prevention messages were also curtailed by competing values, though not to the same extent as in Malaysia. Although Roman Catholicism is an important and central cultural influence, the country also has a tradition of a secular government. The Philippine government thus has in the past enacted policies not consistent with Catholic doctrine or compromises, for example, those that support birth control. In its efforts to prevent AIDS, the messages disseminated in the government-sponsored campaign provided accurate and relatively nonjudgmental information, according to the researchers. However, messages refrained from providing recommendations specific to actual prevention practices: for example, how to make contaminated syringes safer or how to use a condom for safer sexual practices. By focusing on the values that underlie the choice of the interventions' goals and strategies, we can learn how certain goals and strategies were chosen and emphasized, how others were not, and how these choices can be explained by sociopolitical factors. This contributes to a theoretical perspective of the intervention as a social phenomenon. In other words, analytical perspectives view interventions as social change phenomena and explain why particular goals and strategies have been prioritized and others were not even considered.[14]

2. *There may be hidden arguments, implicit claims, or distorted representations embedded in public health communication intervention messages. These are not likely to be attended to in a strategic approach.*

Strategic approaches to research on health interventions are typically based on the assumption that they are justified because the intervention aims to do good and to improve the welfare of the public (Rogers, 1994). Clearly, unless one truly suspects that health interventions ultimately have very different aims or actually intend to do harm,[15] this is unreservedly accepted. Yet even within interventions based on intentions of doing good, other implicit claims and assumptions may be embedded. These can be based on certain moral convictions or political ideologies and can be described as hidden arguments that present taken-for-granted models of causality regarding health and illness. As such, they serve to exclude or minimize alternative explanations (Tesh, 1988).

For example, a prevalent health claim that heart disease can be prevented mainly by individual lifestyle changes is based on a certain definition of the problem (e.g., that people do not exercise because they are not motivated enough). Other factors that may contribute to difficulties in preventing heart disease (e.g., that many people work long hours with minimal leisure time or lack personal control over their job-related tasks) may be deemphasized. Thus, great emphasis has been put on the role of the individual to engage in physical activity, whereas system-related and structural factors in the etiology of the disease or lack of its prevention have been downplayed. Alternative conceptualizations regarding causes of certain health-related problems thus may not be articulated. Consequently, individuals who cannot easily incorporate exercise into their daily routines may be less likely to benefit from an intervention that focuses on increasing personal motivation. These individuals may be more likely to benefit from interventions that aim to promote policy changes in their workplace schedules or to provide more accessible facilities for physical activities. The analysis of public health communication interventions that strives to go beyond how to achieve the goals of the planned intervention can thus have two overlapping ethical missions: It can focus our attention on such distortions (not giving the whole picture or privileging certain perspectives) that may take place in the communicative process of the intervention, and it can enable us to expose hidden arguments embedded in their claims, making their presence "revealed, and their worth publicly discussed" (Tesh, 1988, p. 3).[16] From a critical stance, such analysis can also serve to question taken-for-granted assumptions about the beneficent role of health interventions and their latent or inadvertent outcomes (Salmon, 1989).[17]

Definition of the Problem

The next two propositions concern the notion of the definition of the problem. Interventions for health aim to prevent or solve what policymakers or interventionists have characterized as health-related problems. These propositions suggest that an issue becomes a social problem only after it is defined as such and that the definition depends on values. Definitions of problems are associated with beliefs regarding their causes; the questions we ask about these causes are also value laden, and these values tend to be implicit. Furthermore, definitions, which are seemingly descriptive, are also inherently prescriptive. As such, they intimate particular value-laden solutions (Rhode, 1993-1994).

3. *The way the problem is defined—according to the intervention— represents only one of many ways of framing the health-related issue (Susser, 1974).*

An issue becomes a social problem only after it is defined as such by certain individuals, groups, organizations, or other social entities (Kelman, 1975; Nisbet, as cited in Spector & Kitsuse, 1977).[18] Furthermore, the way the issue is framed tends to reflect the values, priorities, or ideologies of those who frame it. There may be others who differ in their perceptions of what is or is not a problem (Mackey-Kallis & Hahn, 1991).[19] Such differences occur because of differences in values: "Values shape the way problems are perceived; they are crucial to our notion that something is a problem to be solved, rather than a condition to be accepted" (Fleishman & Payne, 1980, p. 45).[20] In other words, if we do not value certain things—for example, if we do not think a clean water supply, a safe habitat for rare insects, or intellectual achievement are necessary or important—lack of these will not constitute a problem. When a health-related issue becomes an "important problem"—for example, by being perceived as a national threat by dominant groups, by getting extensive coverage in the media, or by being promulgated by important constituencies—policymakers may be inclined to feel that it needs to be addressed by a publicly sponsored intervention.[21] The definition of the problem corresponds to explanations of causality; beliefs regarding what has caused it. A striking historical example is the controversy, described by Hamlin (1995), between Edwin Chadwick, Chief Administrator of the Poor Law Commission in Great Britain in the 1830s and William Farr, a physician and pioneer statistician and epidemiologist. Chadwick, a strong proponent of sanitation policy initiatives, framed the problem of high morbidity and mortality among poor people mainly from a biomedical perspective and was a prominent advocate of sanitation measures. Farr, in contrast, attributed death and illness to social causes linked to economics and poverty and advocated a more socioeconomic definition. Although both were highly concerned with the disturbing morbidity rates of the same population, the attribution of cause had important political and economic ramifications. A socioeconomic definition could potentially lead to demands for economic reform; a biomedical definition would more likely lead to addressing the eradication of hosts of specific diseases, mainly through public health measures, such as sanitation. The latter approach was indeed adopted.

The definition of a problem has implications for the whole intervention endeavor. Numerous approaches can be adopted to promote the health of the public (Hornik, 1990); specific solutions, however, are often chosen according to the way problems have been defined.[22] Another example of how the same health-related topic can be framed differently by different stakeholders is illustrated in the case of interventions that aim to prevent adolescent pregnancies. The pregnancies of adolescents have not been viewed as problematic across all cultures or historical times. "The appropriate age for sexual relations and parenthood has always been a matter of cultural definition," argues Rhode (1993-1994, p. 635), who adds that in the United States, it has varied considerably across time, region, class, race, ethnicity, and gender. Currently in the United States, adolescent pregnancy has been proclaimed by public officials as an important social problem that calls for national intervention efforts. Yet this felt urgency is not necessarily linked to its actual prevalence. Rhode notes that the perception of teen pregnancy as a major social problem began in the late 1960s and early 1970s, although the rates of childbirth among females aged from 15 to 19 actually dropped 45% between 1957 and 1983, largely because of liberalization of contraceptive and abortion policies. The reason for the attention to teenage pregnancy, she argues, had less to do with its frequency than with a cluster of "volatile issues involving sexuality, abortion, family values, and wellness policy" (p. 649). Some stakeholders define adolescent pregnancy as a problem because they are mainly concerned with health and welfare issues: Specifically, they are concerned with the health of the baby, basing their concern on evidence that there is a relatively high incidence of morbidity and mortality in babies born to adolescents, or the health of the mother, who may not be mature enough to take care of herself.

A related concern is the well-being of adolescent parents: Having a baby may prevent them from continuing their education, which may be detrimental to their future employment opportunities. This can be extended to concerns for the public good: Society will be deprived of productive citizens. Other stakeholders may be concerned with monetary costs to society. This can be seen as framing the issue from an economic perspective and giving priority to a particular conceptualization of the public good, because adolescent parents are often supported by public assistance funds. Moral beliefs that disapprove of premarital sexual relations or of having babies outside marriage are the main concern of certain stakeholders.[23] Last, some see the main problem of adolescent pregnancy as associated with low self-esteem and low aspirations similar to the way some stakeholders view the problems and solutions related to substance abuse. Underprivileged adolescents are viewed as particularly vulnerable and in need of caring relationships. Those who frame the problem as such are likely to prefer interventions that focus on self-esteem, ethnic pride, mentoring, relationship development, and career opportunities.

Solutions or strategies chosen to address the problem (or problem as defined) are likely to reflect the different types of definitions adopted by different stakeholders as well as their priorities. Those concerned mainly with the welfare of the baby may prefer a solution of comprehensive prenatal care and the provision of parenting education. People who endorse strategies that emphasize the use of contraceptives and sex education in schools clearly frame the problem and solution differently than stakeholders who see the problem as a moral crisis. Whereas those who believe the latter are likely to emphasize that premarital sex is wrong and should be avoided, those who uphold the former may view premarital sexuality as an acceptable aspect of human growth and experience. Both may support an educational approach, but the content of the curricula they would support would be likely to differ substantially. Others, though, may stress the need for providing adolescent parents with resources to take care of their children and would refrain from labeling adolescent parenting as a problem. Instead, they would advocate the need to provide these parents with opportunities to study and pursue rewarding careers. Thus, different stakeholders' perceptions and priorities can lead to different types of problem definitions and consequently to different types of interventions. Inherent in each intervention, therefore, is a particular definition of the problem, and this definition is related to the priorities or ideologies of certain stakeholders. Issues such as adolescent pregnancy, which elicit conflicting definitions because of competing ideologies and political agendas, may result in political compromises. The strategies designated to address them may therefore be inadequate (Rhode, 1993-1994).

The issue of smoking among children also illustrates the importance of problem definition. Glantz (1996), in an editorial in the *American Journal of Public Health*, warns health promoters that by accepting the definition of the problem of cigarette smoking as mainly a problem of smoking among youth, health advocates fall into a trap welcomed by the tobacco companies. The tobacco companies can easily embrace this definition of the problem. In fact, it legitimizes their token gestures that embrace specific restrictions on youth access to cigarettes. They can gladly launch educational initiatives presumably aimed to discourage youth from smoking by saying they do not want youth to smoke and that smoking is an adult choice. These supposed antismoking efforts do little to discourage, and in fact probably encourage, smoking among youth. Glantz argues that framing the solution as programs that encourage youth to resist their peers may result in youth overestimating the rates of smoking among their peers and may increase the desirability of doing it. Instead of falling into what he labels as the "youth access trap" definition of the problem of smoking, Glantz suggests that health promoters should focus on the high profits enjoyed by the tobacco industry, much of them from young smokers. A more effective strategy, he suggests, is to eliminate those profits through taxation and to define the smoking problem as a problem among *all* who consume or are subjected to cigarette smoke.[24]

Definitions of problems and their solutions in the area of drunk driving also illustrate approaches that differ in how the problem and solution to it is framed. Definitions may adopt a disease model by viewing the problem as associated with certain drivers' predisposition to drink excessively and then drive. A more structurally oriented approach would supply definitions that attribute much of the cause to the alcohol beverage industry's marketing and promotion strategies or to societal norms and values that tolerate what critics view as excessive consumption. The first approach is exemplified in the intervention efforts launched by the Mothers Against Drunk Driving organization (MADD), which until recently focused on "blameworthy drivers" as the central culprits (Ross, 1995). MADD's main solution to the problem of drunk driving corresponded to its definition of the problem, which was primarily based on a perception of individual pathology and subsequently emphatically called for individual-level enforcement of strict and punitive legislation (Marshall & Oleson, 1994; Reinarman, 1988).[25] This definitional approach, suggests Ross (1995), was also warmly endorsed by the alcoholic beverage industry, which in turn promoted presumably "safe limits" for alcohol consumption and driving.[26] It was perpetuated, according to Ross, by myths that contradicted actual statistics. For example, evidence indicated that, contrary to the image of the main culprit being a criminal driver who should be taken off the road, most accidents that involved drunk drivers occurred to drivers who did *not* have a prior history of drunk driving arrests. Thus, they did not fall into MADD's category of "evil killer drivers"—habitual law violators who should be criminally persecuted. Alternately, the problem of drunk driving could be explained as a result of the intersection of what Ross considers two important American cultural values: the use of private automobiles and the consumption of alcoholic beverages. The prominence of these values is further fused by the corporate interests of the alcohol beverage and auto industries.

A conceptualization of alcohol-related traffic crashes that calls for population-level solutions and public policy has been reflected in some of the activities of another anti-alcohol-abuse campaign. This was the SMART campaign, which stands for "Stop Marketing Alcohol on Radio and Television," launched by the Center for Science in the Public Interest. Influenced by the consumer movement, it called for corporate accountability and responsibility. Its proposed solutions, aimed at what they considered the structural sources of alcohol-related problems (Reinarman, 1988), were reflected in later efforts of other local and national organizations, including MADD (Marshall & Oleson, 1994; Taylor, 1990).

The value-laden nature of conceptualization of the so-called problem can also be seen in discrepancies between the beliefs and values of target population members and those of the intervention practitioners. Balshem's (1991) account of her experience as a health educator in a cancer prevention program in a white, inner-city working class community provides an illustration of this type of gap. The researcher reflected on how her health education efforts as a practitioner gave primacy and legitimacy to medical and scientific conceptualizations of problems related to cancer. The rhetoric she adopted as a health educator was that of the "magic bullet . . . describing health education's front in the war against cancer [in which] we see the diffusion and elaboration of one of scientific medicine's fundamental metaphors" (p. 164). The community members' views and beliefs about cancer causation differed from those of the interventionists and were related to their perceptions of their lack of control over life circumstances and public policy. These views, however, were discounted by the interventionists as being merely fatalistic, whereas the biomedically based health education model was given priority. The intervention emphasized messages on the role of good nutrition for cancer prevention, whereas socioeconomic factors related to health promotion were neglected. These reflections point to how conceptualizations of the cause or etiology of illness may differ among different stakeholders, but the ones proffered by the sponsors of the intervention are more likely to be adopted as the most authoritative and legitimate.[27]

> Practitioners and researchers who adopt the interventions' definitions of problems and solution, by implication endorse its implicit values. Consequently, inadvertently they may privilege certain institutional arrangements embedded in the intervention and its messages. A value-centered perspective can help explore either the wisdom of such definitions or "whose ends are served by the entire definitional process and by his [the scholar's or practitioner's] participation in that process" (Caplan & Nelson, quoted in Seidman & Rappaport, 1986b, pp. 236-237).

4. Questions about the causes of health-related problems and how to address them are embedded with values.

Normative aspects of the roles of research, theory, and practice become more evident when researchers and practitioners move from asking questions about how to make interventions more effective to questions about values and hidden arguments embedded in the intervention. Tesh (1988), citing Garfinkle, explained that when questions originally asked at an individual level are asked at structural levels, they seem to acquire a value-laden dimension not evident before. For example, "Do junk food advertisements on television affect children's diet?" seems like a neutral question.[28] Its value-laden nature, though, she explained, is hidden, because structural conditions and ideologies (e.g., a marketplace that entitles particular stakeholders) are taken for granted as given. In contrast, the question, "Should there be junk food ads on television aimed at children?" sounds value-laden and political because it moves to question the presumption underlying current structural arrangements and the omnipresent values regarding "free commercial speech" or "individuals' right to choose" (Tesh, 1988). Issues thus get defined differently as "problems" when research questions are asked at different levels of analysis. Strategy-oriented analyses are likely to raise questions from an individual level and examine whether specific teaching techniques indeed get children to be more critical of advertisers' claims. Questions posed on a structural level would expand this analysis by aiming to examine underlying assumptions and ideologies that are embedded in the critical-thinking skills intervention. For example, what factors contribute to having interventions focus on providing students with skills believed to be protective (i.e., from the influence of certain types of messages)? Such interventions could enhance students' critical thinking, which may lead them to question the whole notion of having television programs paid through advertising and subjecting viewers to these types of messages. Clearly, identifying a so-called problem is a more elaborate process by far than is often implied in the statement of research objectives or program design.

Instead of taking the definition of a problem as a given, scholars, practitioners, and the public involved in public health communication interventions can examine the implications of framing or defining certain social issues in particular ways and can also examine the implications of having these issues framed, defined, and prioritized as particular health-related problems. This type of analysis can give prominence to the notion that different stakeholders may have different ways of framing the same health-related issue or may have different conceptualizations on how to approach it. It can also underscore the importance of acknowledging the possibility of alternative or additional explanations for the cause of the problem and alternative or additional approaches to address it.

Values

If we accept the proposition that values have an important role in defining what the problem is, it is also important to examine how scholars and practitioners typically approach values in the public health communication intervention context.

> *5. Typically, values of target audiences are studied for the purpose of developing effective behavior change strategies. The values that underlie the choices of intervention goals and their activities typically are not studied nor are the values of those who sponsor the intervention.*

Research and practice in public health communication interventions tend to treat values as independent variables that may serve as barriers to intervention behavior change goals or as dependent variables that can be manipulated to affect desired behavior change.[29] In contrast, a value-centered approach would analyze values as a basis for the development of a theoretical conceptualization of the intervention process itself (Salmon, 1992). Because health interventions are, by definition, purposeful attempts to influence target audiences' perceptions and behaviors and because they typically use persuasive-interventionist or social-marketing approaches, they are inherently a value-laden enterprise. Values, in the context of social interventions, can be viewed as important factors that underlie social action and as "modes of organizing both the goals of public service and social action programs and the acceptable means of attaining these goals" (Suchman, 1967, p. 33). Suchman argues that it is important to consider values in the analysis of social action programs because the relationships between values and intervention activities "are obviously of tremendous importance in analyzing the objectives and underlying assumptions of any public service program" (p. 33). Warwick and Kelman (1973) explain why this occurs and how it relates to the definition of the problem:

> The role of cultural and ideological biases in the choice of goals is often ignored because the change effort may have a hierarchy of values built into its very definition.

These values may simply be taken for granted without questioning their source and their possibly controversial nature. (p. 390)

The analysis of public health communication interventions can thus not only focus on how to use target audiences' values as motivational factors but can examine values embedded in the entire intervention process, including those of the practitioners: why certain values are emphasized in the choice of particular goals and why these values rather than others are pursued.[30] For example, an examination of the types of policy initiatives considered appropriate by the U.S. National Cholesterol Education Program (NCEP), sponsored by the National Institutes of Health, indicates that the program's endorsement of certain initiatives is compatible with certain institutional values. Specifically, NCEP's policies on food labels and its lack of support of other types of strategies (see Glanz et al., 1995, and Chapter 4) are compatible with the institutions' biomedical orientation to health promotion and with the biomedical professional background of the program's dominant decision makers. Support of incorporating certain data on food labels as an intervention strategy is compatible with a biomedical approach because information about the nutritional value of different food products can potentially inform people on the content of these products. This can help people to comply with recommended medical regimens.[31] Other food-related policies, however, involving proposed changes in the marketplace, workplace, or community sites, which are less compatible with the biomedical orientation and the professional orientation of the program, were not as strongly supported.

Several researchers noted the influence of values on the choice of strategies. Refraining from the use of language considered offensive was motivated by political and value-laden considerations in several AIDS-related campaigns in the United States and other countries. Citing Woods et al., Ratzan, Payne, and Massett (1994) describe how, in one of the early phases of the "America Responds to AIDS" (ARTA) campaign, the Centers for Disease Control and Prevention (CDC) decided to adopt nonoffensive language in the development of public service announcements (PSAs). The result, suggest the researchers, was that audiences were provided with a muddled message. Schoepf (1992) describes a similar example from Zaire, where explicit messages on the prevention of AIDS were not broadcast in the media because they were perceived as using impolite language, and government officials did not want to offend religious leaders. Schoepf explains that mass media campaigns sponsored by the government stressed HIV prevention through marital fidelity and avoidance of commercial sex workers—in accordance with the values they aimed to support. Their messages, however, did not convey explicit advice to people who did not adhere to these values and continued to have multiple sexual partners. Consequently, many men adopted practices they thought would protect them from infection, such as having sexual relations with young girls or plump women believed not to be infected. These practices unfortunately would not necessarily protect them or their partners from HIV infection, especially because commercial sex workers, Schoepf reports, responded by dressing like school girls. They also may have contributed to putting young girls at higher risk. Salmon and Kroger (1992) also observe how values of campaign practitioners—in this case, the value of "doing no harm"—influenced their decision not to use messages that may unduly frighten target audience members in an AIDS prevention campaign. These analyses also allow for the explication of ethical dilemmas—for example, the obligation of interventionists to use or not to use persuasive strategies that may help save people's lives but may offend others or infringe on people's rights (Faden, 1987).

Intervention Strategies and Behavior Change Models

Values have an implicit role not only in determining what is or is not a problem but also in the strategic approach used to solve the problem, once it has been defined as such. Two propositions associated with strategies and intervention models are presented. The first posits that regardless of which health issue is addressed by the intervention, its strategies are value-laden. The second suggests that values influence not only goals and objectives but all facets of the intervention process. This implies that analyses of interventions should examine social conditions and values, which may favor or prohibit certain strategic approaches.

6. *Regardless of the health issue, intervention strategies are value-laden.*

Preventing heart disease, reducing the risk of death from cancer, promoting breast-feeding, preventing the risk of stroke, preventing HIV infection—all these are topics of various public health communication interventions. The mere identification of the issue as a problem, as noted in the preceding propositions, indicates a value judgment. Clearly, by defining the issue as a problem and aiming to intervene to amend the situation defined as problematic, the interventionist aim is *to do good* and promote the welfare of the public by influencing people's behaviors for the purpose of promoting their health.[32] As such, they are inherently value-laden. More so, because many health problems are defined as affected by lifestyle factors, interventions typically aim to influence value-laden behaviors, such as eating food containing fat, alcohol consumption, drug use, or sexual practices.[33] Values emphasized in the intervention, though, may not be fully compatible with values associated with cultural customs, tradition, or some people's conception of what is enjoyable or acceptable (Strasser, Jeanneret, & Raymond, 1987).[34] More so, implicit in the intervention process is the notion of social control (Salmon, 1989),[35] because public health communication interventions typically are based on the assumption that the population targeted *should* and *could* adopt particular behavioral or attitudinal changes and that these changes are likely to be beneficial to them. In fact, in many instances, health promoters can be viewed as change agents, who traditionally have been "outsiders" in relation to a majority of target populations, with their own set of values (Jaccard, Turrisi, & Wan, 1990). Their efforts can be viewed as attempts to control the behavior of target populations. This may represent inherent conflicts between values and priorities of various stakeholders.

   7. *Certain strategic approaches tend to be favored by interventionists, regardless of the interventions' goals.*

   Values and the way health-related problems are defined influence not only goals and objectives of a program but all facets of the intervention process (Hornik, 1990). The choice of intervention strategies (e.g., the use of education or persuasion over engineering or regulation),[36] the intervention approach, and the level at which it aims to promote change (e.g., at an individual or community level), as well as the decision about what populations to target all are influenced by the interventionists' preference for certain values.[37] The relationships between the interventionists and the population also depend on value orientation and the way problems are defined. As Rothman (1979)[38] described in his discussion of three models of community organization, practitioners may be enablers-catalysts and teachers of problem-solving skills, facilitators, or activists-advocates. In this third model, practitioners are more likely to think of their constituents as fellow "partisans" rather than "clients" or (in the context of health interventions) "target audiences." Strategic approaches, such as social marketing or media advocacy, are also clearly value-laden. Media advocacy proponents focus on strategies of facilitation and advocacy for the purpose of raising public awareness regarding institutional and structural causes of health problems and aim to influence policy making on specific health-related issues (Wallack, Dorfman, Jernigan, & Themba, 1993). Those who adopt social marketing may also aim to raise public awareness, but they essentially tend to focus on individual behavior changes. The former tend to define the problem more as a structural issue—for example, limited opportunities of disadvantaged populations—the latter, more as personal motivation or limited personal skills or social support.

Increasingly, public health communication interventions, at both the local and national levels, have been adopting social-marketing strategies (e.g., Solomon, 1989). Many programs, in both academic and nonacademic settings, have included training in social marketing as an important topic in their curriculum. Social-marketing strategies have been noted as potentially highly effective and successful (Gruning, 1989; Manoff, 1985; U.S. Department of Health and Human Services [USDHHS], 1989). Interventions that adopt a social-marketing approach have tended to focus on how to use values and priorities of target audiences strategically to develop more persuasive messages or more effective strategies. Critics have pointed out that the adoption of social-marketing strategies to health interventions has tended to target changes in individual behavior, consequently reducing public health issues to individual-level problems and defining solutions within so-called information-deficit models. The nature of public health problems cannot be reduced to neat, compact individual behavior change problems. Instead, health problems are intricately linked to broader social and political contexts (Wallack, 1989, 1990). A social-marketing approach, add critics, is problematic because it is based on an implicit assumption that people have equal opportunity to participate in the marketplace and the health care delivery system. It ignores or deemphasizes the notion that external social and economic factors that are not individually based are usually the major determinants of health (Blane, 1995). This critique brings us back to the importance of paying attention to how interventionists define and conceptualize problems and at what level (e.g., individual, community, or societal) they believe the intervention should take place.

Public health communication interventions that focus on individual-level rewards carry with them, according to critics (e.g., Wallack, 1989), an implicit assumption that the individual will be rewarded with a personal reward of "good health" for adopting practices that are considered health protective.

Such messages seem to be implied in interventions that adopt value-expectancy models and amplified by social-marketing techniques. An example of this type of message appeared in the brochure, *Blacks and High Blood Pressure,* published by the National High Blood Pressure Education Program, sponsored by the National Heart, Lung and Blood Institute, which promised: "If you follow your doctor's advice and control your high blood pressure, you can live a healthy life." Although the persuasive appeal of such messages may have seemed appropriate by the interventionists, they may also serve to reinforce or reproduce cultural values associated with a Western conceptualization of personal gratification at the expense of other, perhaps more community oriented, values (Burns, 1992).

Different types of messages that draw from different types of behavior change models may emphasize that one should adopt the recommended behaviors because of various reasons that may include responsibility for others, altruism, caring, or group affiliation (Beauchamp, 1988; Burns, 1992; Des Jarlais & Friedman, 1988). Each strategic approach may rely on different ways of framing problems and their solutions or emphasize a particular conceptualization of community and of community involvement (e.g., Hatch & Derthick, 1992), democracy, and citizenship (Bellah, Madsen, Sullivan, Swidler, & Tipton, 1991; McKnight & Kretzmann, 1984; Minkler, 1990). Furthermore, the underlying belief in what the communication *is* and *should be* is clearly value-laden. Should people mainly decode persuasive messages from a benevolent and authoritative source, or is communication a process that can and should encourage self-reflexivity and discourse on the social conditions that influence people's beliefs and decisions and that may privilege certain stakeholders or institutions (Deetz, 1992; Mumby, 1997)? The former perspective would tend to rely on attitude and behavior change models; the latter on critical-thinking or emancipatory approaches. Each is clearly linked with an ideological orientation.[39]

Because current research and practice in health interventions predominately focuses on how to make interventions more effective (Lupton, 1994),[40] a value-centered perspective can help broaden this focus by examining why particular models or strategies tend to be favored by interventionists, analysts, and funding organizations. We can examine why it may be "trendy" to apply certain intervention models and why certain outcomes are emphasized over others. The questions we would ask would be what specific strategies have been or should be used, and also, what are the values and assumptions associated with the value-expectancy models typically used, which include the Health Belief Model, Theory of Reasoned Action, Theory of Planned Behavior Change, social learning, and self-efficacy.[41]

With the proliferation of social-marketing approaches in public health communication campaigns, we may also ask why these have been so enthusiastically adopted and explore the reasons for and the implications of the use of marketing metaphors and techniques that have become dominant in many health-promotion endeavors. Is there an association between the belief that consumption through the marketplace is the optimal means for addressing health-related needs (e.g., the production of low-fat food products) and the adoption of a social-marketing approach in health promotion? Similarly, we may want to examine whether health-related problems and solutions are defined and addressed in certain ways when commercial marketing professionals are recruited to the health-promotion intervention.

Program Evaluation

Program evaluation is an increasingly important enterprise, and evaluations are designed and carried out by either the intervention staff itself or outside organizations. An approach described as *empowerment evaluation* has recently been introduced, which aims to foster improvement and self-determination as part of the evaluation process—clearly, a value-laden goal (see Fetterman, Kaftarian, & Wandersman, 1996). Even small-scale programs carried out by nonprofessionals attempt to incorporate an evaluation component. The following propositions posit that regardless of who conducts the evaluation, the choices of evaluation criteria are inherently value-laden. Program evaluation needs to take the value-laden nature of the strategies used into account in its assessment of outcomes because standard indicators of impact or success may not reflect what was or was not actually accomplished in the intervention.

8. *Choices of evaluation criteria are inherently value-laden.*

Public health communication interventions, like other planned, publicly funded social programs, often are viewed as social experiments that need to be evaluated (Finnegan, Murray, Kurth, & McCarthy, 1989; Rossi & Freeman, 1985; Susser, 1995). When adopting a strategic approach to the study of health interventions, emphasis tends to be on the development and use of evaluation strategies for the purpose of assessing the success of the intervention. This assessment typically is designed to meet formal program objectives. Evaluation, however, as the word implies, is concerned with attaching values to certain outcomes or criteria (Suchman, 1967), and the mere choice of evaluation criteria is value-laden (Scriven, 1983; Shadish, Cook, & Leviton, 1991). Analyses of the evaluation process may therefore examine what has been defined as success, what values are associated with the indicators chosen, and whose definitions of what has "worked" or what has "not worked" in the intervention have prevailed. Analyses can explore, for example, the extent to which evaluation criteria (e.g., the use of biomedical indicators) emphasized in the evaluation reflect values of dominant stakeholders and what types of criteria are not considered (e.g., has the development of caring relationships been considered as an achievement, regardless of changes in health status?).[42] Often, health-related programs adopt biomedical indicators, which may not capture other socioeconomic and cultural factors related to health and illness and their sociopolitical contexts. Merton and Lerne (as cited in Weiss & Rein, 1983) raise ethical concerns embedded in this process and suggest that one of the problems faced by evaluators of social programs is the tendency to adopt the policy assumptions of the program: "So long as the social scientist continues to accept a role in which he does not question policies, state problems, and formulate alternatives, the more does he become routinized in the role of bureaucratic technician." These concerns apply to public health communication analysis as well: Analyses that focus on "solving" strategic tasks tend to adopt sponsors' definitions of problems.

Analyses that adopt a value-centered perspective can explore what evaluation criteria have *not* been applied and which stakeholders are more likely to benefit from the intervention's outcomes. For example, when an intervention focuses on the promotion of the use of mammograms (e.g., Schechter, Vanchieri, & Crofton, 1990), those who are most likely to benefit are women who have insurance that covers mammograms and have access to a convenient site and organizations that manufacture or own and provide the services of this technology. An evaluation, if it aims to assess the success of the program, would get different results if it defined success as increased use of mammograms by all women or only by women who have insurance that covers mammograms. To achieve better success rates, the intervention would need to address making changes in insurance policies or enhancing access to mammogram technology for all women. It is particularly important to identify alternative conceptualizations of the problem because, as noted earlier, there is the tendency to adopt the interventionists' definition of problems and the interventionists' solutions. Analyses can examine who is most likely *not* to benefit from the intervention. For example, in an intervention that aims to increase the number of women who go to get mammograms, if the intervention does not address the issue of limited insurance coverage of mammograms, the evaluation will provide skewed results. Those most likely to benefit from a campaign that urges women to get screened are women who have more ready access to this service, both in terms of monetary cost, proximity, and time. An evaluation of an intervention whose ultimate goal is to increase early detection of breast cancer therefore may provide a more comprehensive assessment of outcomes if it includes criteria for assessing (a) the impact of the intervention on enhancing the women's opportunities for getting mammograms among populations with more limited access and (b) the benefits accrued by particular stakeholders. An analysis of the evaluation criteria that focuses on values can also help to point to trade-offs inherent in the intervention (Priester, 1992a, 1992b) and help broaden evaluation criteria so that they more fully address needs and goals of different stakeholders, especially those who have had little or no say in the intervention (Weiss, 1983). This in turn would address ethical concerns associated with who actually benefits from the intervention or the extent to which the benefits are equitably distributed.[43]

9. Intervention strategies are not necessarily chosen because of their potential effectiveness.

Intervention strategies are not necessarily adopted because they present the most effective solutions to specific health-related problems. As Stanton, Kim, Galbraith, and Parrot (1996) note in a review of the strategies employed in HIV-reduction interventions, "we recognize that sometimes even though investigators are aware that certain intervention designs would be methodologically preferable, political and/or ethical considerations may render these selections impossible" (p. 394). For example, although educational methods are not necessarily the most effective strategy for affecting behavior changes (e.g., Beauchamp, 1987; Salmon, 1989), they are often chosen because they are viewed as the least likely to offend various stakeholders and do not require systematic changes in major social institutions (Wallack, 1990). In public health-related issues assumed to be "sensitive," policymakers have been likely to choose an intervention strategy or message believed to be the least threatening to the status quo or viewed as more attractive because of political consider-ations (Arkin, 1990; Salmon, 1992). This is illustrated in the debate regarding "needle exchange" programs that provide clean syringes to users of injection drugs, which have been shown be relatively effective in reducing the rates of HIV infection in this population. Despite the demonstrated effectiveness of this approach in preventing the spread of infection, according to advocates, support for this approach has met with strong objections by many policymakers who see it as an unacceptable strategy on political or moral grounds (Vlahov & Brookmeyer, 1994). The decision of the New York City Board of Education to require AIDS educators to pledge that they would em-phasize what they consider sexual "abstinence" in their presentations in the classrooms (Hennenberger, 1992) is another example of the adoption of an in-tervention strategy for reasons other than potential effectiveness. This deci-sion was fraught with intense controversy. Whereas proponents of this strategy may have sincerely believed that this message would be effective, health educa-tors, who believed the most effective strategy would be to provide students with information and skills regarding safer sex practices, claimed they would lose their credibility among students if they adopted this position. An evalua-tion of this intervention would have to take into consideration the way the edu-cators compromised and adapted their messages to meet the Board's require-ments. Because the strategies adopted in the intervention were not necessarily the ones most likely to produce the greatest desired outcome, the evaluation of the intervention would need to take into consideration political and ideo-logical factors. A value-centered analysis can help show that the strategies em-ployed were not necessarily chosen because of efficiency or effectiveness. It can also help identify outcomes that are important to evaluate and addi-tional assessment criteria. For example, in one study, it was found that most people contacted in a hypertension screening outreach project in a disadvan-taged community had in fact already been screened. Rather than applying a standard quantitative criterion of the number of people screened for hyperten-sion in this project,[44] alternative criteria might have been more useful, such as the extent to which people in the community developed a sense of trust in the health agency or the extent to which the intervention activities helped create a sense of importance and urgency regarding the issue of hypertension. Further-more, the perspective of members of the target population, in terms of what they expected from the intervention and what was actually accomplished, can be incorporated in the development of evaluation criteria.

Ethical Concerns[45]

Interventions, by definition, are planned, purposeful activities that attempt to bring about changes in individuals or groups or their social environments, and as such, they inherently raise ethical concerns (Zaltman & Duncan, 1977). The final proposition reiterates this position and adds that although ethical concerns regarding infringement on values related to autonomy tend to be raised in the context of persuasive communication interventions, other ethical concerns, associated with values that are more implicit, are less likely to be acknowledged.

10. Because interventions, by definition, are planned, purposeful activities that attempt to bring about changes in individuals or groups, they inherently involve conflicting values and ethical dilemmas, some of which are less obvious than others.

Despite health promoters' intentions of doing good for members of society, interventions raise serious political and moral concerns (Beauchamp, 1987). The most prominent set of ethical concerns typically relates to the use of persuasion and paternalism. Communication interventions often involve promises and persuasive messages. As Forester (1993) explained in the planning context, communication activities in interventions involve announcing, exposing, threatening, predicting, promising, encouraging, explaining, warning, recommending, and other speech acts, each associated with ethical implications.[46] Many public health communication interventions can be seen as marketing initiatives (Goodman & Goodman, 1986) that use persuasive and social-marketing techniques and as such raise concerns regarding the extent to which it is justified to use persuasive strategies to reach the intended health-promoting effect of the intervention if its use may infringe on individuals' rights (Laczniak, Lusch, & Murphy, 1979; Pollay, 1989). Ethical concerns thus range from issues related to persuasion, which can infringe on people's autonomy or privacy (Feingold, 1994; Hiller, 1987; Kleining, 1990), protecting the health of the public, or the notion of justice and fairness, in terms of who is targeted or who benefits most from the intervention (Des Jarlais, Padian, & Winkelstein, 1994). A central concern is the possibility that unintentionally an intervention may cause people harm (Brown & Singhal, 1990; Wang, 1992) by inadvertently stigmatizing members of certain groups by the way it presents a dreaded health-related outcome (e.g., being infected with HIV or having to use a wheelchair).[47]

Interventions may inadvertently serve to make people feel guilty for not adopting their recommendations, especially those who are less economically advantaged, or to deprive them of inexpensive "risky pleasures." This also raises ethical concerns regarding fairness and equity because individuals from higher social classes, as noted by Strasser and his colleagues (1987), can more easily refrain from such risky pleasures than people who are less economically advantaged, because they can substitute them with what are considered healthier habits or substances. Researchers and social critics have been concerned with the phenomenon characterized as the *knowledge gap:* that regarding certain topics, a gap in information acquisition increases rather than decreases between those who are more socioeconomically advantaged and those who are less so (Olien, Donohue, & Tichenor, 1983). This knowledge gap has been noted in health communication research topics, including AIDS, cancer, and cardiovascular disease (Goswami & Melkote, 1997; Salmon, Wooten, Gentry, Cole, & Kroger, 1996; Viswanath, Finnegan, Hannan, & Luepker, 1991; Yows, Salmon, Hawkings, & Love, 1991), and though authors propose different interpretations for the reasons for such gaps, their existence underscores ethical concerns associated with equity.

Becker (1993), a leading proponent of health interventions and one of the developers of the Health Belief Model, a theoretical approach that emphasizes the notion of perceived vulnerability as a basis for behavior change, adds another dimension to this line of critique. He argues that there is a bias in seeing health as a virtue and a "new morality," which has become a value of many health promoters and other members of society. It appropriates notions of uprightness and righteousness, he explains, designating those who are not perceived as appropriately lean or healthy as lacking important virtues. Therefore, interventions' communicative claims can be seen as affecting the production of personal identity.[48] Thus, people who do not adopt the so-called health recommendations may feel guilty or have a low sense of worth because they see themselves as having "weak character" for not being able to follow recommended regimens.[49] Self-incrimination like this supports critics' concerns with the inadvertent contribution of public health communication interventions to victim blaming (Allegrante & Sloan, 1986). By emphasizing lifestyle factors and personal responsibility, interventions implicitly characterize those who do not adopt the recommended practices as unwilling, lazy, or of weak character. Victim blaming is described by William Ryan (1976) as locating the causes of social problems within the individual, rather than in social and environmental forces (Allegrante & Green, 1981; Crawford, 1979; Rakow,

1989; Wikler, 1987).[50] Although health interventions may not explicitly blame individuals for being responsible for their illness, they can be viewed as deemphasizing structural factors, such as work and housing conditions, access to health care, or pollution, factors that can present serious health risks and contribute to the etiology of health-related problems and that warrant institutional rather than personal changes (e.g., Brown, 1983; Coreil & Levin, 1984; Ellison, Capper, Goldberg, Witschi, & Stare, 1989; Glanz et al., 1995; Glanz & Mullis, 1988; Green & Raiburn, 1990; Wallack, 1989; Williams, 1990). Public health communication interventions often do not include information in their messages to the public—for example, how public health risks are intricately vested in the competing interests of powerful organizations, such as the food and tobacco industries, government, or the medical profession (Milio, 1981).[51] Instead, interventions, particularly those that adopt a social-marketing perspective, tend to frame the notion of responsibility for disease prevention as if it were primarily under the control of individuals (Wallack, 1989). Although concerns regarding paternalism and persuasion, which can infringe on an important value in U.S. society—respect for autonomy—have been the ethical concerns most likely to be raised in the context of public health communication interventions, other ethical concerns, associated with other values, are less likely to be pointed out (Duncan & Cribb, 1996). Concerns regarding the potential contribution of interventions to processes of social control, the medicalization of society, or harm caused to individuals by making them more anxious or by labeling them at risk or inadvertently stigmatizing them are less likely to be acknowledged. Similarly, interventionists may be less likely to be aware of the extent to which their activities may privilege certain stakeholders because they tend to be based on middle-class values (Strasser et al., 1987).[52] In the absence of analyses that make implicit values or hidden arguments in public health communication interventions more explicit, the health communication intervention enterprise may inadvertently contribute to privileging the position of dominant stakeholders. The voice and perspective of those who are less privileged may not be heard.

BROADENING THE ANALYTIC APPROACH

Table 1.1 compares what has been labeled here as value-centered to a strategy-centered analytic approach. Each can complement and inform the other.

Table 1.1   Comparison Between Strategy-Centered and Value-Centered Analytic Approaches

Analytic Approach	Strategy-Centered Analytic Approach	Value-Centered Analytic Approach
Locus of analysis	Factors are likely to influence the target populations' beliefs and behaviors.	Factors are likely to influence the choice of goals, design and implementation of the intervention itself as it relates to values and priorities of the sponsors of the intervention.
	The purpose of the analysis is to forward the goals of the intervention.	The analysis views the intervention as a social-change phenomenon and its purpose is to help explain it as such.
Values	Primary concern is with values of target populations.	Values of different stakeholders are explored as grounds for justifications for interventions' goals, strategies, and choice of evaluation criteria.
	Values are studied to design effective messages and are possibly manipulated for the purpose of affecting target populations' attitudes and behaviors.	Analyses examine what and whose values are given priority and social and institutional processes that contribute to this emphasis.
The definition of the problem	Sponsors' definitions are typically taken for granted and guide program goals and objectives.	Analyses explore claims used to justify particular definitions of the problem, alternative definitions, potential distortions, and social processes and values that contribute to the adoption of particular definitions.
	The perspectives of target populations might be incorporated for the purpose of designing more effective interventions.	
Intervention strategies and behavior change models	Behavior change models are reviewed, developed, adapted, applied, and tested to determine how to affect behavior change.	Analyses examine underlying assumptions and values associated with behavior change models and strategies.
	Analyses examine the extent to which particular models or theories explain or can predict health-related behaviors or practices.	Analyses examine the social context that contributes to this emphasis.

Table 1.1   *Continued*

Analytic Approach	Strategy-Centered Analytic Approach	Value-Centered Analytic Approach
Assessment and evaluation	Evaluation criteria are developed and used to assess the success of the intervention, usually according to programs' formal objectives.	Evaluation criteria are examined in terms of what values are emphasized and what are not emphasized in the evaluation criteria.
		Analyses explore the social context that contributes to this emphasis or lack of emphasis.
Ethical concerns	Analyses focus on ethical concerns related to specific strategies, such as the use of persuasion or fear appeals, to issues relating to targeting audiences and efficient use of resources.	Analyses focus on ethical concerns regarding the content of messages as well as inadvertent outcomes, such as framing or attracting-distracting attention to social issues, privileging certain stakeholders, affecting one's self-concept, stigmatization, and labeling.

Strategic approaches can contribute to the planning process of interventions, develop theories and models of behavior change, provide concepts to operationalize and manipulate data, and offer practitioners principles and guidelines to meet goals of public health communication intervention (Freimuth, 1992). Strategic approaches often test conceptual frameworks and behavior change models. They focus on desired strategies and outcomes. Value-centered approaches can contribute to the analysis of such interventions by examining the intervention itself as worthy of study, not only the outcomes associated with it. The analyst's role can be compared to that of the philosopher who can "call attention to neglected features, forgotten relationships, and unforeseen contradictions" and can "aid in better mapping and critically evaluating the conceptual and value commitments involved in particular actions and choices" (Engelhardt, 1986, p. 11). Similarly, the adoption of this kind of framework can help identify distortions (Forester, 1989) that underlie intervention choices of goals and strategies and raise these and others as ethical concerns, which are less self-evident when one is immersed in the design and implementing process.

NOTES

1. For example, income-earning opportunities for women may decrease HIV infection in sites where limited economic power is the main reason they engage in commercial sex work (de Bruyn, 1992).

2. In addition, members of certain marginalized or stigmatized groups were blamed for epidemics, and consequently, this was used as an excuse to inflict torture, expulsion, and often death on them (Tesh, 1988). During the 14th and 15th centuries, Jews were heavily persecuted, and thousands were slaughtered or burned alive in German, Belgian, and Swiss towns (Sutcliffe & Duin, 1992). In Brazil, a 17th-century yellow fever epidemic served as an excuse to constrain women. In England, the Irish were suspected as transmitters of disease; and in India, people blamed the English for the spread of infectious diseases (Tesh, 1988).

3. Cuba is considered the only nation that used the strategy of isolation of infected individuals as an official measure to curtail the spread of HIV infection (Scheper-Hughes, 1993).

4. Turshen (1989) describes the successful campaign to eradicate smallpox in the 1960s and compares it to the failure of the campaign to eradicate malaria. Her analysis attributes these differences to the type of problem and the structural factors associated with the eradication of each disease.

5. The literature that reviews public health communication interventions has been rapidly growing, though only a fraction the of interventions that take place are fully documented in the scholarly literature.

6. These include Andreasen, 1995; Atkin & Wallack, 1990; Backer & Rogers, 1993; Backer, Rogers, & Sopory, 1992; Bracht, 1990a; Donohew, Sypher, & Bukoski, 1991; Maibach & Hotgrave, 1995; Maibach & Parrot, 1995; Rice & Atkin, 1989; Piotrow, Kincaid, Rimon, & Rinehart, 1997; Salmon, 1989; U.S. Department of Health and Human Services, 1992; Wartella & Middlestadt, 1991; Windahl, Signitzer, & Olson, 1992; Winett, King, & Altman, 1989).

7. I am indebted to Brent D. Ruben for this conceptualization.

8. This perspective is based on Salmon's (1989, 1992) writings and is further elaborated later. See also Zook and Spielvogel (1992) on the limitations of a strategic approach in the provider-patient context.

9. See Altman's (1990) analysis in another context.

10. Salmon (1992) presented this conceptualization and described it in more detail.

11. For example, Devine and Hirt, 1989; Flay and Burton, 1990; Flora and Maibach, 1990; Loken et al., 1990; McGuire, 1989; Scherer and Juanillo, 1992.

12. Rogers and Storey (1987) partly attributed the lack of theoretical grounding in this area to the practical nature of communication campaigns and to the diversity of their contexts. Salmon (1989, 1992) suggested that we can gain important theoretical understandings of communication campaigns by analyzing the relationships between values that underlie their choices of goals, strategies, and evaluation criteria.

13. See also Tesh (1988) for a discussion of the role of values in health promotion and health policy. Douglas and Wildavsky (1982), in their discussion of risk and society, discuss the role of values as determinants of conceptualization of risk and how the types of risks a society selects to address are functions of attributes of its social structures. Thus, "each form of social life has its own typical risk portfolio" (p. 8). This can be applied to the context of health: Each society decides what constitutes a health risk and what health-related problems warrant an intervention. I am

indebted to a reviewer from *Communication Theory* for pointing to the connection of Douglas and Wildavsky's work to this context.

14. From a more critical-theory perspective, following Mumby (1997), part of the project of communication studies would be the development of an ethic of communication. This is indirectly raised in Salmon's (1992) discussion on the development of theory "of" and "for" campaigns as a social phenomenon.

15. As a result of negative experiences with official health agencies and the residue of the Tuskegee Syphilis study, a considerable number of African Americans and other minorities often distrust public health professionals and health promotion messages (Dusenbury, Diaz, Epstein, Botvin, & Caton, 1994; Thomas & Quinn, 1991).

16. This topic is further elaborated in the last chapter, in the discussion of distortions.

17. For instance, contributing to the phenomenon of blaming the victim, social gaps, or medicalizing human experience. This is further elaborated in following chapters.

18. Similarly, it has been noted that on the individual level, the way problems are framed is believed to influence personal decision processes (Thompson & Cusella, 1991).

19. The definition of health itself has value-laden and ethical implications (Susser, 1974).

20. Even when it comes to death, perceptions differ according to culture: What our culture considers early death may be seen as timely by others. Maulitz (1988) suggests that perceptions in Western culture that cardiovascular disease and cancer are unnatural causes of death is linked to cultural factors.

21. Seidman and Rappaport (1986b) adopt Berger and Luckmann's (1967) approach and explain how the definition of social problems emerges as particular constructions of reality based on certain expert knowledge, which become widely institutionalized and take on an appearance of objective reality.

22. Tesh (1988) provides an extensive discussion on this topic. See also Best (1989a, 1989b) for an analytic framework on the construction of social problems and illustration of this approach.

23. Joel Best (1989a) used this example similarly to illustrate the construction of social problems. See also Reinarman (1988) for an analysis of the construction of alcohol consumption as a social problem.

24. Similarly, critics suggest the framing of AIDS as a single issue (e.g., as a so-called gay disease) rather than a myriad of socioeconomic factors, or the framing of substance abuse as a problem of limited "refusal skills," have resulted in narrowly conceived and ineffective interventions because of narrow conceptualizations of the problems associated with these issues (Backer et al., 1992; Evans, 1988; Freudenberg, 1990). Such narrow formulations, they say, reflect an ideological position of particular stakeholders "who also like the idea of shifting the burden of responsibility from society to individuals" (Evans, p. 216).

25. MADD was also highly instrumental in supporting federal legislation for raising the minimum legal age for alcohol consumption, which could be seen both as preventive and societal-level strategy (Reinarman, 1988). This legislation, however, can also be seen as an attempt to limit the liberties of youth "for their own good" and as part of an enforcement of a moral approach in which "social control takes precedence over social welfare as the organizing axis of both ideology and policy" perceived as dominant in the conservative Reagan era (Reinarman, 1988, p. 112).

26. In fact, the alcohol beverage industry in the United States had representatives on MADD's board at one point and also contributed money to the organization (Reinarman, 1988).

27. Trostle (1988) provided an analysis of the notion of patient noncompliance, viewed as an important problem from the perspective of health professionals, but which he described as an ideology.

28. This is adapted from Tesh (1988) regarding pollutants in the air and Garfinkle's examples she cites; also see Lau, Hartman, and Ware (1986).

29. See Ball-Rokeach, Rokeach, & Grube, 1984; W. J. Brown, 1991; Grube, Mayton, & Ball-Rokeach, 1994; Gruning, 1989; Fine, 1981; Flora, Maccoby, & Farquhar, 1989; Leichter,

1986, 1991; Manoff, 1985; Solomon, 1989; USDHHS, 1989; White & Maloney, 1990; Wilson & Olds, 1991. Also see Leichter (1986) for a comparative analysis of values and policies in different countries.

30. See Grace (1991) for an analysis of practitioners' beliefs and practices regarding intervention strategies.

31. See Moore (1989), Levine, (1986), and Springarn (1976) on political and ideological factors that influenced the development of health prevention programs, and see Proctor (1995) on the "war on cancer."

32. Doing good is the underlying primary justification for these types of interventions and the basic tenet of the helping professions (Hiller, 1987). This is further elaborated in Chapter 2.

33. Ethical issues, as they relate to the intervention, are discussed later and elaborated in Chapter 6.

34. Similarly, risk taking is typically portrayed in interventions as something that should not be pursued. Yet risk taking is often highly cherished in society (Fitzgerald,1994).

35. Zola (1975), in an article considered to be a classic on this topic, discussed medicine as social control.

36. See Paisley, 1989; Feighery, Altman, and Shaffer, 1991; and Glanz and Mullis, 1988. See Winett et al. (1989) for a discussion of levels of analysis and intervention approaches. See also Green & Kreuter, 1991.

37. See Hornik, 1990; McLeroy, Gottlieb, and Burdine, 1987; and Salmon, 1989.

38. See also Rothman and Tropman (1987) and Minkler (1990). Different conceptualizations of the relationship between interventionists and their target populations are further discussed in the fifth chapter.

39. The topic of different strategic approaches is discussed in the context of models of intervention in the fourth and fifth chapters. An in-depth discussion in which values are linked to epistemological approaches to communication can be found in Anderson (1996), Deetz (1992, 1994), and Mumby (1997).

40. Deborah Lupton (1994, p. 57) explains:

> Health communication scholars, researchers, and practitioners are often hampered in their project by their close links with health promotion agencies largely funded by the state. Consequently the tendency of health communication scholars, researchers, and practitioners has been to accept the prevailing orthodoxy of health promotion ideology, focusing on the planning of health education campaigns, cost effectiveness, and the evaluation of measurable effects, but devoting comparatively little attention to the critical analysis of the ethical and political implications of their endeavors.

41. See Ajzen and Fishbein, 1980; Maibach, Flora, and Nass, 1991; Perry, Baranowski, and Parcel, 1990; and Rosenstock, Stretcher, and Becker, 1988. These models emphasize different factors believed to affect behavior, such as individuals' sense of vulnerability to disease (as in the health belief model), perceptions of people's own and others' health-related social norms (as in the theory of planned behavior change), or an emphasis on individuals' gratifications and of personal competencies (as in social learning). Clearly, each may employ several models or aim to affect both individual and system-level factors.

42. The ethic of care as an important value is discussed in the feminist literature (e.g., Noddings, 1984).

43. As Salmon (1992) suggests, we can ask, does the analysis mainly provide theories *for* or does it also advance theories *of* evaluation?

44. This example is further elaborated in Chapter 4.

45. Chapters 2 and 4 further discuss ethical concerns. For a classic article on the topic, see Warwick and Kelman (1973). See also the 1987 issue of *Health Education Quarterly,* which is devoted to ethics in health promotion, and two books edited by Doxiades (1987, 1990).

46. Forester adopted a critical perspective to analyze planners' work based on the work of Habermas. His analysis can be applied to the health intervention context as well as applications suggested in Chapters 6 and 7.

47. See a discussion by Wang (1992) on the latter and a further elaboration in Chapter 6.

48. See Forester's (1993) discussion. The issue of identity as it is influenced by communication processes can be informed by the symbolic interactionist approach.

49. This was reported in results of focus groups and is further described in Chapters 5 and 6.

50. See the application of this concept to the health context in Beauchamp (1988) and McLeroy et al. (1987).

51. Waitzkin (1989) discusses this in the context of the patient-physician relationship. He maintains that medical encounters are impoverished because practitioners do not discuss with patients any socio-politico-economic factors that may contribute to the etiology of their illnesses.

52. Ellsworth and Whatley (1990) describe films and photos used for health-promotion programs at schools as embedded with the ideological presumption that students can afford costly health-promoting hobbies.

2

Justifications

One has no intellectual problems, no philosophical problems, if one does not worry about giving reasons. However, not attending to reasons and the implications of choices would mean eschewing conversations about moral matters with oneself as well as with others. It would involve acting without concern for consequences. As soon as one wonders whether certain choices are better and how one can tell, the intellectual endeavor is joined. As one attempts to justify actions to others, or to persuade others that their actions are wrong, the intellectual undertaking assumes social dimensions.

—H. Tristram Engelhardt, Jr. (1986, p. 7)

What kind of reasons are given to justify health communication interventions or what claims serve as the moral grounds for intervening in people's course of life or in social institutions?[1] Although few, if any, practitioners or scholars engaged in health communication interventions would say they subscribe to the doctrine that it is justified to use immoral means to achieve beneficent intervention goals, the morality of using particular intervention strategies in specific intervention contexts is not always absolute. Certain trade-offs may be tolerated: Interventionists may disseminate persuasive messages that exaggerate risks. They may decide to refrain from employing highly persuasive means because they believe they are too intrusive, coercive, or manipulative or are morally unjustifiable, although these may help achieve their goal.

Support for particular goals of various public health communication interventions may not be unanimous. Proponents may maintain an intervention's aim is crucial; some may view it as frivolous or even immoral. As noted in the previous chapter, the way the problem gets to be defined greatly influences the way intervention goals and strategies are chosen. What makes a given situation viewed as a problem depends on what is conceived as problematic, and what is conceived as problematic depends on values. For example, the prevalence of a certain medical condition among members of a particular social group might be viewed as natural and normal, thus not problematic. In contrast, this prevalence might be viewed as unfair[2] or as a risk for society as a whole, thus viewed as a problem that needs to be addressed by publicly sponsored interventions. Definitions of problems inherently are shaped by certain values, for example, having a fair and just society or protecting the public from potential harm.

Value-laden reasons vary. Some are implicit and unspoken or seem self-evident. Others are explicit and bluntly stated. Policymakers, advocates, and health administrators often point eagerly to potential economic benefits of health interventions. For example, prevention practices, they argue, can help cut escalating health care costs by reducing illness and diseases associated with behaviors such as smoking, excessive alcohol consumption, preventable injuries, or treatable mental health problems.[3] Some interventions are based on values that appeal to concerns associated with alleviating people's suffering, improving quality of life, and the unfair share of disease among particular social groups and less on a fiscal bottom line. Explications of why interventions are necessary or should be implemented in certain ways are thus based on different prioritizations of values. Our understanding of the intervention process therefore needs to focus on the differential emphasis on certain values.

VALUES AND JUSTIFICATIONS

The word *value* comes from the Latin word *valere*, which means to be of worth or to be strong.[4] Values, as defined by Rokeach (1979), whose seminal work on values has influenced much of social science research on values, are "an enduring belief a specific mode of conduct or end-state of existence is personally or socially preferable to an opposite or converse mode of conduct or end-state existence" (p. 10). Values viewed as individual or shared conceptions of the desirable are considered worth pursuing (Kluckhohn, as cited in Rokeach, 1979; Warwick & Kelman, 1973) or as "any aspect of a situation, event, or object that is invested with a preferential interest as being 'good', 'bad', 'desirable', 'undesirable', or the like" (Suchman, 1967, p. 33). Values have been viewed by psychologists, sociologists, and anthropologists as the criteria people use to select and justify actions and to evaluate people (including the self) and events (Schwartz, 1992), and they transcend specific situations and guide the selection or evaluation of behavior, people, and events (Schwartz, 1994). Suchman (1967) explains the connection between values and social interventions:

> Values are modes of organizing both the goals of public service and social action programs and the acceptable means of attaining these goals. Such values may be *inherent* in the object or activity itself, or they may be *conceived* as being present whether they really are or are not. They may be *operative* as determinants of behavior, or they really are or are not. The relationships between inherent, conceived, and operative values vary greatly from area to area and are largely a matter for empirical investigation. These relationships are obviously of tremendous importance in analyzing the objectives and underlying assumptions of any public service program. For example, any program designed to reduce the incidence of lung cancer by changing the smoking habits of individuals must first establish the inherent value of smoking as a cause of lung cancer, then it must create within smokers the conceived value of the undesirability of dying from lung cancer, which finally must be translated into operative value of giving up cigarettes as a preferred form of enjoyment. As we shall see later, public service values at times may not coincide with people's values. (p. 33)

Valuing is more than attaching a worth, explains Rokeach (1979): Values serve as standards to guide action and as a basis for judgments, choices, attitudes, evaluation, arguments, rationalization, and attributions of causality. Social values, however, are not equivalent entities: A person may hold competing values that may create inner conflicts and dilemmas in different situations. Similarly, the importance attached to certain values may vary widely across individuals, groups, and cultures. When faced with the question whether intervention strategies might be morally justified—even if they might infringe on certain rights or entrenched beliefs—it is values that provide a base for decision making and "as criteria of tolerable and intolerable costs in a given intervention" (Warwick & Kelman, 1973, p. 379). In Western societies, particularly in the United States, core values typically include freedom and fairness. To these, security, peace, responsibility, opportunity, work, family, individuality, social recognition, self-actualization, power, and pleasure are often added as important values (Lappe, 1989; Rokeach, 1979).

For the purpose of developing an analytic framework of values embedded in public health communication interventions, the concept of *justifications* is used. Justifications serve as reasons for choosing certain intervention goals or strategies (Vandeford, Smith, & Harris, 1992). Whether made explicitly or implicitly, formally or informally, justifications serve as grounds for health promoters' claims of legitimacy. By implication, enlisting specific justifications prioritizes certain types of definitions of problems or intervention strategies over other alternatives (Veatch, 1982). Because health communication interventions are planned interventions that—in the name of health—aim to induce changes, the 10 major justifications that follow mainly draw from the bioethics literature, which specifically focuses on values and moral justifications for purposive interventions in the health context. Justifications for interventions, as they are presented in this literature,[5] are often based on ethical principles, which are "fundamental sources from which we derive and justify specific action guides" (Pellegrino, 1993, p. 1161). Values in behavioral studies, in turn, tend to be associated with individual motivational goals or culture and norms. They are likely to overlap, because the majority of the values identified by social scientists as important can be viewed as associated with the justifications specified in this chapter.[6]

Treating justifications as claims that are firmly grounded in moral principles, however, must be tempered with caution, as MacIntyre (as cited in Manning, 1992) reminds us: Justifications may not necessarily be based on what we may think are inherently widely shared values. In certain cases, we may find that "behind the masks of morality [lie] what are in fact preferences of arbitrary will" (p. 69).[7] Likewise, political considerations or personal preferences may play a more important role in decisions about goals, strategies, or evaluation methods of health communication interventions than moral values (Salmon, 1989). Furthermore, in certain contexts, values function to reframe the way in which particular issues are constructed (Kristiansen & Zanna, 1994). The analyst's challenge is to identify them as such, recognize the social context that fostered such decisions, and determine ethical as well as pragmatic implications associated with the intervention's intended and unintended outcomes.[8]

The Justifications

The 10 justifications described in this chapter and subsequently used in the development of an analytic framework (presented in Chapter 3) are mainly drawn from the major ethical principles of doing good, doing no harm, respect for personal autonomy, justice or fairness, and utility. These correspond to values prominent the social science literature. Because the goal of specifying the justifications is to develop a broad analytic framework, each justification may concur with several social values and may be substituted with alternative conceptualizations. For example, included within the justification of doing good is the *ethic of care,* which draws from a feminist perspective, but it can certainly be viewed as distinct and separate. It also needs to be noted that ethical principles that serve as the basis for moral frameworks have been criticized outside the philosophical community as being too abstract, too rationalistic, and too removed from the sociocultural milieu in which moral choices actually take place (Pellegrino, 1993).

The justifications presented in this chapter are not mutually exclusive nor do they include all possible values or justifications in health interventions. Rather, they represent major prototypes and justifications currently dominant in the health intervention literature.[9] Because different approaches to moral reasoning can be applied to each justification,[10] the extent to which certain intervention activities are justified may be determined on the basis of the consideration of likely consequences or outcomes. Justifications that mainly consider potential outcomes as the rationale for their goals and strategies would follow ethical theories associated with consequentialism, which is a moral approach in which the worth of actions is assessed in terms of their results or the situation. The most noted ethical theory of this type is utilitarianism, in which moral decisions are based on the greatest balance of good over bad, for everyone considered (Mappes & Zembaty, 1991).[11] In contrast, the underlying justifications for the intervention may rest on considerations of the importance of adherence to certain duties or overriding moral rules.

This second approach represents what are known as *deontological ethics*[12] in which what matters most are not results or outcomes but the integrity and the duty to act according to a moral principle such as truth telling or promise keeping—whatever the consequences (Seedhouse, 1988).[13] Furthermore, the same justification, for example, the notion of autonomy, may carry profoundly different understandings of its meanings among people who differ in their political or value orientations (Lappe, 1989). Despite the profound differences among the approaches and the application of ethical principles to actual cases, the ethical principles and core social values offer a basis for implicit and explicit values embedded in the intervention phenomenon. Following is a description of the 10 justifications subsequently used to develop a value-centered analytic framework, as they relate to major ethical principles and social values and their application in the health communication intervention arena.[14]

Beneficence or "Doing Good"

Under the belief that by preserving or bettering the health of intended audiences or clients one is promoting their welfare, the aim of interventions for health is certainly benevolent. By implication, a fundamental justification for these interventions is beneficence or the ethical imperative of doing good. Beneficence is the basic tenet of the helping professions: the obligation of the health professions to benefit their clients by actively pursuing their positive states of health (Hiller, 1987) or by preventing or removing potential harm (Veatch, 1982). The principle is called *beneficence,* explains Seedhouse (1988), rather than *benevolence* "because it makes the point that we should try in practice to do good and not evil, not merely that we should wish to do so" (p. 136).

The principle of beneficence or doing good serves as the ethical foundation of the profession of medicine and other health professions and is considered a *prima facie* principle synonymous with the Hippocratic obligation to act in the best interest of the patient (Pellegrino, 1993). Although this principle seems self-evident, it is nevertheless problematic: It may be difficult to determine what is actually in the client's or intended audience's best interest and, even if this is known, whether the practitioner has the right to impose or to use persuasive strategies to accomplish the goal of doing good (Veatch, 1982). The duty to do good entails the obligation to carefully weigh potential risks and harms against possible benefits to be gained from the intervention and also requires not engaging in unwarranted paternalism. The latter involves the assumption that the provider or professional knows what is best for the client or patient: Because he or she is acting in the client's best interest, they are therefore justified in denying their client a fully autonomous decision.

The example in which adolescent pregnancy is framed as a social problem, discussed in the previous chapter, can serve to illustrate the tension between the values placed on doing good and other ethical obligations—specifically, the notion of *paternalism.* An effective intervention that would succeed in getting adolescent girls to adopt the use contraceptives may depend on the use of highly persuasive strategies. Strategies may employ persuasive messages that warn girls from getting pregnant by portraying those girls who do get pregnant as irresponsible, ruining their lives and the lives of significant others. Presumably, the use of these type of messages will help adolescent girls avoid a situation perceived as detrimental to their physical, social, economic, and mental well-being. However, first, such messages may serve to stigmatize girls who have already become pregnant, many of whom may have low self-esteem and are already shunned by certain segments of society. Second, for particular adolescent girls, having a baby might be highly beneficial: Taking care of a child might enhance their self-esteem, help them feel more responsible or nurturing, or provide an opportunity to be loved and love and care for another. Some girls might actually become more motivated and work harder to achieve educational or employment goals. For these particular girls, antipregnancy messages are not necessarily beneficent. Furthermore, such messages may serve to stigmatize them or contribute to a low self-image. The taken-for-granted assumption that the intention of doing good justifies the use of persuasive tactics needs to be challenged by the possibility that the intervention may infringe on people's right to autonomy or may in fact be doing some harm by casting them in a negative light. Thus, even the seemingly purely beneficent justification of doing good is fraught with potential tensions and value contradictions.

Care: Drawing on feminist theory and Gilligan's (1982) work on different moral approaches to ethical decision making (e.g., Manning, 1992; Noddings, 1984, 1990),[15] alternative perspectives on doing good and conceptualizing justice can serve to expand or replace traditional Western ethical principles. Although articulations of the ethic of care differ, it is mainly presented as a critique of traditional ethical theories of rights and justice (Cole & Coultrap-McQuin, 1992) and is predominantly a contextual rather than principled approach to moral reasoning.[16] Compassion for others plays an important role in moral decision making, and such decisions are also based on personal experience and self-reflectiveness rather than on the application of abstract ethical principles. The emphasis in the ethic of care is on relatedness between people, receptivity, attachment, and a person's responsiveness to others, as well as on the importance of trying to fulfill others' needs, regardless of specific rights or obligations (Manning, 1992).[17] The justification of care as grounds for doing good (e.g., the importance of relational aspects) may differ from the grounds used to claim the rightness of a beneficent approach for providing treatment and service based on biomedical criteria. Differences in ways beneficence is applied are manifested in the training and decision-making processes of different health professionals, such as traditional nursing care compared to traditional medical training.

In what ways does the ethic of care apply to health communication interventions? Would an emphasis on the ethic of care as a justification for health communication interventions affect the way we define problems or solutions? Clearly, having the ethic of care as a justification for an intervention can result in a different conceptualization of doing good, of assessing desired outcomes, and in the application of different strategic approaches. Fostering connectedness and focusing on relational needs can lead to conceptualizations of doing good that differ from those that focus on biomedical definitions of health or psychomotor functioning. The care ethic, suggests Braithwaite (1994), permits partiality and emphasizes the importance of direct relationships in the moral life of individuals. In contrast to ethical theories of justice, it offers a justification for preferential concern for individuals in need. This can serve as an alternative to concerns associated with justice when deciding to design a community-based intervention for the underserved in a multi-problem-ridden and diverse population. Analyses that aim to understand the social context and its influence on the design and implementation of a communication intervention can benefit from examining the way the notion of good is constructed in the intervention, as well as the types of criteria used by the caregivers to provide care and caring. The complexity of the justification of doing good and the ways its definition may be linked to particular social values can be better examined. Moral as well as practical implications may also be discussed. The notion of doing good can be expanded beyond a service-provision model or traditional needs assessment approaches to perspectives that give more prominence to relational and situational aspects. Incorporating the ethic of care in our analysis can help examine the extent to which the intervention is being justified on the basis of connectedness, relationship development, and nurturing or the extent to which attending to particular needs of people with whom one has a special relationship are used to justify the intervention, instead of or in addition to principles such as efficiency, equity, or the good of the public as a whole.

Nonmaleficence or to Do No Harm

Even when particular health-related situations are identified as problems, there are many instances in which no interventions or only ones relatively limited in scope take place. The reasons for refraining from intervening altogether or for only using less effective strategies are frequently influenced by consideration of the ethical principle of *nonmaleficence*— the fear of causing possible harm. Doing no harm is often considered as the foremost ethical principle or maxim for health providers. It is the obligation to bring no harm to one's clients or the persons one serves as a professional.[18] It reiterates the popular medical ethos, *primum non nocere* (first of all, do no harm), and instructs health providers not to risk or cause harm to the populations they serve. The obligation of the health provider is to ensure that, at minimum, the actions they intend to carry out with the intentions of promoting health are not likely to cause any harm to the individuals involved (Hiller, 1987). An example of this obligation is stated in the pledge given by nurses, formulated by Florence Nightingale, the founder of modern nursing in the latter half of the 19th century, in which the nurse pledges to abstain from whatever may be deleterious to the patient (Barry, 1982).

Medical care or treatment, however, may involve certain risks for the patient. These may include physiological side effects that result from potent medications or actual pain and suffering. It may lead to an iatrogenic condition, which is a disorder caused by medical practice.[19] For example, a patient may contract unexpected serious complications as a result of undergoing certain medical procedures or from staying at a medical facility and being exposed to infectious diseases there. Such complications may in fact be more detrimental to the patient's welfare than the medical condition for which he or she had been treated.

Health promotion and disease prevention activities can also place individuals at risk: A person may suffer injury as a result of engaging in physical activity or have a life-threatening reaction to a vaccination. Certain treatments or preventive activities may be promoted even when they may be associated with certain risks when the potential of doing good is believed to override the risk of potential adverse consequences. Sometimes, the intended good may be for the sake of other individuals (e.g., when an individual donates a kidney to another person who is ill, which can put the donor at risk) or for the public as a whole, whereas the individual may not be the one to personally benefit. The potential for doing harm is a serious consideration among health professionals when deciding what treatment or course of action to take to help the patient. Beneficence, remind us ethicists, "assumes an obligation to weigh and balance benefits against harms, benefits against alternatives benefits, and harms against alternative harms" (Beauchamp, 1994, p. 32). Clearly, the justification of doing good may conflict with considerations of potentially doing harm. Those engaged in providing medical care and research are often acutely aware of the risks of harm presented by their interventions and constantly see the need to weigh possible harm against possible benefits.

But what about the potential of doing harm in the context of health communication interventions? In the example of an intervention that aims to reduce teenage pregnancies and uses persuasive messages, potential harm lies in the risk of stigmatizing the adolescent mother or mother to be. Thus, even presumably benign persuasive messages can cause considerable harm. The following examples illustrate how this justification had been given at least some consideration in making strategic decisions in two public health communication campaigns. Refraining from doing harm was interpreted as a justification for deciding not to use fear-arousal messages in a U.S.-government-sponsored AIDS prevention campaign (Salmon & Kroger, 1992). It was also used as a possible objection to promoting contraceptive implants among adolescent girls from low-income populations. In the case of the implant idea, one of the interventionists' considerations was the traditional medical concern about possible harmful physiological side effects, but a more subtle fear, as stated by health providers, was related to a very different kind of potential harm: They worried that although implants may be an effective method for preventing unplanned pregnancies among adolescent girls, those who would use them may be less inclined to insist on using condoms when they engaged in sexual intercourse. Consequently, these girls may be less protected from sexually transmitted diseases, including HIV (Lewin, 1992).

The prospect of iatrogenesis, a central consideration in decision making in clinical medicine, has received only scant attention in discussions of social interventions (Seidman & Rappaport, 1986b). The possibility of doing harm, whether physiological, psychological, or cultural, does not seem to be a serious concern among those involved in public health communication interventions. Perhaps it is presumed that because public health communication interventions mainly use educational or information dissemination strategies, in contrast to invasive clinical procedures, there is little risk that they would cause significant harm because they do not invade people's bodies. Ivan Illich (1975) expands the notion of iatrogenesis beyond mere physical damage. In his severe critique of institutionalized medicine, he describes both social and cultural iatrogenic effects. Modern medicine, he argues, deprives people of control of their bodies and spirituality and society from its cultural and moral means of dealing with human suffering and death.[20] Illich's critique echoes other critics' concerns with the medicalization of life, which they suggest increases as more and more of life domains become incorporated within medical definitions and control (Fox, 1977; Zola, 1972).[21] The preoccupation with biomedical definitions of disease thus takes a social, cultural, moral, and existential significance that may not be easily resolved, even as the medical profession loses some of its monopoly on health care delivery (Fox, 1977).[22] Such concerns regarding possible social iatrogenic effects can be applied to the context of public health communication interventions as well: Interventions may further promote medicalization or enhance the power and dominance of particular institutions. Furthermore, as Marshall Becker (1993), a prominent health promotion scholar, has forcefully warned, health promotion interventions may turn the pursuit of health into a crusade with moral overtones, which may harm people more than it may do them good.[23]

Autonomy

By aiming to influence people's attitudes or to get them to modify their behaviors, public health communication interventions risk interfering with personal freedom, thus violating one of the most prominent principles in Western bioethics: respect for autonomy. The principle of respect for autonomy is rooted in liberal Western tradition, which places high importance on individual choice, both regarding political life and personal development. Historically, the word *autonomy* comes from ancient Greece, where the notion of self—*autos*—and rule or law—*nomos*—were combined to refer to self-governance in the city-state (Beauchamp, 1994). The underlying premise of this principle is that all competent individuals have the intrinsic right to make decisions for themselves on any matter affecting them, at least so far as such decisions do not bring harm to another party. Respect for personal autonomy provides the foundation for the development of important medical care codes, such as patient's rights, informed consent, and confidentiality. Health care providers are obligated to honor the self-respect and dignity of each individual as an autonomous, free actor (Hiller, 1987). The justification of autonomy can be associated with values of freedom, self-determination, power, and control (see Rokeach, 1979).

John Stuart Mill (1863/1978), a strong proponent of the centrality of the principle of individual autonomy, argues that only the individual can know his or her own particular good. According to the principle of respect for autonomy, one should refrain from interfering with, or attempting to interfere with, autonomous choices and actions of others by either subjecting them to various forms of control, influence, or coercion or manipulation of information (Childress, 1990). Pellegrino (1993) explains why the principle of autonomy, which is highly consistent with the "individualistic temper of American life that emphasizes privacy and self-determination" (p. 1160), directly contradicts the traditional authoritarianism and paternalism of the Hippocratic ethic. The latter eschewed patient participation in decision making. Pellegrino adds that many clinicians are still not fully convinced of the soundness of autonomy as a primary principle in medical care and fear its absolutization may override good medical judgment and work against the patient's best interest.

In the context of public health communication interventions, threats to autonomy clearly emerge when there are planned attempts to induce particular lifestyle practices through behavior modification or persuasive methods. Furthermore, as in the provider-patient context, failure to respect autonomy can range from manipulative undisclosure of pertinent information to outright coercion (Beauchamp, 1994). Whereas certain health-related outcomes are desirable from the health promoters' perspective, employing communication strategies that may be manipulative or even deceptive can be seen as violating respect for individual autonomy (Hiller, 1987). This concern was voiced by Kelman (1969) in his discussion of social-change interventions. He argues that the most important question change agents face is to what extent do the change strategies they employ inhibit or nurture freedom of choice. The principle of respect for autonomy places the burden of moral justification on those whose intervention activities would restrict people's activities or influence their decisions. This principle also serves as the rationale for democratic forms of government and increasingly serves as a justification for increasing the involvement and participation of community groups and residents in the health intervention process, from goal setting to implementation and evaluation (Bracht, 1990a, 1990b).

Community Involvement and Participation: Respect for autonomy extends beyond the level of the individual and includes communities and nations. In the context of health interventions, having community residents define what the problems are that face their community and what social problems should be addressed and how to address them, rather than having such decisions imposed by experts or public agencies, can be viewed as another dimension of autonomy. Increasingly, involvement or participation of community members in health intervention has become a cornerstone of many initiatives, many of which have articulated an ideology of community capacity building and the notion of empowerment. Community involvement and empowerment can be seen as an important autonomy-related justification: It has been increasingly presented as the underlying principle of community-based interventions and as a reflection of democratic ideals[24] or a promising tactic for disease prevention and the promotion of health (Eisen, 1995; LaBonte, 1994).

Privacy: Another facet of individual autonomy is respect for privacy.[25]

> Everyone has the right to respect for his privacy and family life, his home and his correspondence. There shall be no public interference by a public authority with the exercise of this right except such as is in [the interest] of national security, public safety or the economic well-being of the country, for the prevention of disorder or crime, for the protection of health or morals, or for the protection of the rights and freedom of others. (Knox, 1987, p. 67)

As this definition implies, the right to privacy is conferred by society. Conflicts between what is considered the good of the public as a whole and individuals' rights to privacy or autonomy are inherent. One such conflict is whether the individual is entitled to engage in behaviors that damage the welfare prospects of others. John Stuart Mill (1863/1978), in his famous essay *On Liberty,* argues against restricting individuals in the name of benefiting them without their consent. He maintains that the only justification for exercising power over members of society against their will is to prevent harm to others. According to Mill, the state cannot legitimately require the individual to take care of his or her own safety (Beauchamp, 1987), and individuals may do whatever "mischief" they wish to do to themselves, as long as this does not interfere with their duties to others (Mill, 1863/1978). Similarly, Dworkin (as cited in Hiller, 1987) argues that restricting a competent individual's liberty—even for his or her own good—should be done only when attempting to prevent far-reaching, potentially dangerous and irreversible outcomes. Dworkin contends that those who impose paternalistic interventions on others should demonstrate clearly why such actions were taken and ensure that they were the least restrictive measures necessary to reduce the risks.

Truth telling,[26] although it may be considered a virtue, is also presented by some as an important ethical principle (e.g., Seedhouse, 1988) affiliated with the principle of autonomy. Truth telling is clearly associated with persuasive messages: Messages that distort information, do not fully disclose all the facts, or make claims that may not be totally true deprive people of making autonomous decisions. In the example of the intervention to prevent adolescent pregnancy, health promoters face a dilemma of whether—by using highly persuasive strategies when targeting adolescent girls—their strategy infringes on these girls' autonomy or whether it is justified because these girls are believed to be too immature to make autonomous decisions. This raises the issue of paternalism, which cuts across intervention topics, professions, and populations. The problem of paternalism, explains Tom Beauchamp (1994), is generated by a conflict between principles of respect for autonomy and beneficence. Each of these principles has been conceived by different parties as *the* overriding principle in cases of conflict. One approach that justifies a form of paternalism is based on the notion of the social contract (Dworkin, as cited in Daniels, 1985). In certain cases, individuals who value their autonomy realize that sometimes their competency to make rational decisions is temporarily or permanently undermined. They may engage in self-destructive behaviors that run counter to their true interests. Had they been fully competent, well-informed, and acting truly voluntarily, it is believed they would in fact avoid these behaviors. To protect themselves against hazardous outcomes, people can thus choose to authorize others to act on their behalf, even if this may appear to be contrary to their expressed wishes. This delegation of authority allows for an initial autonomous choice and provides a rationale for a particular kind of paternalism. Its application, though, is constrained and depends on the specific type of the intervention. It also requires a careful determination of whether there is indeed a limitation in competency and how the intervention will restore, where possible, the individual's diminished autonomous decision making. These conditions can serve as assessment criteria for when to enact regulations that restrict individual choices for the purpose of disease prevention or health promotion.

Associated with respect for autonomy and the notion of paternalism are two interrelated contentious issues. The first refers to the tension between a restriction that is good for society but that may conflict with individual freedom. Similarly, individuals' needs and desires may conflict with what is viewed as good for society. Democratic societies may thus need to "reconcile and balance the good of the individual with the good of the whole" (Beauchamp, 1987, p. 70).[27] A democratic society, according to this view,

includes some legitimate forms of paternalism [that] is based on the view that government must reconcile two main ends: the rights and interests of the individuals taken separately, and the good of individuals together—the community—even for life-style risks. (Beauchamp, 1987, p. 70)

The second issue concerns the extent to which the individual should be allowed to take voluntary risks. Does the principle of autonomy imply that individuals have the right to take voluntary health risks of their choice? Some emphatically answer in the affirmative: Individuals should be able to take whatever risks they choose, as long as they do not harm others. But some question whether the adoption of certain ill-health-promoting practices by certain people represents truly voluntary choice, because people may be subjected to highly persuasive appeals or institutional constraints (Pinet, 1987). Bioethicists are typically very cautious about supporting regulations that might infringe on personal choice and autonomy, but some also concede that individual choices are not necessarily made under conditions that allow their choices to be truly free (Daniels, 1985). Daniels explains why the notion of individuals making free choices regarding behaviors considered hazardous is problematic:

> Even a view that holds the individual to be the best architect of his ends and judge of his interests rests on important assumptions about the information available to the agent, the competency of the agent to make these decisions rationally, and the voluntariness of the decisions he makes. It is because these assumptions are not always met that we require a theory of justifiable paternalism. (p. 157)[28]

Manipulative or coercive interventions are justified as corrective and thus are viewed as benevolent by those who adopt the latter position. Others, however, may see them as unjustifiably paternalistic (Salmon, 1992).[29] Clearly, the principle of respect for autonomy is a paramount value that serves as a foundation for the notion of democracy. Its conception, however, may become distorted, as Minkler (1989) implies. Minkler cites the sociologist Aaron Antonovsky's observation that there is a strong tendency in the U.S. to equate "sense of control" with "being *in* control" in terms of being able to personally order and determine events that influence one's life and correspondingly, one's health. Minkler, a proponent of community-level interventions, explains that the American obsession with personal control is an important cultural and ideological underpinning of American health promotion efforts, because it has contributed to the dominance of the individual focus of many health interventions to the exclusion of others.

Market Autonomy

For some, closely related to valuing individual autonomy and personal choice is the value placed on market autonomy. Although it is not considered an ethical principle, among certain stakeholders, market autonomy is seen as a highly valued mode for operating society and a compelling reason for prohibiting regulatory efforts. Prioritizing market autonomy as a value is deeply seated in strong beliefs that a market economy free from restrictions is warranted by the principle of autonomy or free choice. Proponents of the free market system believe a free market economy is ultimately the best way to maximize human enterprise and to distribute materials and social goods in society and the optimal method for balancing economic contribution and economic rewards. The fewest regulations and restrictions possible, they argue, should be placed on the marketplace. This openness, they believe, works as the primary method to motivate individuals to contribute to society, enables members of society to choose the goods and services they want, and ensures a healthy economy. Proponents of marketplace autonomy also believe consumer demand will drive producers to provide healthier food products or other health-promoting consumer goods and services at competitive prices (Garret, Baillie, & Garret, 1989).

Even its proponents, however, concede that the adoption of a presumably free-market system allows for inequalities in distribution of goods in society (Garret et al., 1989). In addition, the notion that a regulation-free marketplace indeed ensures equal opportunities to all members of society to compete in it, even in supposedly free-market capitalist economies, is strongly challenged. Critics present evidence that different sectors of the population have unequal privileges regarding access to marketplace resources, including government support or protection (Bellah et al., 1991; Deetz, 1992; Milio, 1981; Schiller, 1989). In the health care context, because of marketplace conditions, providers are often drawn or driven to practices and geographical locations that do not necessarily serve the needs of all populations. Fear of losing health insurance has prevented people from changing jobs (Braithwaite, 1994), thus restricting their occupational choices. Furthermore, the corporatization of managed care shows increasing evidence of decreasing rather than increasing people's health care options and choices. Restrictions, in the name of health, can also be made on marketing certain activities or the distribution of products, which though not illegal are considered hazardous or disease promoting.[30] Proponents of putting restrictions on the marketplace for the purpose of promoting health suggest that such restrictions are highly appropriate not only as strategically effective but may actually present fewer infringements on individual rights than the supposed free-market system (Beauchamp, 1987). For example, restrictions on marketing and promotion of cigarettes and alcohol products are proposed by government agencies and health advocacy groups as effective means to reduce the use of these substances and can be viewed as less punitive of individual behavior. It is not surprising that these policy initiatives are highly opposed by the tobacco and alcohol industries and portrayed by them as threats to individual freedom. The government that enforces them has been depicted as unwieldy and interfering in parental rights in child rearing (Davis, 1996). The prominence of the notions of market autonomy, "marketplace democracy," or "market justice" that underlie the consumer society is also reflected in the dominance of health promotion interventions that focus on changes on the individual level and conceive people's behaviors as resulting from personal choices. Critics add that inherent in such a market model is attention to individual behavior and inattention to the preconditions of that behavior (Minkler, 1989; Wallack, 1989).

Personal Responsibility or Virtue

Does the right to autonomy also entail obligations? Most people would answer that it does, though perceptions of what responsibilities individuals should have toward their society, which grants them certain rights, and what responsibilities they have for significant others are likely to vary (Beauchamp, 1987; Campbell, 1987). Are people responsible for other people's behavior? Most people, suggest ethicists, will agree that people have moral obligations toward others that arise out of special relationships, as well as duties that flow from one's membership in the moral community as a whole. There is no agreement, however, over the exact nature or relative strength of these obligations, although being a "good Samaritan" seems to be expected from members of society and is even protected by law (Douard & Winslade, 1994).

First, we can view personal responsibility as a moral duty to protect others, which rests on the claim that others have on us when they are dependent and vulnerable. In certain situations, therefore, if our inaction is likely to result in a significant amount of harm to others, we are obligated to act (Douard & Winslade, 1994). In most societies, parents or guardians have legal obligations to care for children, and health providers have professional obligations to provide certain care for their patients. But moral responsibility regarding care for others extends beyond legal requirements. Ethicists point out that we express moral disapproval and even outrage at people who do not warn, protect, or come to the aid of others who are at risk of being harmed, even if they are not related to them. We also praise as heroes people who, at great risk to themselves, go out of their way to protect strangers (Douard & Winslade, 1994).

What, then, is the moral imperative that underlies one's duty to help another person? Is one obligated to help one's spouse who has been told to lose weight? Are people to be held responsible if they do not succeed in helping? For example, what should one do if the overweight spouse insists on purchasing foods high in calories and saturated fats? Clearly, the ethical imperative of benevolence, as it is associated with one's obligation to help another in need, can conflict with the threat of infringing on the other's autonomy. Another type of conflict may arise from a person's preference to choose a course of action that is independent of the needs and desires of others. This can also be seen as a variation of the notion of freedom, which can conflict with one's duties toward or connection with others (Douard & Winslade, 1994).

Second, personal responsibility can be linked to the notion of fairness: the notion that a person should not needlessly encumber others. A responsible person, this implies, will do his or her utmost to refrain from taking risks that may result in injuries for which others may have to pay in money, time, or effort. With growing emphasis on individuals' lifestyle behaviors as risk factors for ill health, personal responsibility has become a highly prominent theme in many public health communication interventions. These interventions urge individuals to take responsibility for their own health, to adopt what is recommended as health-promoting behaviors, and to refrain from hazardous practices. The emphasis on individual responsibility presumably is based on the assumption that specific health-related lifestyle behaviors, characterized as high risk, are freely chosen or at least under the control of the individual. This argument is extended by some to suggest that people who take what are considered voluntary risks with their health impose unfair burdens on others (McLeroy et al., 1987; Veatch, 1982). According to this perspective, personal responsibility includes not only responsibility for doing things for oneself but also responsibility to others. Thus, individuals who smoke or who drink what are considered excessive amounts of alcoholic beverages or who ride motorcycles (Rowland et al., 1996) are perceived as liable for increased costs they might place on the health care system if they become ill or cause injury to others. Grounds for this claim are that people's voluntary risky acts may cause an unfair burden to others.

Several authors distinguish between voluntary and nonvoluntary risk-taking behaviors and suggest that potentially risky behaviors, such as smoking, drug abuse, or working in dangerous places, are influenced more by structural factors than free will and therefore are not truly voluntary. Consequently, individuals who engage in them would be exempt from full responsibility. Other activities, such as skiing or skydiving, are seen as truly voluntary, and therefore, the individuals would be held responsible for the possible adverse consequences of their undertakings (Veatch, 1982). Yet certain risky behaviors are not only sanctioned by society but admired; these include risks taken by firefighters and athletes or those taken in combat (Fitzgerald, 1994). Third, engaging in responsible behavior may be associated with virtue or with abiding by moral obligations that emanate from a person's or society's beliefs regarding how a good and righteous person conducts himself or herself. Virtue has been defined as an internal disposition to habitually seek moral perfection or "to live one's life in accord with the moral law, and to attain a balance between noble intention and just action" (Pellegrino, 1985, p. 243). The notion of virtue implies that one has obligations beyond what strict duty might demand, and the person is expected to do what is considered right and good even at the expense of personal sacrifice and legitimate self-interest. Doing what is good contains the ideas of service, responsiveness to others with special needs, fidelity, compassion, kindliness, and promise keeping, which are also associated with the ethic of care. Pellegrino (1985) notes, though, that there are dangers from overzealousness or misguided observance of virtuous behavior, which, he warned, can easily lapse into self-righteous paternalism or an unwelcome overinvolvement in the personal life of others.

Responsibility and virtue can also be seen as closely affiliated with some of the social values specified by Rokeach (1973), which he characterizes as *instrumental values*. These include being courageous, helpful, honest, obedient, responsible, and self-controlled. In the context of public health communication interventions, one may need courage to act in a way that may not be initially popular in order to be a role model, or one may need courage to behave in what is considered a responsible manner. Similarly, one may need self-control and practice self-restraint to help avoid one's own and others' risky practices.

Promise keeping, which can also be perceived as a moral virtue, is viewed by some as an important ethical principle, as well (e.g., Seedhouse, 1988). In the context of public health communication interventions, promises that interventionists make to target audiences about participation in the intervention process, intended outcomes, and support in the future are an important part in the integrity of the program. This is particularly important in cases where the intervention is viewed as a field experiment, and target population members may feel they are being used for research purposes and afterward, left with un-kept promises of long-term continuation or substantial changes.

Utility, Effectiveness, or the Maximum Good

Considerations of efficiency, such as who should be targeted or what methods should be used to the greatest advantage, typically rely on justifica-tions associated with utility. Stressing the usefulness of method to maximize a desired outcome can be associated with an ethical approach that places its main emphasis on consequences. According to this perspective, the primary obliga-tion of the interventionist is to maximize the greatest utility from the health promotion efforts (Hiller, 1982). Criteria for justifying actions or policies, therefore, may be assessed as right or wrong according to the extent to which they contribute to promoting human welfare of all those concerned and bring the greatest good to the greatest number (Rayner & Cantor, 1987). One of the underlying premises for this type of justification is that society has limited re-sources, and these should be used to maximize their effectiveness. Another value reflected in this justification is the notion of efficiency, characterized by Simon (1976) as a "master premise" in decision making, particularly in organi-zational contexts. This pits principles of justice (discussion follows) against utility. One may ask whether it is ethical to waste society's limited resources, for example, by targeting an intervention to people who are not likely to adopt its recommendations. But one may also ask how fair it is to allocate society's limited resources mainly to those who are more likely to benefit and also more likely to be its privileged population (Veatch, 1985). Another problem with ap-plying utilitarian principles as the primary justification for public health com-munication interventions is that economists have shown that preventive mea-sures are not necessarily cost-effective, though moral justifications may prevail (Russell, 1986, 1987).[31]

Justice or Fairness

What health-related topics should a communication intervention ad-dress? Who should be the intended audiences? The ethical principle of justice (which includes the notions of fairness or equity)—although perspectives on what it means vary widely (Braithwaite, 1994)—is a central justification both for conceptual and strategic decisions in the design and implementation of many public health communication interventions. The principle of justice or fairness suggests that all human cases should be treated similarly and fairly regarding the distribution of goods and harms within the society (Warwick & Kelman, 1973). From the point of view of the health promoter, justice is the obligation to treat one's intended audience members fairly in terms of health-related burdens (e.g., monetary costs, accessibility, distribution of risk) and benefits (Hiller, 1987). Moral perspectives on justice differ, however. Some take a different view on the way costs and benefits of health-related resources should be distributed.[32] Whereas one approach may center on having equal availability of resources to everyone, another may prefer to allocate scarce health promotion resources to those perceived as bearing the greatest need. Critics of the latter suggest that

> the principle of evaluating any distribution scheme by its effect on the least disadvantaged is dangerously vague. Whose judgment and what criteria should be used in evaluating the effect on the least advantaged? If the advantaged are to be the judge, justice as fairness puts the fox in charge of the chicken coop. (Garret et al., 1989, p. 78)

Another criticism proposes that this perspective ultimately denies the dignity of the individual by labeling certain individuals as disadvantaged (Garret et al., 1989). An additional criticism is that the emphasis on need may conflict with a utilitarian approach or libertarian approaches that base their justification on merit or outcome (Hiller, 1987).

Some authors argue the principle of justice demands an obligation to provide health care in such a way that everyone will have the opportunity to be as healthy as others. As Whitehead (1992) suggests, "equity in health implies that ideally everyone should have a *fair opportunity* to attain their full health potential and more pragmatically, that none should be disadvantaged from achieving this potential, if it can be avoided" (p. 433).[33] Many contemporary discussions on justice in the literature refer to Rawls's (1971) work on this topic. Rawls argues that we hold society responsible for guaranteeing the individual a fair share of basic liberties, opportunity, and means, such as income and wealth, needed to pursue individual conceptions of the "good." Individuals are responsible for choosing their ends in such a way that they have a reasonable chance to satisfy them under just arrangements. Justice, Daniels (1985) is careful to point out, is not an obligation to satisfy citizens' desires; instead, just social institutions provide individuals with an acceptable framework within which they may pursue happiness.

According to Whitehead (1992), one's sense of injustice is heightened when social or health problems appear to cluster together and reinforce each other among certain populations or when gaps in mortality and in experience of illness are glaring.[34] People's sense of injustice would be felt when discrepancies in ill health are related to situations such as the following: Individuals from lower socioeconomic groups tend to consume less nutritious diets because of their lower income or lack of access to an adequate food supply; they engage in less physical activity because of lack of leisure facilities or lack of time to make use of them; and there is disproportionate promotion of health-damaging products targeted at them (such as tobacco products, alcoholic drinks, and fast food products offering meager nutritional value). Other hazards, such as skiing injuries, are not likely to invoke the same sense of injustice because the activities that led to the injury are viewed as voluntary.

The distinction between illness and disease presumed to be caused by voluntary in contrast to involuntary behavior is important in discussions of health interventions and justice (Veatch, 1982). People who take what are considered voluntary risks with their health can be seen as imposing unfair burdens on others (McLeroy et al., 1987; Veatch, 1982). The critical issue, therefore, is to what extent are potentially risky behaviors, such as smoking, drug abuse, or working in dangerous work sites, chosen freely and to what extent are they influenced by life circumstances that are not under the control of the individual. The latter would justify or even mandate having publicly sponsored interventions. This issue is further addressed in the discussion above of the justification of personal responsibility.

When reasons pertaining to justice are used to justify health communication interventions, two issues that are central, though often taken for granted, need to be considered: (a) Is health a special social good, and (b) if so, how do we consider fairness in its distribution? The argument, drawing from Daniels's (1985) discussion of justice and health, is that to apply theories of justice to health care, we need to know what kind of a social good health care is; what are the social functions and effects of health, and why do we think health has a particular moral importance that may distinguish it from other aspects that can potentially improve our quality of life. Health care is typically seen as special in our society, and many believe that it should be treated differently than other social goods. The argument is that even in societies that tolerate or even glorify inequalities in the distribution of most social goods, many people feel that it is only fair that health care should be distributed more equitably. An alternative approach, even one that does not see health, on its own, as a social good, nevertheless also strongly links health and justice. Because disease and illness affect one's chances to obtain other social goods, health, it is argued, "is of direct relevance to worries about justice because it contributes directly to the distribution of opportunity in society" (Daniels, 1985, p. 176).

How do considerations of justice relate to public health communication interventions? The answer depends on the role delegated to them in addressing inequities in the distribution of disease and illness in society or in equalizing access to and use of health care services. Associated with justice are questions such as these: Does dissemination of information on how to improve one's health afford the same opportunities to all audience members? Should the intervention target particular populations who are more in need? What topics should the intervention focus on?[35] Should the intervention focus on changing structural factors that influence people's opportunities to adopt health-promoting practices? Last, it should be noted, public health communication interventions may have different goals and apply different strategies, depending on their conceptualization of justice.

Applying principles of justice to the example of adolescent pregnancies raises several issues. First is the framing of the issue as a problem: Adolescent pregnancies can be seen as a problem of a particularly vulnerable population with special needs, which therefore justifies a special intervention. Second is the types of options offered to the adolescents: Contraceptives may not be easily accessible or may be relatively expensive and therefore not consistently used by adolescents with limited financial means. Adolescents may also be limited in their access to health care providers who can counsel and advise them confidentially. Therefore, they may not have a fair opportunity to avail themselves of effective preventive measures. Another issue is of targeting particular groups to encourage their adoption of particular contraceptive measures, such as implants, and even introducing legislation that would try to compel women on welfare to use these measures. This may possibly stigmatize them or deprive them of other types of options ("Birth-Control Implant," 1992). It may be impossible for a public health communication intervention not to face issues associated with justice and fairness, especially when they target one group and not another or when benefits of the intervention are not likely to be shared by all, particularly by individuals who do not have equal opportunities to take advantage of them.

The Public Good

One important justification for engaging in health promotion activities is that they are likely to benefit the public or the community as a whole. This corresponds to highly cherished social values, such as security and social integration, societal stability, political order, social integration, promoting the welfare of society, national development, and national security (Rokeach, 1973; Warwick & Kelman, 1973). A typical example of how the benefit to the public may outweigh the benefit to particular individuals is immunization: Not only the person who is immunized to personally avoid a particular disease is likely to benefit, but others will benefit from eradicating the cause of the disease. In fact, there is a chance that the individual who takes the immunization might suffer from potential harmful side effects, but the risk of this potential harm is seen to be balanced by the potential benefit that many others will gain. Furthermore, for the public as a whole to be protected, only a certain percentage of the population needs to be immunized (Clark & Knox, 1993; Garret et al., 1989; Veatch, 1982). Prioritizing the public good may thus serve as a justification for infringing on individual autonomy and mandating certain practices that restrict individuals' freedom. For example, parents who may prefer not to have their children immunized, nevertheless, do so to comply with the law. Justifications that appeal to the notion of the public good may be grounded in moral approaches that emphasize the importance of the community or the nation and the duty of individuals to contribute to the welfare and well-being of the collective. Appeals can thus be linked to values such as national development, tradition, and national security. The claim that the public as a whole should benefit is often defended on utilitarian grounds or reduced monetary cost: Intervening can save society economic resources (Veatch, 1982). In the case of immunization, it can be justified as an efficient way to decrease the spread of a disease in a large population. The famous British Chadwick Report in 1842, which advocated substantial public health intervention measures, was based on this justification. Chadwick's major assumption was that improving the health of the masses, particularly eliminating disease among the poor, would reduce government expenditures (Tesh, 1988). Thus, health promotion activities, particularly prevention programs, are often presented as cost control measures for society as a whole. However, this view has been challenged by economists, who suggest that preventive activities are not necessarily cost-effective and should be justified on other bases (Russell, 1987). Critics, thus, maintain that the notion of the public good should not be solely based on monetary considerations but should be grounded in valuing good social institutions and a good society (Bellah et al., 1991).

Self-Actualization

Self-actualization, although it might be seen as a variation of the ethical principle of respect for autonomy, can also be seen as a more proactive maxim that calls for enhancing human potential.[36] It also reflects some of the values mentioned in the literature of social science, which include personal growth, creativity, a sense of accomplishment, stimulation, inner harmony, happiness, and spirituality (Rokeach, 1979; Schwartz, 1994). Freedom, suggest some bioethicists, does not need to be only defined negatively, as noninterference with one's wishes. Its definition can also include a positive obligation to enhance human potential (Campbell, 1987). If we accept that values associated with autonomy include the obligation to maximize human potential, then its enhancement can serve as an important justification for interventions (Seedhouse, 1988). The enhancement of human potential or self-actualization, although related to autonomy, can also be viewed as a distinct moral goal. Seedhouse suggests that this is implicit in the World Health Organization's broad definition of health, which includes social well-being. Seedhouse argues that "the most moral form of endeavor is one which aims at producing more of what human beings are for, more enhancing human potential" (p. 25) because work for health can "release more or less of the potential of individuals" (p. 27). This justification corresponds to self-actualization, the ultimate human need in the famous Maslow (1954) hierarchy, and to values of having an exciting life, sense of accomplishment, pleasure, self-respect, social recognition, and spirituality, specified in the work of Rokeach (1973) and others.

Science

Science is viewed as an important driving force in health interventions. Health planning in the United States, explains Barry (1982), had been shaped largely by two traditions: (a) the Western belief in the rationality of science, in which planning is viewed as the institutionalized application of the methods and findings of science to social affairs, and (b) the tradition of social reform and the public health movement that flourished at about the turn of the century and viewed social or political action as the main means for improving the health of the public. Medical practitioners and scientists often value scientific methods as the only reliable source of knowledge or means for making decisions about the appropriateness of intervention goals and strategies. Only those they find acceptable serve as the basis for defining what a medical problem is, what legitimate and effective ways of addressing such health problems are, and the extent to which their prevalence warrants interventions (e.g., according to epidemiological data).

Science has been used to justify the choice of goals of health interventions by framing and defining certain medical conditions as health risks. For example, elevated blood cholesterol has been declared by official health agencies as a health problem when scientific analysis suggested that it is causally linked to higher risk of heart disease. Science was used to justify the adoption of certain definitions of the problem in a national health intervention sponsored by the U.S. National Heart, Lung and Blood Institute (NHLBI): "The NCEP's education efforts are based on scientific evidence of relationships between diet, high blood cholesterol levels and cardiovascular heart disease" (from the National Cholesterol Education Program's *Communication Strategy,* 1992). Similarly, what the authors considered as the current state of science served as the basis for a national depression awareness campaign sponsored by the U.S. National Institute of Mental Health (Regier et al., 1988).

Science may also be used to explain the choice of intervention strategies. Science was used as a justification for pursuing the problem through educational strategies in the National High Blood Pressure Education Program (NHBPEP). This is illustrated in an explanation given in a 1992 press conference by Horan, Associate Director for Cardiology at NHLBI, which sponsors several public health communication interventions:

> The Institute [NHLBI], which has a broad mandate that includes both research and education, is in a unique position to assure that the [intervention] Program's educational activities are backed by appropriate science. In fact, it's the science . . . that drives the [National High Blood Pressure Education] Program's educational initiatives.

Evaluations of intervention efforts also clearly tend to adopt science-based criteria. Public health communication campaigns, especially when they serve as demonstration programs or are grant funded, often aim to implement as rigorous as possible experimental designs (e.g., a randomized control trial) to prove that the intervention strategies are what have brought about the desired change rather than secular trends (Fisher, 1995; Luepker et al., 1994; Susser, 1995).

Table 2.1   The Justifications, Associated Ethical Principles or Frameworks, and Examples of Corresponding Social Values

Justification	Ethical Principles or Framework	Social Values
Doing good	Beneficence, ethic of care	Doing good, relatedness, connectedness, care, humanism
Doing no harm	Nonmaleficence	Doing no harm, care, humanism
Autonomy	Respect for autonomy, privacy, truth telling	Privacy, empowerment, freedom, self-determination, dignity, power, control, individualism, antipaternalism
Justice	Justice; fairness, equity	Justice; fairness, equity
Personal responsibility	Beneficence, virtue	Virtue; care; service, responsiveness to others with special needs, fidelity, compassion, kindliness, and promise keeping; courage, helpfulness, honesty, obedience, self-control
Public good	Public good, utilitarianism, communitarianism	Good of the public; national security; social integration; societal stability; political order; social stability; promoting the welfare of society, national development
Self-actualization	Respect for autonomy	Personal growth; creativity; a sense of accomplishment, stimulation; inner harmony, happiness; spirituality; excitement in life; pleasure, self-respect; social recognition
Utility	Utility, pragmatism	Effectiveness, efficiency
Market autonomy	Respect for autonomy	Free choice, effectiveness, efficiency
Science		Rationality, objectivity

Adopting the scientific method may have its limits, however, because it can only grasp as much as its tools allow and will measure only what it is designed to measure (Barry, 1982). Our knowledge of the phenomenon is thus limited to what the scientific tools are designed to show. Consequently, we may miss additional factors that explain the health-related issue and means to address it.

Exclusive reliance on a scientific method may result in a reductionist attitude, a belief that the whole can be understood completely by analyzing its parts, or that a process can be explained as the result of earlier, simpler stages. It also may downplay sociopolitical factors and the role of social reform in health.

TOWARD THE DEVELOPMENT OF AN ANALYTIC FRAMEWORK

The 10 justifications presented in this chapter represent some of the major ethical principles or moral grounds for intervening in people's courses of life or in their social institutions. These justifications, each of which may consist of a series of different types of rationales or ethical approaches, can help identify corresponding social values embedded in an intervention and its components. These justifications can be identified in the official goals and explanations given as to why a publicly sponsored communication campaign has been launched and why particular populations are targeted by it. As such, the justifications serve as a major facet in the analytic framework presented in the following chapter. Table 2.1 presents the justifications and ethical principles or approaches associated with them and examples of corresponding social values. The framework developed in the next chapter draws on how the justifications can be applied to each facet of the intervention. Because the justifications presented in this chapter primarily represent a Western approach to morality, this becomes one of the framework's limitations and needs to be noted.

NOTES

1. Campbell (1990) began a chapter titled "Education or Indoctrination?" with the question "Is health education justifiable?" (p. 15). This question has been adapted here to the context of health communication interventions. The purpose of this chapter is not to make a case for why health communication interventions are justified but to describe the kinds of values emphasized implicitly or explicitly and used as justifiable reasons for implementing such interventions.

2. The notion of fairness carries different interpretations. This will be further discussed in the elaboration of the justification of justice and fairness, which follows.

3. The monetary benefit cost justification for prevention, although often presented as a compelling argument by proponents of health prevention programs, is disputed on economic grounds by some who claim, for example, that having people live longer is not necessarily a benefit from an economic perspective.

4. Since the time of the Greeks, philosophers have written about the theoretical side of values. Today, the word *axiology* (from the Greek *axis,* meaning "worthy") is used to refer to the study of

the general theory of values. The study of ethics is a specialized field in the study of values in human conduct and focuses on the nature of morality (Barry, 1982).

5. Some authors prefer to use the terms *medical ethics* or *biomedical ethics.*

6. Clearly, there is an overlap, and the values discussed by Rokeach (1973) and others address some of the same core constructs. Because the context of interventions is purposeful change in the name of health, the focus here is on justifications or moral reasons why a change should be undertaken within one's social context. Additional or alternative constructs of values can be added to the framework, the purpose of which is to serve as a heuristic tool to examine values embedded in interventions.

7. Manning (1992) adds that justifications are usually self-serving. Analyses of the choice of intervention strategies might reveal that certain strategies are chosen because the planners or implementers are familiar with them or like them, rather than because they believe they are the most effective.

8. Among reasons cited for using theory in the design of health interventions is that without theory, one would tend to apply one's favorite methods, and the assessment of the success of the intervention would be limited (Leviton, 1989). Similarly, specifying values and making justifications explicit would be important: They can be scrutinized and used as criteria for judgment of worth and evaluation.

9. The literature reviewed in this book is mostly confined to the United States context.

10. The purpose of normative ethical theorizing is to introduce clarity and ways of thinking and making decisions about morality. Ethical theory thus consists, according to some authors' definitions, of the philosophical reasons for or against a set of reflections about morality. *Morality* is the tradition of what is believed to be right and wrong in human conduct and is seen as a social code, grounded in a historical context, rather than as an individual belief (Beauchamp, 1994).

11. Contemporary discussions of consequentionalism tend to distinguish between two kinds of utilitarianism: *act utilitarianism,* according to which people ought to act to produce the greatest balance of good over evil, everyone considered, and *rule utilitarianism,* according to which a person ought to act in accordance with the rule that, if generally followed, would produce the greatest balance of good over evil. These discussions mainly discard another type of consequential theory, called *ethical egoism,* in which the basic principle is that a person ought to act to promote his or her own self-interest (Mappes & Zembaty, 1991). Mill's (1863/1978) book on Utilitarianism is considered to have had a major influence on the development of this theory. Mill's work diverged from Jeremy Bentham's (see Beauchamp, 1994), also a major writer on this topic (and who was Mill's teacher), whose justification of utility was based more on self-interest. Mill's conceptualization of utility put more of an emphasis on the belief that most people have a basic desire for unity and harmony with each other rather than purely desiring gratification of personal interest (Beauchamp, 1994).

12. The word *deontology* comes from the Greek *deon,* meaning obligation or necessity, and deontology is the ethics of duty (Rayner & Cantor, 1987). An ethical theory provides an ordered set of moral standards or a framework that can be used to assess what is morally right or wrong and that can be used to help people determine what they morally ought to do. In contemporary ethical discussion, ethical theories usually are grouped into two basic and mutually exclusive types: teleological and deontological (Mappes & Zembaty, 1991). Although distinctions are made between the two major types of approaches, distinctions are also made between different types of approaches within them, as well.

13. Deontological principles typically are those that cannot be reduced to interests in achieving particular goods or values, and teleological ones, those that can be so reduced (Engelhardt, 1986). According to John Rawls (as cited in Engelhardt, 1986), what distinguishes between them is that a deontological theory either does not specify the good independently from the right or does not interpret the right as maximizing the good. Within teleological theories, "the good is defined independently from the right, and the right is defined as that which maximizes the good" (p. 24). Within deontological approaches, there are variations in the consideration given to

the consequences of action according to the way principles and rules are viewed. Some follow Kant's philosophy of moral imperatives or universal laws, focusing on whether duties and rights can be seen as absolute standards or as strong prima facie moral demands—a duty that is always to be acted on unless it conflicts on a particular occasion with an equal or stronger duty—depending on circumstances or competing moral claims. The question is whether there are some ethical principles that are more basic or carry more weight than others (Beauchamp, 1994).

14. This is not an attempt to provide even a brief overview of ethical theory. Numerous articles and books are devoted to the subject.

15. Some authors note different types of contextualist ethics of care held by other cultures or certain groups of African Americans (Stack, 1993).

16. It may also be possible to associate care with the justification of responsibility and virtue discussed later, although Pellegrino (1993) distinguishes between a virtue-based and a care-based ethic. Nevertheless, if we accept the notion of care as a special kind of commitment in which one feels compelled (thus obligated) without formal ethical imperative, and if this feeling is not based on formal demands, then care can be seen as akin to a certain conceptualization of virtue.

17. Pellegrino (1993) suggests that the ethic of care is an attractive alternative ethical approach for health professionals but because it is subject to wide interpretations, it needs further grounding in rules or principles.

18. Doing no harm, or nonmaleficence, is not always treated as an independent principle and may be set in the larger context of doing good. As T. L. Beauchamp (1994) explains, "the range of duties requiring abstention from harm and positive assistance may be conveniently clustered under the single heading of the principle of beneficence" (p. 30). Some bioethicists see the principles as distinct, with philosophical reasons for separating the passive "do no harm" from the active "do good," which may conflict. Some even see an actual hierarchical order between them; this may be problematic, however (see Beauchamp & Childress, 1994; Veatch, 1982; or Beauchamp, 1994, for a discussion).

19. The word *iatro* comes from the Greek *iatreia,* which means healing; combined with *genic, iatrogenic* means an adverse condition that comes from or is caused by healing or medical treatment.

20. The ethical dilemmas on inadvertent harm in Chapter 6 further elaborate the notion of causing potential harm and Illich's (1975) notion of social and cultural iatrogenesis.

21. This is expanded in numerous other places, including the literature that draws on a feminist perspective.

22. Illich (1975) extends the concept of iatrogenesis to include what he calls clinical, social, and cultural iatrogenesis. See a series of essays that demonstrates how iatrogenesis can take place among various health professionals (Morgan, 1983). Seidman and Rappaport (1986a) explain that "the very problem definitions that provide sanction for 'helping' may be at the root of iatrogenic effects of every variety because how we see the problem will determine how we try to solve it" (p. 6).

23. The potential iatrogenic effect of health as a value is further elaborated in Chapter 6.

24. See Wallerstein and Bernstein (1988), two issues of *Health Education Quarterly* (Volume 21, Numbers 2 & 3), and an issue of *Health Education Research* (Wallerstein & Bernstein, 1995) devoted to this topic. Rappaport has also written succinctly on this topic (e.g., Rappaport, 1981). An elaboration of a duality that may be embedded in the justification of community involvement is presented in Chapter 5.

25. Though note that legal interpretations may vary, and several authors make certain distinctions between them.

26. Telling the truth is an important type of contractual agreement between people in society in general and in the development of relationships of trust between health providers and their clients. Some providers believe it is best not to tell certain clients what they consider the truth about their prognoses. This implies that the practitioner knows what "truth" is and raises the issues of how truth is defined and whose knowledge base provides the real truth. In the case of health, should the

so-called truth include various institutional aspects, for example, explanations of how certain policies were formed, the role of insurance companies, the politics and regulations involved, and so on?

27. Dan Beauchamp (1987) argues that a "chief purpose of public policy is to cope with what Brian Barry calls the standard liberal fallacy: the fallacy that what is in the interest of the individual is also in the interest of the community" (p. 70).

28. Much of Daniels's (1985) discussion is in the context of risks at the workplace, though he also refers to the area of prevention in health in general. His argument is that individuals who work in sites that are known to put them at relatively high risk for safety hazards are likely to have chosen their jobs because of limited opportunities, although they might say they have freely chosen them.

29. See also Bok (1978) on paternalism and lying in medical and other contexts.

30. The discussion of coercive or regulative strategies in the next chapter further elaborates these issues.

31. Although smoking cessation may decrease the cost of treating certain smoking-related diseases, some, perhaps cynically, argue that the relatively early death of smokers is beneficial financially because companies and the government will have to pay less for their retirement and social security.

32. See Braithwaite (1994) on the differences between egalitarian and libertarian approaches to justice.

33. This, according to Whitehead (1992), is adapted from an unpublished report of the World Health Organization.

34. Whitehead (1992) distinguishes between inevitable or unavoidable health differences and those that are unnecessary and unfair, and he identifies seven main health determinants: (a) natural or biological variation, (b) freely chosen health-damaging behaviors, (c) transient health advantages as a result of health practices that allow the less advantaged to catch up fairly soon, (d) health-damaging behavior where the degree of choice of lifestyle is severely restricted, (e) exposure to unhealthy stressful living and working conditions, (f) inadequate access to essential health and other public services, and (g) health-related social mobility, where sick people move down the social scale. Societies would not be held responsible in terms of justice or fairness for health differences of the first three categories, but inequalities resulting from the next three categories would be considered as avoidable and the resultant health differences as unjust. Regarding inequalities associated with the seventh category, the original cause for ill health might be seen as unavoidable, but the outcome can be seen as preventable and thus unjust.

35. An important issue in health promotion is resource allocation. Facing limited resources, decisions need to be made regarding what kinds of services should be provided by the system and what kinds should be prioritized. Critics of the current U.S. health care system argue that it is biased in favor of high-technology acute care and tends to ignore preventive measures, and that policymakers tend to be more willing to

> impose cutbacks on a program most of whose recipients are poor young women and children, or to cut back on preventive measures, like nutritional programs in the schools, or environmental protection and enforcement, than to alter our practices with regard to the chronically ill and dying elderly. The issue here is not just one of old versus young, but reflects a prominent view in our class-divided society about who are the "deserving" poor. (Daniels, 1985, p.15)

This concern can be applied to the context of health interventions; what topics should be covered, and are the interventions funded adequately and fairly?

36. Schwartz (1994), in a study based on Rokeach's work, proposes a distinction of eight types of motivational values derived from universal human needs for existence associated with the physical survival of the individual and its dependence on social interaction: prosocial, restrictive, conformity, enjoyment, achievement, maturity, self-direction, security, and power. Others focus on values such as compassion, materialism, and religiosity. From a different perspective, Warwick

and Kelman (1973) identify four core values as central to the American tradition: freedom, justice, welfare, and security. The first two can be seen as analogous to the ethical principles of autonomy and justice discussed as major justifications in the discussion to follow; welfare corresponds to the ethical principle of beneficence, and security or survival can be seen as related to autonomy. They also mention truth telling and duty (which can be associated with personal responsibility); political power (autonomy); private enterprise (market autonomy); political order and social stability (the public good); and cultural styles, traditions, religious values, and kinship (the public good and social integration, or perhaps in a category of its own, which can be characterized as the justification of culture and tradition).

3

"They Are Always There"

Values in Intervention Facets

They are always there, the value judgments: the choices in policy decisions, in deciding what it is you are going to study, and deciding what it is that is a problem that needs the attention of the public health department, or the CDC, or whatever. There are always choices made. You can't avoid them. I guess the argument I would raise is that perhaps in a lot of these situations we would be better off if only we would pay attention to the values that seem to drive those choices, or to influence those choices in some situations. We ought to make them explicit.

—Reinhard Priester, formerly at the Center for Biomedical Ethics,
University of Minnesota (personal communication, 1993)

The purpose of this chapter is to present a perspective and conceptual tools for examining embedded values in public health communication interventions. Two major assumptions guide the development of its analytic approach. The first is that values are embedded not only in interventions' goals and objectives but in every component of the intervention process (Hornik, 1990; Paisley, 1989; Salmon, 1989, 1992; Warwick & Kelman, 1973). The second is that, as Suchman (1967) explains, value orientations "do much to determine the objectives of public service programs, the kinds of program operations that may be established, and the degree of success achieved by these programs" (p. 33). In other words, values determine the choices of goals, strategies, and evaluation criteria.

What can help us think about intervention goals in analytic terms as they relate to social values? Rogers and Storey (1987) suggest that for analytic purposes, it is important to identify the locus of the intervention: whether the intervention aims to change individual beliefs or behaviors or influence societal or structural processes. Another important facet of the intervention is the type of strategy adopted to carry out the goal of the intervention, which Rogers and Storey characterize as the locus of strategy: specifically, whether the intervention aims to affect changes through mandatory (i.e., regulations) or voluntary practices. A third important facet is what stakeholders are most likely to benefit from the intervention, or as Rogers and Story suggest, the locus of benefit derived from the intervention's outcomes: whether the main beneficiaries of the intervention are individuals, particular groups, organizations, or society as a whole. This analytic approach is illustrated in Figure 3.1. Each facet is presented as an axis and can be considered as a continuum. The locus of the change is defined according to whether the desired change is to occur on the individual or societal level. The locus of the strategy specifies whether the intervention strategy uses mandatory or voluntary practices. The locus of the benefit is again defined according to which level of stakeholders is likely to gain from the intervention's outcomes (e.g., individuals, groups, organizations, or society). To this, a fourth axis is added, the locus of evaluation, drawing from the work of Warwick and Kelman (1973; see discussion to follow) regarding the extent to which the assessment of outcomes or the determination of success focuses on individual-level or on organizational or societal-level indicators. A specific intervention can be located at any point in the four-dimensional space.[1]

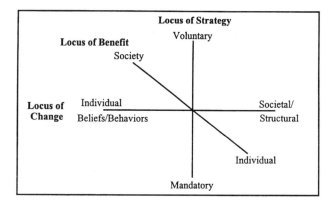

Figure 3.1. Dimensions of Intervention Objectives
SOURCE: Adapted from Rogers and Storey (1987).

Warwick and Kelman (1973) make similar distinctions between four facets of social interventions, which correspond to Rogers and Storey's (1987) locus of the intervention. The four facets they outline are (a) the choice of goals to which the change effort is directed, (b) the definition of the target of change, (c) the choice of means used to implement the intervention, and (d) the assessment of the consequences of the intervention. Their discussion introduces an additional consideration: ethical concerns. Each intervention aspect, they explain, raises major ethical issues that may involve conflicting values, thus raising questions about what values should be maximized at the expense of others. Values are thus a pivotal factor in each of the intervention components and influence all stages of the intervention process:

> Value systems do not merely influence program goals and objectives. They influence all stages of the intervention process. Thus, the intervention strategy that one chooses (e.g., a persuasive strategy vs. a coercive strategy) will be influenced by one's values (balancing of freedom and social welfare), as will the decision to target an intervention on only a segment of the population (equal opportunity and accessibility versus pragmatism), and so on." (Jaccard et al., 1990, p. 105)

INTERVENTION FACETS

The analytic framework developed in this chapter consists of six major facets: (a) *justifications:* why were certain goals, solutions, or evaluation criteria chosen; (b) the *locus of the problem:* at what level was the problem conceived; (c) the *locus of the solution:* what did the intervention aim to change; (d) *strategies:* what methods were employed; (e) the *locus of the evaluation:* what were the criteria for success; and last, (f) *ethical concerns:* what ethical concerns were associated with the intervention. Table 3.1 presents the six main intervention facets and examples of value-laden aspects associated with them.

Locus of the Problem

Because, as reiterated in the previous chapters, health-related problems are not problems until they are characterized as such, identifying how a problem is defined *by the interventionists* is analytically of primary importance.[2] For example, even the way a specific disease is defined can have profound implications for particular populations. This has been illustrated in the changing definition of AIDS, which has expanded from being restricted to symptoms

Table 3.1 Dimensions of Intervention Objectives and Examples of Value-Laden Aspects

Intervention Facets	Examples of Value-Laden Aspects
Justifications	What are the implicit and explicit claims or moral grounds for intervening?
	What ethical principles or social values serve as the basis for these claims?
	What values are prioritized in the use of these justifications? What values are not prioritized?
	Are there other cherished values that conflict with those used to justify the intervention?
Locus of the problem	What values are associated with the way the problem has been conceived by dominant stakeholders?
	Who is mainly perceived as entitled to be helped?
	What social factors are believed to be the cause of the problem and thus require an intervention?
Locus of the solution	What and whom does the intervention aim to influence, and what values are associated with this?
	What does the intervention *not* aim to influence, and what values are associated with this?
	Who will mainly benefit from the intervention?
	Whose rights may be infringed upon?
Methods and strategies	What are the costs and benefits associated with each method in terms of values?
	Why were specific strategies chosen and others not, and what values are associated with these choices?
Locus of the evaluation	What are the grounds or justifications for the intervention and its methods?
	What indicates whether the intervention was successful; what is considered important, and what values are associated with this?
	What unintended effects may have occurred, and how are they identified?
	Did the intervention contribute to advancing important social values?
Ethical concerns	What ethical concerns are associated with each facet of the intervention?
	How do the ethical concerns relate to widely held social values associated with the intervention?
	What ethical concerns are acknowledged and addressed and how?

associated with the manifestation of the disease in males to including symptoms particular to women. This expansion finally allowed the provision of official benefits to women, who were previously denied them (Clarke, 1994).

Social problems are time, place, and context bound. The way the health issue is framed as a problem (or not) is likely to reflect certain priorities or ideologies of the more dominant stakeholders (Mackey-Kallis & Hahn, 1991; Seidman & Rappaport, 1986b). The mere identification of the problem itself presents a value judgment: the particular view of the ideal state is what determines what is considered problematic, thus requiring action (Warwick & Kelman, 1973). Is the problem conceived as poor motivation on the part of individuals who do not adopt recommended practices? Perhaps the problem is a result of structural socioeconomic conditions, such as limited access of smokers to smoking-cessation programs. Alternately, the locus of the problem (e.g., drug abuse) may be associated with a high prevalence of families in the community with what are considered dysfunctional relations among their members. Causes of health problems can thus be characterized according to different levels, ranging from the individual to the societal.

Seven levels have been defined for the purpose of developing this framework: (a) individual, (b) family, (c) organizational, (d) community, (e) marketplace, (f) societal-structural, and (g) cultural or normative (adapted from Hornik, 1990; Paisley, 1989; Rogers & Storey, 1987; Salmon, 1989; Winett et al., 1989). They are specified in Table 3.2 and described in the discussion to follow. The distinctions between the different levels help to explicate embedded values and theories. The use of the word *values,* when making distinctions between intervention levels, serves to remind us that there are divergent positions on what interventions *should* and *can* do (Winett et al., 1989). For example, the locus problem can be identified at different levels, as a lifestyle issue versus an issue mainly associated with societal structures and distribution of resources. This has "not only theoretical importance but strong political and economic connotations" (p. 41). Because the definition of problems and solutions is essentially a value-laden process, it carries with it the following implications:

> Approaching problems in certain ways can have great impact on societal priorities, policies, and resource expenditure. Defining a problem and placing the problem in a value and conceptual context brings a continual and unending tension in the field. There is no one correct position. For example, for every problem there are likely to be individual, interpersonal, organizational, environmental, and institutional mechanisms. Focusing on one level—one definition of the problem and a set

Table 3.2   Locus of Problem and Solution Types: Example, Cigarette Smoking

Problem Locus	Example of Presumed Causes	Solution Locus	Example of Strategies
Individual	Peer pressure on youth to smoke; addiction of smokers unable to quit on their own	Individual	Teaching refusal skills among youth; providing smoking cessation activities
Family	Smoking among family members; lack of support for smokers who want to quit	Family	Providing education on the effects of smoking on significant others, especially children; providing training in social support
Organizational	Workplace routines that allow for smoking breaks as a way to segment the work pace; high prevalence of employees who smoke; no restriction on smoking in the workplace	Organizational	Banning smoking in the workplace; allowing for non-smoking breaks; providing group support activities; establishing an incentive plan for smoke cessation; providing alternative breaks in work routines
Community	Many commercial outlets in the community where kids can purchase cigarettes; extensive promotion of cigarettes in the community	Community	Banning billboard advertising and point-of-purchase marketing; providing school education programs; promoting legislation to limit marketing and distribution of cigarettes in the community
Marketplace	Sophisticated marketing strategies of tobacco companies particularly aimed at children and youth, women, and minorities	Marketplace	Using excise taxes; banning vending machines accessible to children; restricting promotional activities; providing incentives for alternative products
Societal	Large profits from tobacco products, which support individuals, corporations, and government activities	Societal	Legislating taxes of tobacco products; restricting advertising in mass media; eliminating subsidies for tobacco growers; supporting alternative ways to use tobacco or substitute it with other crops
Cultural-normative	History of tobacco products as part of the identity of certain geographical areas and populations; cultural tendencies to indulge in addictive substances and to view smoking as a personal right	Cultural-normative	Aiming to influence norms regarding tolerance of promotional strategies of the tobacco companies and changing attitudes regarding regulatory policies; influencing norms and beliefs regarding ways to cope with personal stress and stressful life conditions; stressing the violation of the rights of nonsmokers

of theories and values—may undermine the viability of other analyses. (Winett et al., 1989, p. 41)

Having a framework that outlines pertinent levels or loci of intervention and analysis[3] can help analysts and practitioners identify where the intervention mainly identifies the source of the problem, how its main causes have been framed, and the extent to which the strategies employed correspond to the way the problem has been defined.

1. *Individual:* Identifying the locus of the problem at the individual or interpersonal level assumes a primary cause of the problem is rooted in the way individuals think, behave, or interact. For example, the assumption would be that people engage in what are considered high-risk behaviors either because they are not aware of the danger they entail, they lack personal motivation to engage in health-promoting practices, or they have peers who are likely to induce them to engage in risky practices.

2. *Family:*[4] Identifying the locus of the problem at the family level assumes a main cause of the problem is rooted in what occurs at the family level. For example, risky behaviors are a result of lack of family support of health-promoting behaviors, or living in families with dysfunctional relationships induces the consumption of hazardous substances.

3. *Organizational:* Identifying the locus of the problem at the organizational level assumes a main or major cause of the problem is rooted in organizational arrangements or practices. For example, the problem is associated with people not having the time or facilities at their work sites to engage in physical activities or that food offered at work site is low in nutritional value and high in calories and saturated fats.

4. *Community:* Identifying the locus of the problem at the community level assumes that a main cause of the problem is rooted in what occurs at the community level: for example, the assumption that there is a high prevalence of substance abuse in certain communities because of their limited educational, recreational, and employment opportunities for youth.

5. *Marketplace:* Identifying the locus of the problem in the marketplace. For example, analysis may indicate food products high in calories and fats are more profitable and thus more heavily marketed, whereas more nutritious food products, such as lower-fat meats are more expensive, thus less accessible.

6. *Societal-Structural:* Identifying the locus of the problem at this level assumes that much of the problem is rooted in societal or structural processes. For example, it is believed that (a) poorer health outcomes are causally linked to disparities in employment and housing opportunities, (b) the political power and economic wealth of certain industries or corporations are believed to ensure the dominance of particular products and their prolific marketing within and across nations, (c) discriminatory norms and practices regarding certain populations and limited access to health care resources of particular populations result in adverse health outcomes for these disadvantaged populations, and (d) an economic and political system that gives preference to corporate interests creates unsafe physical and social environments.

7. *Cultural or Normative:* Identifying the locus of the problem in cultural or normative processes assumes a main cause of the problem can be found in cultural or normative customs or beliefs and values. For example, people's beliefs about causes of health and illness or role expectations influence their use of screening activities and adherence to treatment recommendations. Cultural practices may be associated with practices perceived as harmful by others, such as taboos regarding discussing certain topics, or cultural traditions regarding gender roles and family relations may affect people's health-promoting behaviors.

Once definitions of problems and the factors associated with them are accepted, and even institutionalized, certain types of problem definition and strategies are likely to be given priority over other alternatives by researchers or the intervention practitioners. By specifying the level in the Locus of the Problem and Solution facets, we can make more explicit some of the implicit value-laden assumptions or hidden arguments, following Tesh's (1988) articulation, about the causes of the problems and the value-laden priorities embedded in them.

Locus of the Solution

As in the Locus of the Problem, the way solutions to the problem are defined is also linked to values. These can be characterized along the same seven levels, as well:

Individual: Identifying the locus of change or solution at the individual level assumes that an appropriate way to address the problem should be done at the individual level. For example, children should be taught refusal skills to withstand peer pressure regarding substance abuse.

Family: Identifying the locus of solution at the family level assumes that an appropriate way to address the problem should be done at the family level. For example, family members should be helped to develop social support skills to help a family member quit smoking, or family dynamics should be modified to reduce friction and abuse.

Organizational: Identifying the locus of solution as involving organizational factors assumes that a central way to address the problem should be done at the organizational level. For example, interventions should help workplaces implement smoking cessation programs, develop policies regarding smoke-free work sites, or provide nutritious lunch menus.

Community: Identifying the locus of solution with community aspects assumes that an appropriate way to address the problem should be done at the community level, for example, working with community members and policymakers to promote legislation that restricts cigarette vending machines in the community, enhancing community resources associated with activities for children and youth after-school activities, and working toward economic growth and a wide availability of jobs in the community.

Marketplace: Identifying the locus of solution in the marketplace assumes that an appropriate way to address the problem should be done at the marketplace level, for example, increasing taxes on and restricting marketing strategies of disease-causing products, decreasing subsidies associated with the growth or production of these substances,[5] offering incentives for health-promoting products or services, and mandating health insurance to adopt policies that would encourage the implementation and practice of certain preventive procedures.

Societal-Structural: Identifying the locus of solution with societal or structural factors assumes that an appropriate way to address the problem should be done at the societal level, for example, changing the way corporations influence the legislative process, changing the organization of health care insurance, and influencing the causes of socioeconomic differences.

Cultural or Normative: Identifying the locus of solution with cultural or normative factors assumes that the problem should be addressed through cultural or normative processes, for example, reinforcing social norms regarding protecting those who are vulnerable, nonsupport of excessive alcohol consumption, or support for the enactment or enforcement of restrictive policies.

Many public health communication interventions aim at individual, interpersonal, or family levels of intervention. Critics maintain that the success of programs that exclusively focus on these levels is inevitably limited in scope, although many individuals may benefit from such programs. They may even become victim blaming if they do not address other levels of intervention, such as those associated with marketplace, organizational, or structural factors. Environmental or social conditions are likely to impose too many obstacles, particularly to those who are less economically and socially advantaged, to adopting, and more so, to maintaining, recommended practices (E. R. Brown, 1991). For health interventions to be both successful and equitable, individuals need—in addition to education about topics such as nutritious foods or the hazards of smoking—social and environmental conditions that provide them with the necessary opportunities to enable their long-term adoption of the recommended behaviors (Daniels, 1985; McLeroy et al., 1988).[6]

The locus of change is not a static dimension. It may differ at different stages of the intervention, or several loci may be pursued simultaneously. These changes may be interrelated, as Rogers and Storey (1987) suggest, because even small changes at the national level require individual-level changes on a relatively large scale, to get people to think of their own behaviors in the larger context of the national good. Table 3.2 illustrates how the issue of smoking can be conceived as a problem located on different levels, ranging from individual to societal factors, and how solutions to it can also be conceived on different levels of intervention. Unfortunately, despite the recognition of multilevel causes, proposed solutions often concentrate on narrower levels of intervention. Although it is understandable that many interventions cannot aim to address broad structural causes, if they are not taken into consideration in design and analysis, the intervention is likely to result in limited effects and skewed evaluations.

Strategies

Various methods or strategies can be employed for the purpose of achieving the goals of a public health communication intervention. Strategies may include the use of fear arousal appeals, asking individuals to put social pressure on others, or teaching people skills such as the use of self-monitoring devices, conducting self-early-detection exams, or managing persuasive social interactions. Values clearly play a central role in the choice and application of such strategies (Hornik, 1990; Wallack, 1989; Warwick & Kelman, 1973), and as Warwick and Kelman suggest, values that underlie particular strategies may conflict:

> Questions about the morality of coercion, manipulation, deception, persuasion, and other methods of inducing change typically involve a conflict between the values of individual freedom and self-determination, on one hand, and such values as social welfare, economic progress, or equal opportunity, on the other hand. (p. 380)

The following categories can help distinguish between intervention strategies (adapted from Hornik, 1991; Paisley, 1989; Salmon, 1989; Schmid, Pratt, & Howze, 1995; Winett et al., 1989): (a) engineering or environmental control, (b) power-based or enforcement, (c) incentives, (d) persuasion or education, (e) collaboration, and (f) facilitation or empowerment.

Engineering and Environmental-Type Solutions: Environmental and engineering-type solutions are strategies that emphasize measures that control or modify the social and physical environment to foster and maintain behavior changes (Schmid et al., 1995; Schmitt, 1996) or so-called built-in mechanisms that influence target audiences' behaviors. These may include safety caps on medications, road design that channels traffic in ways that prevent collisions, or seat belts that automatically engulf the passenger (see Paisley, 1989) or "passive" restrictions on movement to promote increased physical activity, such as restricting downtown centers to pedestrians and bicycle traffic, connecting residential and business areas with walking paths (King et al., 1995), or fortifying foods or water with particular additives to ensure that people will consume them (e.g., fortification of food products with folic acid to increase the chance that pregnant women will consume enough to prevent a common birth defect; Kolata, 1996). Some environmental-level interventions center more on making products or services aimed to promote people's health more available or accessible, such as securing physical sites for local residents to exercise or have walking clubs (Schmid et al., 1995, Schmitt, 1996).

Power-Based or Enforcement-Type Strategies: Power-based strategies typically rely on regulations and their enforcement to influence people's behavior or on the restriction or regulation of the availability or production of certain substances or products. Their enforcement tends to depend on a threat of some kind of punishment, sometimes referred to as disincentives. Regulatory methods may consist of fines, loss of privileges (e.g., loss of driving license; loss of commercial sales license), bans (e.g., no smoking allowed in certain areas), taxation or regulations regarding the content and restriction of marketing methods for certain products, and restriction of access to certain products or limiting participation in certain activities (e.g., minimal age requirements for purchase of alcohol and tobacco products).

Incentives for Actions or Behaviors: Incentives operate on the flip-side assumption of coercive approaches; it is presumed that people will be more likely to adopt or avoid specific practices if they believe the action will be accompanied by a desired reward or if they are provided with a specific enticement to make it more attractive. Similarly, incentives can serve as a means to reinforce and maintain the health-promoting behavior. Incentives can include taxation, subsidies, decreased fees, and revenue policies that favor those who adopt the recommended behavior or practice, or they can take the form of prizes, bonuses, or monetary, symbolic, or other types of rewards.[7] For example, work sites may offer rewards for workers who have managed to quit smoking or companies may be provided with subsidies for the development, production, and marketing of particular health-promoting products, such as protective helmets or low-fat food products. Norway, for example, has successfully implemented a nutrition and food policy that incorporates incentives.

Persuasion or Education: Dissemination of persuasive messages and information that explains why one should adopt recommended practices, or avoid those considered hazardous, are at the heart of most educational interventions. Educational strategies can range from presenting data on estimated risk from particular diseases and providing messages to counter what are considered risk-promoting persuasive appeals (e.g., alcohol and cigarette advertisements) to teaching the acquisition of particular skills (e.g., self-exams; advocacy skills). Although the messages of educational efforts may often seem as if they are neutral, they typically can be viewed as a persuasive endeavor, even if they do not seem to use blatant persuasive appeals. The mere selection of certain facts and their presentational style encompasses persuasive elements. Furthermore, educational messages often use fear appeals or present a recommended concrete plan of action. Educational efforts may employ interpersonal and mass media channels and rely on strategies ranging from the use of peer educators to public relations and advertising techniques. Educational activities can employ a variety of communication channels. These include interpersonal communication, group interactions, lectures, community events, flyers, posters, products, warning labels on commercially manufactured products, and messages disseminated in the mass media through ads and news and entertainment programs.

Collaboration: Increasingly, interventions are a collaborative effort. This is particularly evident when interventions are implemented at the community level, even when launched by national organizations or national or state agencies. This requires collaboration with local or community-based agencies. Similarly, a not-for-profit organization may enlist the support of a for-profit organization to collaborate on the dissemination of particular messages, as illustrated in the collaboration between the American Health Association's campaign with several food-producing companies or the National Cancer Institute's collaboration with Kellogg, a cereal-manufacturing company (Freimuth, Hammond, & Stein, 1988). Another type of collaboration often takes place when several organizations share an interest in certain intervention topics and decide that it would be more efficient to work together. For example, organizations that work to promote women's health may collaborate on an intervention to promote early breast cancer screening, or organizations whose mission is to promote the health of children may work together to promote a children's immunization campaign.[8]

Facilitation or Empowerment: The major assumptions underlying most facilitation or empowerment approaches are that people can and should be given the means to make decisions about what should be done to promote their well-being and that they should be able to accomplish these largely on their own. A prerequisite for this accomplishment is for those who are in decision-making or helping positions to make changes in the social and physical environments of the target population that will facilitate this type of activity. Facilitation and empowerment can thus take place through what has been characterized in the community development and health education literature as capacity building. This approach has strong ideological undertones but may draw from divergent sources ranging from psychological theory that focuses on constructs of self-efficacy to social movement and social change theories.[9]

The strategies specified in this framework are not mutually exclusive; several types of strategies may be used in the same intervention to attain particular goals (Hornik, 1990; Winett et al., 1989) or may be employed at different stages of an intervention. Most interventions, however, emphasize certain strategic approaches. Table 3.3 provides examples of activities associated with each strategy type.

Ethical Concerns and Justifications Embedded in Strategies[10]

The use of any of the particular strategic approaches raises ethical concerns. Engineering, enforcement, incentives, and even educational, collaboration, and facilitation strategies raise concerns regarding the use of coercive or persuasive measures that may infringe on personal autonomy or privacy. Engineering strategies may be justified on the basis of utility and the public good. As Schmid et al. (1995) maintain, it "is unreasonable to expect large proportions of the population to make individual behavior changes that are discouraged by the environment and existing social norms" (p. 1207). Their wide use, however, can infringe on the principle of respect for autonomy. Similarly, strategies that restrict access to substances considered harmful, such as tobacco or alcohol, are viewed as highly effective preventive measures for particularly vulnerable populations, such as children (Sweanor et al., 1992). As such, these restrictive strategies may be viewed as morally justified. Other restrictive policies, however, may raise our objections. For example, Japan's governmental decision in 1992 to restrict access to oral contraceptives—despite positive recommendations of its own medical advisory committee and their use in other countries—would have been likely to raise reactions of disapproval, at least in U.S. culture, on the basis that this restriction violates citizens' rights to choose their

Table 3.3   Intervention Strategies and Examples

Strategy Type	Examples
Engineering	Built-in mechanisms; product design, such as "childproof" caps for medications; workplace food facilities that offer mainly low-fat meals; speed bumps on roads to slow traffic; air bags in motor vehicles; pathways and stairs that direct employees to walk from one site to another rather than use elevators; road dividers
Regulation-enforcement	Policies and laws regarding point-of-purchase activities, such as limiting the sale of single cigarettes; regulation regarding advertisements of alcohol, such as limiting ads on billboards in school vicinities; bans on promotion, such as bans on promotional products for tobacco that would appeal to kids; excise taxes on anti-health products, such as foods with higher fat content or alcohol and cigarettes; mandates, such as the requirement to wear a helmet when riding a motorcycle or bicycle or to use seat belts in an automobile, or to use infant car seats
Incentives	Subsidies for products considered health promoting, for example, physical activity equipment or safety helmets; tax breaks or low-interest loans for producers of products considered health promoting, such as food products rich with fiber and safety or disease-prevention products; tax and revenue policies regarding the provision of health and medical care services
Education-persuasion	Dissemination of messages through various communication channels, including interpersonal interactions, group activities, written materials, and mass media: for example, messages on the benefits of screening for diseases such as breast or colon cancer or educational programs on how to adopt certain practices, such as walking, for the purpose of increasing cardiovascular activity, or warning labels on the potential hazards of alcohol, or safety instructions on the operation of equipment
Collaboration	Working with other organizations to promote health: for example, collaboration between churches and voluntary organizations that work to prevent high blood pressure and health organizations that counsel and treat people with this medical condition; organizations can actually participate in the activities or can actively refer their members to another organization, which can provide them with information or services
Facilitation	Helping to enable the adoption of health-promotion activities or adaptation of the social and physical environment through capacity building of an organization; helping constituencies or enabling local residents to define and address health-related problems

method of contraception. According to several authors, one of the main justifications for the Japanese government's policy was that this would promote the use of condoms. The government was hoping that making the use of condoms the most viable option for contraception would help prevent the spread of sexually transmitted diseases, particularly AIDS (Jitsukawa & Djerassi, 1994; Weisman, 1992).[11]

Legislative regulatory measures tend to restrict the freedom of individuals or groups or the activities of producers and marketers of products, if their activities, though not illegal, are viewed as causing ill health (Campbell, 1987). Despite serious concerns regarding such regulatory or restrictive strategies, their proponents argue that these types of strategies are potentially more effective in achieving the goals of the intervention than educational strategies: "One stroke of effective health legislation is equal to many separate health intervention endeavors and the cumulative efforts of innumerable health workers over long periods of time" (McKinlay, 1975, p. 13). Lobbying for legislation that mandates smoke-free environments can be viewed as having a potentially larger impact on the smoking behavior of a large number of people than individual antismoking education (Hornik, 1990). Similarly, engineering-type solutions can be seen as effective health-promoting strategies (E. R. Brown, 1991). For example, redesigning roadways and improving the safety engineering of cars can significantly reduce automobile accidents and fatalities, independent of the actions of the drivers, and perhaps the Japanese government will indeed succeed in increasing the use of condoms for AIDS prevention.

Even incentives for actions or behaviors that are backed by legislative power or authorities may be viewed as potentially coercive. This is particularly true in work organizations in which members may feel compelled to adopt recommended practices. Yet the use of incentives may also be seen as leaving relatively more room for personal choice. Proponents of regulatory-type solutions claim that because individuals are surrounded by persuasive antihealth messages and environments, they are not really freely choosing unhealthy behaviors, and it is therefore justified to use more coercive strategies (Pinet, 1987). People's options for health-promoting choices could thus be increased by offering low-fat foods on restaurants' menus. These would further be supported by incentives. Restrictions on high-fat food, in contrast, may be justified on the basis of both utility and doing good, because these strategies would act to reduce barriers to good nutrition (Glanz et al., 1995).

An argument that seems counterintuitive but that is forcefully made by some proponents of regulatory strategies is that strategies that restrict access to practices considered unhealthy may be in fact *more* ethical than educational strategies. First, based on considerations of the ethical principle of *utility*, enforcement can be relatively more efficient. It has been documented that interventions that applied bans on cigarette vending machines or raised taxes on alcohol and cigarettes have proven to be relatively more effective compared to those that adopted only educational approaches (Beauchamp, 1988; Clayton, Cattarello, & Johnstone, 1996; Ennet, Tobler, Ringwalt, & Flewelling, 1994; Jason, Ji, Anes, & Birkhead, 1991; Kahn, 1994; Warner, 1986). As proposed in the first chapter, intervention strategies are not necessarily chosen because of their potential effectiveness, and they may be chosen as a political compromise or because they have a stronger link to certain social values over others. These kinds of considerations exasperate some advocates of regulatory policies, as alcohol abuse prevention advocates maintain: "Enormous and sustained sums would have to be spent on education to achieve even a fraction of what will follow from ecological interventions aimed at access, and from greater enforcement of drinking countermeasures" (Edwards, Anderson, Babor, Cassewell, et al., 1996, p. 479).

Second, in contrast to presumed common sense, regulatory strategies may be viewed as relatively *less* intrusive and less infringing on individual autonomy or privacy than some persuasive strategies. Regulations and restrictions may be viewed as minimally intrusive to individuals by placing restrictions on the marketplace as a whole or protecting the environment; thus paradoxically, their application may adhere to values associated with respect for privacy. They may be less likely to stigmatize particular individuals because they often consist of controls placed on the marketplace or the use of market goods in the public realm. Thus, their application aims to distribute the restrictions to all members of the population (Beauchamp, 1987). Dan Beauchamp goes on to explain that this minimal intrusion occurs because commercial regulations "and regulating public space operate generally and at a distance, not singling out one particular individual or another for moral improvement" (p. 77). Last, regulations can also effect distributive justice by working to redistribute resources and opportunities previously inequitably distributed in society (Daniels, 1985), thus advancing values associated with justice and equity.

Paternalistic measures are fraught with ethical concerns and raise questions regarding how justified it is to intervene in people's lifestyle choices that may affect health. Do people indeed suffer from diminished capacities to make rational decisions to such an extent that they need to be coerced to use seat belts while using cars or to wear protective helmets while riding on motorcycles? Many of the behaviors considered unhealthy or hazardous are associated with leisure activities or practices that are desirable and gratifying for individuals. Thus, "to intervene in these behaviors would require independent evidence that the behavior is the result of diminished capacity to make decisions, or in some specifiable way not voluntary" (Daniels, 1985, p.158). As grounds for making claims to justify the ethical basis of enforcement strategies, researchers and practitioners increasingly present evidence of what they consider manipulative persuasive and marketing strategies of tobacco and alcohol products—in particular, how these industries target children who are considered especially vulnerable and not fully competent to make autonomous choices.[12]

Milio's (1981) argument in support of public policies to promote health is similar to that of Daniels (1985) and draws on both the justifications of *justice and equity* and the requirement to afford people the opportunity to live in environments that foster health and minimize risk. This also echoes values associated with self-actualization as well as the public good. Health policy should not focus on health as an individual goal pursued according to personal desires of individuals but should be viewed in the context of providing citizens with environments that reduce what are perceived as risks for their health:

> The obligation of health policy, if it is to serve the health interests of the public, does not extend to assuring every individual the attainment of personally defined "health." In a democratic society that seeks at least internal equanimity, if not humanness and social justice, the responsibility of government is to establish environments that make possible an attainable level of health for the total population. This responsibility includes the assurance of environmental circumstances that do not impose more risks to health for some segments of the population than for others, for such inequality of risk would doom some groups of people—regardless of their choice—to a reduction in opportunities to develop their capacities. (Milio, 1981, p. 5)

Educational strategies, often the cornerstone of many public health communication campaigns, also raise ethical concerns regarding the use of persuasive techniques because the use of persuasion, by definition, reduces the ability of individuals to freely choose among options (Faden & Faden, 1978). Educa-

Illustration 3.1. Example of an ad on mammography.

tional strategies also raise ethical concerns regarding the extent to which their use may privilege those who have more resources and opportunities or the extent to which they may inadvertently stigmatize or negatively label those who do not adopt the recommended practices.[13] For example, messages calling for a yearly mammogram for women over a certain age may frustrate women whose health insurance only pays for such a test for every 2 years. Women who hear the message and would like to adopt its recommendation may feel they cannot personally afford the expense of the procedure.

Collaboration strategies also raise ethical concerns because they may privilege certain agencies or groups while excluding those who are marginalized. Groups with connections to funding organizations would be able to increase their resources, whereas others without these connections would be disadvantaged even further. Furthermore, collaborative efforts may in fact exploit the resources of voluntary organizations, which may find themselves providing services that should be provided by publicly funded agencies (Green, 1989).[14] Even facilitation strategies, which presumably embody values of autonomy and justice, can raise ethical concerns. For example, those who have been "empowered" may adopt goals that are incompatible with the public's good, or those who gained power through the facilitation process may not necessarily represent all other members of the community.[15] Examples are summarized in Table 3.4.

Locus of the Outcomes

Rogers and Storey (1987) suggest that an important dimension of the outcome of a campaign is its locus of benefit: Who is intended to gain from the intervention outcomes and who actually does. Beneficiaries of the intervention's

Table 3.4   Intervention Strategies: Examples of Potential Benefits From the Use of Strategies and Ethical Concerns Associated With Their Use

Type of Solution or Strategy	Examples of Potential Benefits	Examples of Ethical Concerns
Engineering	Prevents harm *[doing good]*	Restricts free choice *[autonomy]*
	Effects felt by most people *[justice-fairness, utility, the public good]*	Privileges certain stakeholders (e.g., those whose products are favored) *[justice-fairness, market autonomy]*
	Efficient *[utility]*	
	Avoids personal blame *[refraining from doing harm]*	
Enforcement-Regulation	Prevents harm *[doing good]* efficiently and effectively *[utility]*	Restricts personal choice by limiting people's and organizations' activities *[autonomy, market autonomy]*
	Affects marketplace availability rather than penalizing individuals *[justice-fairness, care]*	May unfairly penalize the economically or socially disadvantaged who have limited alternative gratifications *[justice-fairness]*
	Benefits the public as a whole *[the public good]*	
	Avoids personal blame *[refraining from doing harm]*	
Incentives	Promotes pro-health practices *[doing good]*	Restricts personal choice by introducing a highly persuasive appeal *[autonomy, market autonomy]*
	Affects marketplace availability of pro-health products or services *[justice-fairness, utility]*	May privilege those who are already economically or socially advantaged but is less available to those who are not *[justice-fairness]*
	Allows for relatively more choice than power-based methods *[autonomy]*	May provide a distraction from considering institutional factors that may affect the behavior and its causes *[framing, justice-fairness, utility]*
	Benefits the public *[the public good]*	

(continued)

Table 3.4   Continued

Type of Solution or Strategy	Examples of Potential Benefits	Examples of Ethical Concerns
Persuasion or education	Prevents harm or hazards that can adversely affect people's welfare [doing good]	Highly persuasive appeals restrict choice [autonomy]
	Allows for relatively more personal choice than power-based strategies [autonomy]	May privilege those who are economically or socially advantaged [justice-fairness]
	May benefit the public as a whole [the public good]	May contribute to blaming the victim or may provide a distraction from addressing institutional factors [doing harm, framing]
		May be less effective than other strategies [utility, public good]
Collaboration	Allows for choice [autonomy]	May privilege those who already have connections and resources [justice-fairness]
	Enhances resources [utility]	
	Benefits the public [the public good]	May deplete the resources of organizations or individuals [doing harm]
Facilitation-empowerment	Allows for choice [autonomy]	May adopt goals that conflict with the public good [public good]
	Enhances resources [utility]	
	Increases the power of those who were disenfranchised [justice-fairness]	May mainly enhance the power of those who already have relatively more power [justice-fairness]

NOTE: Values or ethical principles are in brackets and italicized.

outcomes, as in the definition of the problems and solutions, can be categorized according to the same categorization used when focusing on the locus of change: individuals, families, communities, organizations, the marketplace, or society as a whole. Table 3.5 provides examples of evaluation criteria according to different loci of analysis in the context of prevention of substance abuse.

Just as value-based judgments are embedded in the definition of the problem, they are also embedded in the assessment of the intervention's outcomes or its effectiveness. Warwick and Kelman (1973) explain the rationale for this

Table 3.5   Examples of Evaluation Criteria According to Locus of Analysis

Locus of Outcome-Evaluation	Examples of Evaluation Criteria Related to Substance Abuse Prevention
Individual	To what extent did children or youth acquire particular refusal skills; have more children and youth adopted anti-substance-abuse attitudes; have more enrolled in prevention programs?
Family	To what extent have family relations that contribute to substance abuse been modified; is there less tolerance for substance abuse within the family unit?
Organizational	To what extent have new substance abuse prevention policies been adopted; have prevention and treatment programs and facilities been established or improved?
Community	To what extent have community-based organizations supported or adopted the goals of substance abuse prevention in the community and found ways to work together on this issue; have policies such as the banning of alcohol advertising on local billboards been proposed and enforced; have educational and attractive leisure and employment opportunities for youth been developed and implemented?
Marketplace	To what extent have policies such as restricting point-of-purchase marketing in local commercial outlets and alcohol beverage server regulations been adopted and enforced; are fewer products being sold or consumed?
Societal-institutional	To what extent have structural conditions and the provision of opportunities for economically and socially disadvantaged populations taken place; to what extent have employment and labor conditions that create stressful conditions for workers taken place; have policies regarding the marketing and distribution of substances (including legal ones) been adopted and implemented?
Cultural-normative	To what extent have social norms regarding regulations and policies to restrict the production and promotion of substances and policies to support people who need treatment services been changed; to what extent have norms that support the consumption of substances been modified?

assumption: "Our assessment of the consequences of an intervention depends on what values we are willing or unwilling to sacrifice in the interest of social change" (p. 380). Using the analytic framework described in this book and a careful analysis of the stakeholders involved (Guba & Lincoln, 1981, 1989)[16] can help identify who does *not* benefit from the intervention or who benefits from an *ineffective* campaign (Salmon, 1989).[17] For example, alcohol and tobacco abuse prevention campaigns often rely on educational strategies. Yet interventions that employ engineering or enforcement-type strategies, such as the elimination of cigarette vending machines or further imposition of excise taxes, tend be more effective in decreasing the consumption of these substances (Feighery et al., 1991; Peterson, Zeger, Remington, & Anderson, 1992; Winett et al., 1989). The tobacco and alcohol industries may actually gain from interventions' emphasis on educational strategies (Salmon, 1989). In fact, these industries actively support educational efforts and messages that urge people not to drink and drive. It is not surprising, therefore, that these industries also support efforts to distribute messages to parents and children that suggest that children should not smoke or drink, with messages that such practices are associated with adulthood or may be risky. Clearly, these are not necessarily deterring messages for youth who strive for the trappings of adulthood or thrive on risk taking. These industries also support organizations that lobby for punitive legislation against drunk drivers viewed as criminals but vehemently oppose interventions that aim to restrict marketing and distribution practices (Glantz, 1996; Reinarman, 1988). Despite their denials, these industries, according to health advocates, specifically aim their marketing activities toward a teenaged target audience—the future market for their products (DiFranza et al., 1991).

The assessment of the intervention focuses on outcomes viewed as pertinent and important. Although they typically draw from the official goals of the intervention, the type of indicators chosen for evaluation may or may not correspond to the factors identified in the definition of the problem (Masergh, Rohrbach, Montgomery, Pentz, & Johnson, 1996).[18] For example, whereas a problem may be defined as mainly on the structural level, the strategies adopted may mainly address the individual level: Structural changes may be seen as beyond the scope of the intervention's goals and resources. The evaluation of the intervention may need to resort to indicators that do not necessarily represent an actual solution to the roots of the problem but perhaps represent efforts to contain or cope with it within the system or to help specific individuals who may be able to personally benefit from it. Evaluation criteria, therefore, need to be sensitive to the limitations of the intervention and what it is actually doing within its constraints. Broader social-change values may need to be substituted with a harm reduction approach or with a variation of the ethic of care to understand and assess the actual impact of the intervention and for planning future goals and strategies.

Values are critical when choosing what types of indicators reflect successful outcomes. A particular indicator that may serve to gauge the success according to one value-laden goal may not be adequate for another. In the example of an intervention to prevent adolescent pregnancy that chose the strategy of persuading adolescent girls to use a contraceptive implant, a likely evaluation criterion would be the relative frequency of pregnancies before and after the intervention in the target population. For stakeholders who define the problem as based on sexual promiscuity or for those who believe the girls engage in abusive sexual relationships because of low self-esteem, however, this criterion would be irrelevant because these adolescent girls may continue to engage in premarital sex and may have simply adopted enhanced contraceptive practices. Stakeholders who are interested in preventing youth from being infected with sexually transmitted diseases are also not likely to find this criterion satisfactory. The contraceptive implant may protect the adolescents from pregnancy, but they may continue to be exposed to infection. The type of criteria chosen to evaluate a program reflects particular priorities and values, which a value-centered analysis can help make more explicit.

Ethical Concerns[19]

The mere suggestion of intervening in someone else's life or in the functioning of social institutions raises ethical concerns. Ethical concerns in health promotion can include the infringement on each of the ethical principles typically raised by bioethicists as relevant to the context of health care. These include doing harm, threats to autonomy, justice, utility or the maximum good, and the good of the public, some of which have already been mentioned in the context of the choice and implementation of intervention strategies. Because the purpose of this framework is to provide a conceptual approach to analyze public health communication interventions, a preliminary framework for identifying ethical concerns is adapted from the articulation of Brown and Singhal (1990) and is further developed in the following chapters. Brown and Singhal discuss ethical dilemmas in the context of the use of entertainment television for social development and distinguish between four main types of concerns:[20] (a) content of the messages, (b) equality associated with the targeted populations, (c) prosocial development through the use of communication channels as a persuasive tool to guide social development, and (d) unintended effects, which can range from specific behavioral outcomes to the reinforcement of particular cultural or ideological positions. A fifth aspect is (e) control, particularly as it is reflected in the notion of the production and reproduction of privilege and dominance, which are important constructs in communication theory (Deetz, 1992).[21]

Content: Ethical concerns can be raised regarding the extent to which the content of the messages in the intervention may be viewed as relevant to diverse members of the population served by the intervention, the extent to which it employs what may be considered unwarranted persuasive appeals or creates an appearance of truth, urgency, or necessity, and the extent to which it affirms mainly individual-level solutions, thus by implication deemphasizing other potential loci of change (e.g., see an analysis of messages by Farrant and Russell, 1987, and by Duncan and Cribb, 1996). Ethical concern can thus be raised regarding the following:

Target Population: Does the intervention reach those who are considered hard to reach, or does it mainly enhance the health of those who have the greatest opportunities to adopt its recommendations?

Channels: To what extent do the messages in the intervention justify the use of government, public, and commercial outlets to carry health promotion messages, or what are the ethics of infusing intervention messages into entertainment programs and other types of programming?

Control: To what extent does the intervention contribute to the legitimization of certain social institutions as experts or authorities (e.g., medicine) or serve to control people's behavior (e.g., restrict their choice in the types of behaviors they may want to engage in)?

Unintended Effects: Does the framing of certain conditions or issues as problems needing medical attention[22] contribute to what critics describe as the medicalization of life, and do certain messages in the intervention frame particular behaviors in such a way that they may affect the self-concept of the individual in a negative way (Barsky, 1988)? Concerns may also be raised regarding the extent to which interventions may contribute to so-called health gaps and reinforce inequities in society or perhaps unduly raise consumer expectations regarding health care from what critics argue is an already overburdened and inequitable health care delivery system.

Table 3.6 presents these concerns as a series of questions that can serve to guide inquiry, analysis, and practice of health interventions from a normative perspective. Ethical concerns are further elaborated in Chapters 6 and 7.

A VALUE-ANALYTIC FRAMEWORK: FOCUS ON THE LOCUS OF INTERVENTION

The analytic framework presented in this chapter is based on the assumption that particular values and justifications are emphasized or given priority in every component of the intervention process. The purpose of the framework is to provide a heuristic approach rather than to prescribe particular constructs. This framework can be modified and adapted with a conceptual approach that may focus on types of goals rather than levels of intervention. Additional or alternative justifications or strategic approaches can be added. Table 3.7 lists the major facets of the analytic framework, notes the focus of each, and provides examples of embedded values and claims.

The analytic framework developed in this chapter consists of the five facets outlined earlier. Each facet can relate to a range, the extent to which there is a high or low emphasis on the particular concern. In each of the intervention facets, choices were made regarding the level of intervention. Because the framework uses justifications that mainly draw from ethical principles as they are presented in the biomedical literature, not all moral approaches are represented, and it may not encompass the whole phenomenon of the intervention and its social culture. Other kinds of values may be relevant, and moral frameworks of ethical principles based mainly on Western philosophy may not reflect the complex and pragmatic moral issues embedded in health care and may not encompass alternative ethical perspectives that exist among people from other cultures (Pellegrino, 1993).

The framework is presented in Figure 3.2 as a mapping sentence, which is a formal way of relating the content and its domains to a particular range (Brown, 1985). Mapping sentences are described in Borg and Shye (1995) and Shye, Elizur, and Hoffman (1994) as a formal presentation of expressing facets of a research area by assigning an element of the range (e.g., to which extent they have been used) to an element of the domain (a focus; e.g., which type of strategy). Such mapping provides an opportunity to develop an analytic framework that can, in turn, contribute to the design of specific research questions

Table 3.6   Examples of Research and Practice Questions Drawing From Ethical Concerns Associated With Public Health Communication Interventions

Area of Concern	Examples of Questions Associated With Ethical Concerns
Content	Do the messages include strong persuasive appeals?
	Do messages frame particular behaviors in a way that may stigmatize certain behaviors or populations?
	Do messages emphasize and affirm mainly individual-level solutions, thus implying that other intervention levels are less important to target or cannot be addressed or serve to distract attention from them?
Target	To what extent does the intervention include diverse perspectives on how the problem and solutions are perceived?
	To what extent does the intervention reach different segments of the population?
	To what extent may it serve to widen the gap between those who have more opportunities and those who have less?
	To what extent does the intervention emphasize issues that are more relevant to certain cultural groups than to others?
Control	Do intervention stakeholders consider whether the intervention privileges or legitimizes certain institutions or stakeholders?
	In what ways can the recommendation to adopt certain attitudes or behaviors be related to attempts to control individuals or certain populations?
Channels	Does the design and analysis consider ethical implications regarding the use of particular media and the means for getting the intervention's messages effectively disseminated?
	Does the design and analysis consider the nature of collaboration of those involved in the intervention with other organizations?
Unintended effects	Do intervention stakeholders consider whether the intervention may contribute to the gap in usage between those who have more and those who have less access to resources?
	Do intervention stakeholders consider the extent to which the intervention may stigmatize certain individuals or groups?

SOURCE: Adapted from by Brown and Singhal (1990).

**Table 3.7   Major Facets of the Analytic Framework and Their Foci
With Examples of Embedded Values and Claims**

Facet	Focus	Examples of Embedded Claims
Justifications	What are the moral grounds for having the intervention take place? What kinds of claims are made to justify the goals of the intervention and its strategies?	Intended population viewed as vulnerable and needing protection from life-threatening, preventable diseases *(doing good)* Perceived unequal distribution of the disease in different population groups *(justice-fairness)* Economic cost of treating particular medical conditions is high, thus warranting prevention activities *(utility)*
Problem	Where is the locus of the problem defined or at which level of analysis is the problem identified?	Individuals are not aware of being at risk *(individual)* The community lacks resources *(community)* The marketplace does not produce health-promoting products *(marketplace)* Vulnerable populations are limited in their access to preventive care *(societal level)*
Solution	At which level is the solution identified?	Informing people they are at risk *(individual)* Changing workplace environments to reduce specific hazards *(organizational)* Addressing economic opportunities on a national level *(societal)*
Strategies	What methods are used to address the problem? What methods are not?	Changing individual behavior through educational strategies *(education)*
Outcomes	What is the locus of the outcome or at which level are outcomes specified? What are the criteria for success?	Knowledge and awareness of risk among individuals or groups *(individual, organizational)* Workplace safety policies *(organizational)* Community norms *(community)* Institutional arrangements regarding access to care *(structural-institutional)* Reduction of morbidity on a national level *(societal)*

(continued)

Table 3.7   Continued

Facet	Focus	Examples of Embedded Claims
Ethical concerns	Are there value conflicts? What ethical principles may be infringed upon as a result of the intervention?	Use of persuasive strategies that may infringe on individuals' freedom of choice *(content)* Restrictions on the marketplace that may infringe on marketers' rights to promote their product *(target)* Privileging certain stakeholders over others *(target, framing)* Harming individuals who have or fear certain medical conditions *(identity)*

NOTE: Intervention levels and values or ethical principles are in parentheses and italicized.

and can help us conceptualize the multitude of relationships that can take place between the different facets and compel us to think about theoretical explanations for particular types of relationships (Shye et al., 1994).

Applications

This framework, which focuses on levels of analysis, can be adapted to serve several types of interrelated analyses. First, it can serve as a basis for identifying embedded values in public health communication interventions. It can help identify what values are officially declared as formal justification for a particular intervention as well as what values are not specified but are nevertheless heavily embedded in it. Specifically, it would examine how they are manifested in the way problems are defined, what is taken for granted as important, the types of strategies chosen, and what seems to be less highly regarded. One way this type of analysis can be accomplished is by developing a list of values or justifications and using it as a checklist when analyzing the intervention. An example of how this can be applied is presented in Resource A, Work Sheets A.1 and A.2. Another approach could use the questions summarized in Table 3.8.

To what extent are embedded in the intervention the considerations of

A. Justifications
a. 1. Doing good, care
a. 2. Doing no harm
a. 3. Autonomy, as justifications for intervening at a(n)
a. 4. Market autonomy
a. 5. Personal responsibility
a. 6. The public good
a. 7. Justice, fairness
a. 8. Utility, efficiency
a. 9. Science
a. 10. Self-actualization

B. Locus of the Problem
b. 1. Individual
b. 2. Family
b. 3. Organizational level treated at a(n)
b. 4. Community
b. 5. Marketplace
b. 6. Structural, institutional
b. 7. Cultural, normative

C. Locus of the Solution
c. 1. Individual
c. 2. Family
c. 3. Organizational level of intervention
c. 4. Community
c. 5. Marketplace
c. 6 Structural, institutional
c. 7. Cultural, normative

D. Strategy Type
d. 1. Engineering
d. 2. Enforcement
d. 3. Incentives, disincentives assessed at a(n)
d. 4. Education
d. 5. Collaboration
d. 6. Facilitation

E. Locus of the Outcome
e. 1. Individual
e. 2. Family using
e. 3. Organizational, level, each raising ethical concerns regarding
e. 4. Community
e. 5. Marketplace
e. 6. Structural, institutional
e. 7. Cultural, normative

F. Ethical Concerns
f. 1. Content
f. 2. Target
f. 3. Channel
f. 4. Control
f. 5. Unintended effects

with

Range
Very low
|___|___|
emphasis
Very high

Figure 3.2. Mapping Sentence of a Value-Centered Analytic Framework That Focuses on Levels of Analysis
NOTE: Samuel Shye helped construct an earlier version of this Mapping Sentence, and Ruth Guttman helped with this version.

Table 3.8   Description of the Analytic Process of Identifying Which Values or Justifications Are Emphasized in Each Facet

Analytic Facets	Analytic Questions
Problem	What is the problem? At what level is the problem mainly identified? Who has defined the problem (what stakeholders)? What was the process for defining the problem (e.g., expert committees, survey of stakeholders)? What are the main criteria for making the problem a "problem"? Who is mainly going to benefit from the intervention? Who is not?
Justifications	Why is the intervention needed? Why is it important? Which justifications are formally specified? Which are embedded but not specified (taken for granted)? What are the moral grounds for having the intervention take place? What are moral grounds or competing claims for not doing the intervention or for modifying its original intentions? What are the moral grounds for deciding on a particular strategic approach to address the problem? What are the moral grounds or competing claims for not choosing alternative strategic approaches (which may be more efficient)?
Solution	How does the intervention address the problem? Which types of strategies seem optimal? Which types of strategies were selected? At which level is the solution mainly identified? Which social values are associated with the choice of the solutions (and rejection of others)? Which sociopolitical factors are associated with the choice of the solutions (and rejection of others)?
Strategies	Which specific methods are mainly used to address the problem? Which are not? How do these relate to the skills and experience of the intervention practitioners? Which social values are associated with the choice of the strategic approach (and rejection of others)? Which sociopolitical factors are associated with the choice of strategic approach (and rejection of others)?
Outcomes and evaluation criteria	What are the main outcomes? At what level are outcomes specified? What criteria indicate success and failure? Which social values are associated with the type of criteria emphasized? Which values are associated with criteria not emphasized?
Ethical concerns	Are there any value conflicts? Which ethical principles may be infringed upon, throughout the intervention process and in each facet? Which stakeholders benefit the most? Which stakeholders benefit the least?

Developing and Adopting an Analytic Approach

This chapter concludes with suggestions for further adaptation or application of the analytic framework it has outlined. The analytic process includes identifying values and inherent ethical dilemmas in overall goals and specific aims, in the presumed function of the intervention, in each of its facets, and in possible alternative strategic approaches. Following is a series of guidelines that can serve to identify and classify embedded values that may not be included in the justifications or the analytic constructs employed earlier.

1. *Adopt an analytic framework that provides meaningful constructs that allow for differentiating between value-laden aspects of the intervention.* The following questions can guide the identification and differentiation task: What are shared core social values? What is the vision of a good society? What are the core social values in the social context of the intervention? How do these core values relate to the intervention context? What can serve as an indication of different embedded values in the intervention system? What conceptual dimensions can serve as an indication of different ideological commitments or different worldviews?

2. *Identify intervention sponsors' preferences regarding certain goals and outcomes that indicate their preference of certain values.* For example, find out what factors they praise or blame, what strategies they choose or criticize, and what they believe is a necessary "price" to pay for achieving intervention goals and objectives. Find out what the intervention practitioners or the materials they produce say should take place—what the ideal should be. Identify what one's own preferences would be regarding goals and compromises.

3. *Find out what is officially used to justify certain behaviors and actions and what specific claims are made and what are not.* For this purpose, a framework that specifies a range of justifications or values may be crucial in helping identify what is *not* used (i.e., less valued) and what is taken for granted (i.e., embedded in a pervasive ideology). Identify what justifications one finds as acceptable or necessary and what may be viewed as unnecessary and having potentially adverse moral implications.

4. *Identify values embedded in each facet of the actual intervention.*

5. Examine the extent to which the strategies used in the intervention correspond to the ideal. Identify what interventionists believe constrains the ideal from taking place and what compromises they have been willing to make. Relate these to normative justifications and social values identified with the ideal of the intervention.

The analysis can be guided by the following procedure: First, the values are made more explicit, and then, a comparison is made across the facets to see what values are emphasized or deemphasized in each intervention facet. Work Sheet A.1 in Resource A can be used for this purpose. This type of analysis can be used to examine the extent to which there is correspondence or discrepancies between the way problems are defined and the way they are addressed by the intervention. For example, it can help identify gaps in such cases as where the problem is defined as the vulnerability of children to tobacco marketing initiatives but the solution emphasized is education on the hazards of smoking and social skills training, with minimal emphasis on activities aimed to restrict tobacco companies' marketing activities. Another example is when the main problem is identified as limited access to nutritious foods on a community level,[23] but the solution focuses mainly on nutrition education. Similarly, the analysis can indicate the extent to which justifications emphasized in the definition of the problem have been overridden by other justifications embedded in the strategies adopted to solve it. Incongruity between the justifications in the two facets may point to ethical concerns and may also help explain situations where intervention outcomes differ from what has been expected. For example, if an intervention's goals (e.g., to reach minority populations) are justified on values of caring or justice and equity but its strategies emphasize utility or efficiency, populations that are harder to reach may not be given the opportunity to benefit from the intervention. Work Sheet A.3 in Resource A can be used for this purpose.

Explanation

The comparison between the justifications or values and levels of interventions emphasized in the different facets can raise the question of why certain values that are emphasized in the definition or locus of the problem (e.g., justice) are not emphasized in the solution. The latter seems to emphasize other justifications (e.g., utility).

The comparison can help point out why particular interventions in particular social contexts emphasize certain justifications and strategies, and interventionists can use this framework to test their assumptions. Alternatively, the comparison can point to discrepancies that call for theoretical explanations. The analysis of the discrepancies or correspondence between the values emphasized in the way problems are defined and those emphasized in the solutions or types of strategies used to address them can be used to develop theoretical explanations. The specification of justifications in each intervention facet and identification of key stakeholders can also contribute to a better understanding of which stakeholders *should* be the actual target of the intervention (e.g., those who are considered gatekeepers or policymakers), as well as who its actual main beneficiaries are (e.g., those who live near the facility that provides the services, those who have the time or resources), whether by intention or by default. This framework can also be used to discuss how decisions are made in sponsoring organizations that develop and implement health communication interventions: the extent to which various value-embedded considerations influence the choices made regarding the way they construct goals, the types of strategies they choose to use, and the evaluation criteria they emphasize. By making the justifications explicit and making distinctions between the ways they are emphasized in each intervention facet, this framework can serve as a response to Tesh's (1988) challenge that values of health interventions be made explicit.

The comparison can also contribute to the evaluation process: If problems are defined at one locus of intervention and are addressed mainly in another, the intervention may not address important aspects of the problem. If the evaluation criterion is too narrowly defined, it may not capture the complexity of the intervention effects, and evaluations may conclude that certain programs did not have the desired effects because the measures they used attended mainly to design and criteria favored in biomedical contexts that may not be appropriate for the complexity of communication interventions (Hornik, 1997). This is often a commonplace complaint of practitioners who feel that evaluations that use population-level impact indicators are not sensitive to the effects their activities have had on organizational processes or relational developments.

Comparing Across Interventions

Once an intervention is mapped or described using the analytic framework, interventions can be compared to one another. The comparison across interventions allows us to note similarities and make distinctions among interventions that aim to achieve the same goal (see Gorman & Speer, 1996) and how different interventions may emphasize the same values in their definition of the problem but apply different strategic approaches or different criteria to assess outcomes. The analysis can indicate how this relates to values embedded in these interventions. This type of comparison can use the method presented in Resource B, Work Sheets B.1 to B.4.

By using this framework we can broaden our analysis. Not only would we be concerned with how we or others can get the public to adopt certain health-related claims (e.g., certain health-related recommendations), but we will also engage in critically examining the process of claim making and the claims themselves. For example, we can examine the extent to which an intervention gives prominence to certain dominant groups' or experts' definitions of problems and solutions and what levels of intervention are preferred by what stakeholders. This can show us to what extent the locus of problems and solutions in the intervention is defined on the individual level and the extent to which it may deemphasize other levels. Because the same values can be emphasized in different ways in different types of interventions, we may also want to distinguish between different intervention types and to identify their particular characteristics. For example, what different types of relationships are likely to take place between the intervention constituencies (see Rothman & Tropman, 1987) who mainly may benefit and what social institutions may be privileged. This type of analysis is described in the next chapter.

NOTES

1. This representation, however, may imply that different strategic approaches are on a continuum, whereas they can be viewed as distinct or complementary. This is examined in the typologies presented in Chapters 4 and 5.

2. This corresponds to the discussion of the definition of the problem elaborated in the first chapter.

3. For analytic purposes, these constructs can serve as a framework to identify what level is seen as the main source of the problem, and other types of levels can be adapted or expanded according to different contexts.

4. Physician and anthropologist Robert Like (personal communication, June 1994) suggested adding this level to the framework.

5. For a review of policy-related strategies, see Brownson, Koffman, Novotny, Hughes, and Eriksen (1995).

6. In current assessments of the prevention of cardiovascular disease interventions, the authors conclude that to achieve equitable and meaningful preventive behavior changes, there is a need to address structural factors (Viswanath, Finnegan, Hannan, & Luepker, 1991). This is also

implied in the conclusion of a review of the outcomes of large publicly funded systematic health communication campaigns: "Despite the multiple cardiovascular disease activities during the 1980s, the disparity in risk factors and mortality between the upper and lower socioeconomic status groups increased" (Winkleby, 1994, p. 1371), a disparity that was documented in three major cardiovascular disease prevention demonstration projects sponsored by the U.S. National Institutes of Health conducted in California, Minnesota, and New England.

7. See Winett et al.'s (1989) discussion of incentives; see also Glanz et al.'s (1995) discussion of economic strategies.

8. Different models of collaboration may emerge. Chapter 5 further elaborates this topic.

9. Alternative conceptualizations of facilitation as they relate to community involvement are discussed in Chapter 5.

10. See further elaboration to follow and in Chapter 6.

11. In addition to the issue of autonomy, an ethical concern is whether the government provided adequate opportunities to obtain condoms, for example, by ensuring that their cost is low enough, that there are sufficient and convenient outlets to purchase them, and that social norms encourage their purchase and use. If these conditions are not fulfilled, it may frustrate those who would like to use them but feel they cannot.

12. For example, see Atkin, 1989; Botvin, Goldberg, Botvin, & Dusenbury, 1993; DiFranza, Norwood, Garner, & Tye, 1987; Grube & Wallack, 1994; Pierce & Giplin, 1995.

13. These points are further elaborated in Chapter 6 in the persuasion dilemma discussion.

14. This issue is further elaborated in Chapter 6 in the discussion of the exploitation dilemma.

15. A discussion of empowerment as an intervention strategy is further elaborated in Chapter 5.

16. See Levy and Stokes (1987). The notion of stakeholders is further developed in Chapter 5.

17. Guba and Lincoln (1981, 1989) distinguish between three broad classes of stakeholders: (a) the agents involved in the intervention; (b) beneficiaries, those who profit in some way, directly and indirectly; and (c) victims, those negatively affected (e.g., groups systematically excluded, politically disadvantaged, or who suffer opportunity cost).

18. See also a study that compared the perspectives of different stakeholders on evaluation criteria (Masergh et al., 1996).

19. See Chapter 6 for further elaboration.

20. The framework is further developed and adapted to the context of health communication interventions; this is presented in the sixth and seventh chapters in this book.

21. This draws on the influential work of Watzlawick, Beavin, and Jackson (1967), further adapted by others (e.g., Burgoon & Hale, 1984), as well as work with a more critical perspective (Deetz, 1992).

22. The concerns regarding content, equity, and channel are adapted from Brown and Singhal (1990); the concerns regarding framing, legitimacy, and identity are adapted from Forester (1989, 1993) and discussed further in Chapters 6 and 7.

23. This was found in focus groups reported on in an unpublished report (see Guttman, 1994).

4

Even When They Apply the Same Justifications, Interventions Are Not the Same

The Personal Responsibility Typology

> By investigating the function of theory in life as it encounters the world, we can arrive at more fruitful ways of thinking about theory. Allow me to suggest three basic functions: *directing attention, organizing experience,* and *enabling useful response.* Can we see differences that make a difference? Can we form and recognize patterns that specify what things are and how they relate? Can we make choices that not only enable us to survive and fulfill needs but also to create the future we want?
>
> —*Stanley A. Deetz (1992, p. 71)*

Consider two interventions: Both aim to increase immunization rates in a low-income population. Both provide information to parents on the benefits of child immunization, and both emphasize the same value: personal responsibility. The first recruits community residents as lay educators to disseminate messages about parental responsibility for childhood immunization. The lay educators are successful in increasing immunization rates among families they have contacted. The second also features the importance of childhood immunization and parental responsibility, but interactions between practitioners and parents focus on the role and ability of parents to influence the allocation of health care resources in their community. These two interventions clearly differ—although both emphasize the justification of *responsibility* as a prominent value and both are concerned with the promotion of childhood immunization. The use of typologies as an analytic approach can provide a framework for making meaningful distinctions.

Because different interventions may seem to emphasize the same values or use the same justifications, the analytic framework presented in this chapter aims to make distinctions between interventions according to whether they emphasize a particular value as a *goal* or *strategically.* In other words, even when interventions emphasize the same value, they may differ in aspects that are socially significant. Creation of typologies that differentiate between interventions according to the extent to which they emphasize certain values can serve to direct our attention to and organize processes within the intervention phenomenon and across interventions (Deetz, 1992).

The typologies in this and the following chapter are constructed by examining whether a particular value prominently emphasized in the intervention is emphasized as a goal or is mainly strategical.[1] For example, Intervention A may emphasize community involvement or participation mainly strategically to get various organizations to work together to achieve intervention objectives determined by a sponsoring agency. In contrast, Intervention B, which views participation as a core value, may prioritize activities believed to lead to participation, neglecting to focus on activities linked to achieving the official health-specific objectives. In this intervention, the value of participation overrides the specific predetermined health objective. Each of these interventions can represent a different type; thus different patterns of relationships between the interventionists and the population are likely to emerge. To illustrate this conceptual approach, two typologies are presented in the following discussion. The first centers on the justification of *personal responsibility*—a nearly omnipresent theme in public health communication interventions. The second focuses on the widely used justification of *participation,* or as referred to here, *community involvement.* This justification draws from the ethical principle of autonomy and serves as a primary justification for a substantial number of public health interventions' goals and strategies, many of which are sponsored by government agencies and foundations.

		GOAL	
		Low	*High*
STRATEGY	*Low*	A Justification X low both as goal and as stragegy	B Justification X high as goal but low as strategy
	High	C Justification X low as goal but high as strategy	D Justification X high both as goal and as strategy

Figure 4.1. Framework for Creating Typologies: Differential Emphasis on the Same Justification in Different Intervention Facets

The models in the typology are presented as prototypes[2] and characterized according to whether there is a high or low emphasis on particular justifications or values in the intervention's goals or strategies. The purpose of this analytic approach is to show that interventions, although they may emphasize the same justification, may represent very different value-laden approaches. Thus, when Intervention B emphasizes justification X in its goals but not in its strategies, it will differ from intervention D, which emphasizes the same justification X in both. Both differ from intervention C, which emphasizes justification X only in its strategies, or from A, which does not emphasize justification X at all. This presents us with a typology of 4 models per justification, as illustrated in Figure 4.1. Each quadrant represents an intervention type, but actual programs may fall in between these clear demarcations. Over time, as the dynamics of the program and its circumstances change, it may belong to a different model.

ANALYTIC DIMENSIONS

To describe, analyze, critique, and compare the intervention types described by the models, the following three dimensions can serve as analytic constructs:

   1. Content: The types of messages emphasized, taken for granted as important, or believed to be true, in contrast to those not given credibility or marginalized. For example, certain treatment or prevention recommendations are rejected because they are not based on what the intervention sponsors consider scientific evidence. Instead, particular medical procedures accepted by official authorities are emphasized in the intervention. Certain stakeholders are believed to be entitled to preferential access to services—those officially targeted by the intervention—or are more likely to benefit from the intervention's activities because of their situations, resources, or circumstances, whereas others are not. For example, those whose insurance covers the type of early detection screening recommended by the intervention, those who can afford to purchase the recommended products, or those who have the time to carry out the recommended activities are likely beneficiaries of the intervention, whereas those who cannot, are not. The former are more likely to avail themselves of early detection, to purchase lower-fat meat products, or to engage in physical activity in a commercial gym. Analysis of the content can thus help identify what stakeholders are likely to gain by the intervention. For example, certain professions or organizations may be given the opportunity and preference to provide health-related services recommended by the intervention. This allows for these organizations and individuals to gain commercial opportunities or, for those viewed as experts, to benefit from consultation or use of their services. By compiling a comprehensive list of stakeholders and of the messages emphasized in the intervention, the analysis can compare those who are privileged by the intervention to those who are not.

Table 4.1 lists examples of stakeholders that may be directly involved in a public health communication intervention or may be privileged by its activities or inactivities.[3]

2. *Relationships: The type of relationships or roles developed and sustained within the intervention system and the distribution of power and control in the intervention context.* For example, those who make decisions and control resources are considered as experts. Each model also describes the kind of relationship that would typically exist between the intervention practitioners and those targeted by it: Is the relationship characterized as a client-professional relationship, or as a consumer-service provider relationship? Does the interventionist serve as a teacher, guide, or consultant? Alternatively, are target population members treated as colleagues, peers, or perhaps even as adversaries?[4]

3. *Context: The type of structures and systems that the activities associated with intervention promote, sustain, or reproduce.* Anthony Giddens

Table 4.1   Examples of Potential Stakeholders in Public Health Communication Interventions

Intended Audiences
- Audience members identified as at risk or with special needs
- Members of particular ethnic, cultural, or socioeconomic groups
- Underserved populations
- Organizations that provide services or goods to target audiences
- Information professionals or specialists
- News media professionals
- Opinion leaders, gatekeepers
- Legislators, policymakers
- Indirect or secondary target audience members (e.g., parents, teachers of youth)
- Potential collaborators and sponsors of future campaigns

Professionals, Practitioners
- Medical professionals
- Allied health care and health care professionals
- Public health, health education professionals
- Social work professionals
- Behavioral and counseling professionals
- Community organizers
- Biomedical researchers
- Social science researchers and practitioners
- Politicians, legislators
- Mass media professionals
- Public relations and marketing professionals
- Lobbyists, advocates

Commercial Industries and For-Profit Organizations
- For-profit medical organizations
- Biomedical and pharmaceutical industries
- Food products manufacturers and distributors
- Health insurance carriers
- Medical equipment and supplies industry
- Fitness supplies and facilities industry
- Alcohol and tobacco industries
- Work organizations
- Mass media organizations
- Advertising and public relations organizations
- For-profit health organizations
- Complementary and alternative health outlets
- Telecommunication and electronics industry
- News media outlets

Table 4.1   *Continued*

Public and Not-for-Profit Organizations
Funding organizations, foundations
Biomedical and academic research organizations
Advocacy groups
Consumer groups
Self-help groups
Medical institutions and organizations
Professional associations and societies
Federal government health-related institutions & agencies
State government
Local government
Local government health agencies
Not-for-profit and voluntary health promotion organizations
Not-for-profit health services organizations
Labor unions
International health organizations
Not-for-profit insurance carriers
Community organizations and groups
Schools, educational institutions
Colleges and universities
Libraries
Religious, faith organizations
Not-for-profit media organizations
Political organizations
Charities

(1979, 1984) explains how institutionalized social structures are mostly produced and reproduced by the perceptions and practices of their members. This process, which Giddens characterizes as *structuration,* takes place as social actors' interpretations of events are affected by their differential access to resources and by ideological frameworks that serve to legitimize the institutionalized practices or structures. Systems of practices are often invisible, but as they get reproduced, they can serve as bases of power and influence. Intervention activities can thus reinforce particular institutional practices. For example, interventions may recommend schedules that support a medically oriented bureaucratic culture. Similarly, health insurance companies may sustain reimbursement policies that reinforce particular practices and channel income to particular professionals but not to others. Last, the intervention can reproduce ideological frameworks, for example, by greatly valuing efficiency in organizational operations and viewing for-profit medicine as a more efficient system. Also, interventions that rely on the use of voluntary agencies may serve to reproduce the notion that the use of voluntary organizations, rather than government agencies, is the best vehicle to promote health. This contextual dimension of the model can help identify what types of practices, and consequently beliefs and values, are promoted or reproduced—often inadvertently—by particular types of interventions.

A discussion follows, on the application of the typology framework with the justification of personal responsibility, a prominent theme in many health promotion interventions. In the next chapter, a typology is developed based on the justification of community involvement, another prominent theme in current health promotion efforts.

PERSONAL RESPONSIBILITY

Personal responsibility and health go back in history. Illness and death in ancient times, sometimes those of people's children, were often attributed to people's bad deeds or evil thoughts. People were also believed to affect the health of others by casting spells on them or by defying the will of gods. Personal responsibility plays a central moral and pragmatic role in contemporary health promotion as well (Ziff, Conrad, & Lachman, 1995). As Louis Sullivan, former Secretary of Health and Human Services, in his introduction to *Healthy People 2000*, reiterated, "First, responsible and enlightened behavior by each and every individual truly is the key to good health" (USDHHS, 1990, p. v). Similarly, the former Surgeon General, C. Everett Koop, in a *Message From the Surgeon General* to the public on AIDS—which was literally distributed to all households in the United States—called on the public to "practice responsible behavior based on understanding and strong personal values" (USDHHS, 1988). Another manifestation of a blunt call for personal responsibility is manifested in the theme of the 1994 U.S. CDC campaign on AIDS, which declared, "*It's your move: prevent AIDS*" (USDHHS, 1994).

In most societies, parents or guardians have legal obligations to care for young offspring, and health providers have professional obligations to care for their patients. But a moral responsibility regarding care for others spans beyond legal requirements. Ethicists point out that we express moral disapproval of and even outrage at people who do not warn, protect, or come to the aid of

Understanding AIDS

A Message From The Surgeon General

T his brochure has been sent to you by the Government of the United States. In preparing it, we have consulted with the top health experts in the country.

I feel it is important that you have the best information now available for fighting the AIDS virus, a health problem that the President has called "Public Enemy Number One."

Stopping AIDS is up to you, your family and your loved ones.

Some of the issues involved in this brochure may not be things you are used to discussing openly. I can easily understand that. But now you must discuss them. We all must know about AIDS. Read this brochure and talk about it with those you love. Get involved. Many schools, churches, synagogues, and community groups offer AIDS education activities.

I encourage you to practice responsible behavior based on understanding and strong personal values. This is what you can do to stop AIDS.

C. Everett Koop, M.D., Sc.D.
Surgeon General

Este folleto sobre el SIDA se publica en Español.
Para solicitar una copia, llame al 1-800-344-SIDA.

Illustration 4.1

others who are at risk of being harmed, even if they are not personally related to them. We also praise as heroes people who—at great risk to themselves—go out of their way to protect strangers or their nation (Douard & Winslade, 1994). What, then, is the moral imperative that underlies one's responsibility for and toward others, in the context of health promotion? Is one obligated to help one's spouse who has been told to lose weight? Are people to be held responsible if they do not succeed in preventing their spouses from purchasing foods high in calories and saturated fats, for example? Should a spouse employ highly persuasive methods that may infringe on the rights of the at-risk spouse? In other words, what is their obligation to actively promote the health of another presumably autonomous person, and when are they not held accountable for failing to do so?

it's your move

prevent AIDS

AMERICA
RESPONDS
TO AIDS

 DEPARTMENT OF HEALTH AND HUMAN SERVICES
Public Health Service

Illustration 4.2

Many public health communication interventions address modification of lifestyle behaviors identified as risk factors for ill health. These interventions' messages urge individuals to take responsibility for their own health, to adopt what they recommend as health-promoting behaviors, or to refrain from what are characterized as hazardous practices. Justifications for such messages can be associated with two aspects of the notions of obligation or duty. The first formulation of obligation calls for taking care of one's own health for the sake of significant others, to enable the person to provide for them. The second formulation suggests that one may be held accountable for one's behavior and has an obligation to not become an unfair burden on others and society as a whole by engaging in risky behaviors that may lead to injury. The notion of accountability in this context can be linked to one's actions' impact on others' well-being (Niebuhr, 1978; Veatch, 1982).

Engaging in responsible behavior may be associated with virtue or with abiding by moral obligations that emanate from a person's or societal beliefs regarding how a good and righteous person conducts himself or herself (Pellegrino, 1985). The notion of virtue implies that one has obligations beyond what strict duty may demand. The person is expected to do what is considered right and good, even at the expense of personal sacrifice and legitimate self-interest. Doing what is good contains the idea of service, responsiveness to others with special needs, fidelity, compassion, kindliness, and promise keeping, which are also associated with the ethic of care (Noddings, 1984). Pellegrino (1985) cautions that there are dangers from overzealousness or misguided observance of virtuous behavior, which can easily lapse into self-righteous paternalism or an unwelcome overinvolvement in the personal life of others.

Responsibility and virtue can also be viewed as closely affiliated with some of the social values Rokeach (1973) specifies as *instrumental values*. These include being courageous, helpful, honest, obedient, responsible, and self-controlled. In the context of public health communication campaigns, one may need courage to act in a way that may, at least initially, not be popular, to act in a way considered responsible, or to serve as a role model. Similarly, one may need self-control to practice self-restraint to help curb one's own and others' attraction to and inclination to engage in risky behaviors. The obligation to care for and promote the health of others, particularly those who depend on one, individuals with whom one has a special relationship, or those for whom one has a special capacity to help, can also be included in the notion of personal responsibility (see Douard & Winslade, 1994). Obligation, as a component of responsibility in contrast to accountability (Agich, 1982), has a forward-looking dimension: a moral charge to help another person or to act in a way considered virtuous or caring. With the heightened awareness of health costs to organizations and society and the causal connection made between individuals' lifestyle behaviors and health, virtue and morality seem to be coupled with behaviors associated with promoting good health. Whereas one may not label a person who is considered overweight or who smokes as immoral, it seems more difficult nowadays to envision them as virtuous. Health behaviors thus accrue a moral undertone as they become increasingly associated with personal responsibility.

What is considered virtuous clearly depends on one's moral orientation (Baier, 1993; Pellegrino, 1985) and social prescriptions. This forward-looking notion of responsibility in health promotion suggests that an emphasis on personal responsibility in intervention messages need not necessarily result in blaming the victim (Rosenstock, 1990)—a frequent critique of interventions that use personal responsibility as their major theme. Rosenstock uses Brickman et al.'s (1982) typology that distinguishes between situations in which one is not perceived as responsible for one's health problem but is responsible for the solution to it, to bolster the following argument: saying that people are responsible for solving a health problem does not necessarily mean that they are blamed for causing it. Furthermore, promoting responsibility at the individual level is not negated, even by practitioners and scholars who advocate community empowerment, as long as it does not come instead of community-level activity. In fact, empowerment on the individual level, which corresponds to the notion of *agency,* is viewed as a necessary condition for social transformation (Bernstein et al., 1994).

What are necessary conditions for being able to be responsible? Following Harmon (1995), responsibility incorporates a combination of three basic components: agency, accountability, and obligation (p. 19). Agency implies the following requirements: that one has the ability to exercise one's own will, has received a moral education to be able to make moral choices, can actively interpret what is happening, is knowledgeable of potential consequences of action (or nonaction), is acting intentionally, and is in charge of one's own action (Bellah et al., 1991; Harmon, 1995; Niebuhr, 1978). Both accountability and obligation presuppose the idea of agency. The assumption is that the person "is both self-aware and in possession of the necessary means to cause an event or action to occur" (Harmon, 1995, p. 25) or, if we may add, is free *not* to engage in actions deemed potentially hazardous and therefore deemed irresponsible.[5] If we accept agency as a necessary aspect of responsibility, intervention models that stress responsibility as a goal need to include activities that enable agency in its full sense. In other words, to be able to urge people to be responsible, we would also need to ascertain that they possess knowledge and skills to make responsible decisions about the intervention topic. They would need to act intentionally, to have received a relevant moral education, to be able to interpret or be knowledgeable about potential consequences of action (or inaction), and to be in charge of their own fate (Harmon, 1995). In contrast, responsibility emphasized as a strategy implies a more strategic application of the notion of obligation. It would be used mainly as a powerful persuasive appeal to encourage individuals in the intervention population to adopt specific behaviors or as a persuasive rationale for why they should refrain from engaging in pleasureful but risky practices.

MODELS OF PERSONAL RESPONSIBILITY

The four types of models relating to personal responsibility are shown in Figure 4.2. The purpose of naming the models is to simplify the discussion: instead of referring to the "low strategy, low goal" model, it is referred to as the Environmental Model, labeled as such because there is stronger reliance on the environment to guide people's behavior than, for example, personal motivation. The other three models are the Invocation Model, where the emphasis on goal is high but that on strategy is low and where the notion of being responsible is heavily evoked as an important end in itself; the Instrumental Model, where the emphasis on strategy is high but that on goal is low, where the notion of responsibility is used strategically to achieve particular health-related goals, and the Deliberative Model, where the emphasis on both aspects is high and where what is considered being responsible becomes part of the discourse.

Emphasis on Personal Responsibility as a Goal

In the Deliberative and Invocation Models, in which responsibility is emphasized as a goal, the goal of the intervention is to get members of the target population to make what the interventionists consider responsible decisions. These are believed to lead to better personal health and healthier social and

	GOAL	
	Low	*High*
Low	*Environmental:* Responsibility low both as goal and as stragegy	*Invocation:* Responsibility high as goal but low as strategy
High	*Instrumental:* Responsibility low as goal but high as strategy	*Deliberative:* Responsibility high both as goal and as strategy

STRATEGY (label at left, between the two rows)

Figure 4.2. Emphasis on Personal Responsibility as Strategy of Goal Models

physical environments. Responsibility, therefore, is appealed to as an important value by invoking core social values that would support it. Such values would delineate moral implications of being responsible for one's self, significant others, and society (Knowles, 1977). To meet the requirement of providing a basis for responsible choices, the intervention, following the stipulations of responsibility, also needs to supply the targeted population with a basis for moral reasoning. Moral, or in this context, responsible reasoning, explain Harron, Burnside, and Beauchamp (1983, p. 4), involves deliberation and choices made between competing yet compelling options, which do not necessarily lead to clear-cut answers about what is right or wrong.[6] These contemplative processes are more characteristic of the Deliberative Model, which emphasizes personal responsibility both in its strategies and its goals, and less of the Invocation Model, in which personal responsibility is emphasized as a goal but is less prominent in the strategies employed.

Content

A message from the Surgeon General (see Illustration 4.1) in which he urged readers to "practice responsible behavior based on understanding and strong personal values" (USDHHS, 1988) illustrates the kind of messages associated with the models that emphasize responsibility as a goal: Responsibility would be portrayed as a basis for behavior. But people also need to hear why responsibility is so important and what it consists of. Some of these issues can be found in messages to parents about drug abuse prevention, the responsibility of parents toward the upbringing of their children in general, and what this responsibility consists of. As stated in a pamphlet to parents (Johnson, 1991), "We all share the responsibility for a generation of young people at risk for AOD [alcohol and other drug]-related problems" (p. 4). The individual child, we are told, is vulnerable to a multitude of drug abuse enablers and should not be blamed if she or he succumbs to them. The problem of drug abuse, according to this pamphlet, should not be placed at the individual level but should be viewed as caused by the social environment. The parents, who are the intended readers of the pamphlet, are also therefore responsible for rendering the social environment antidrug and drug free (Johnson, 1991).

Prompted by concerns regarding values in the 1960s, educators developed a strategy called *value clarification* (see Simon & Kirschenbaum, 1973; Smith, 1977), which is mainly a descriptive means of identifying and illuminating one's values and how they affect one's judgments (Hiller, 1987). The process involves techniques designed to help identify core beliefs and behaviors people prize or feel strongly about, to consider pros and cons of the consequences associated with various alternatives, to compare the extent to which one's actions match one's stated beliefs and when they do not, and how to reconcile this gap. Health educators have traditionally adopted the value clarification approach and often use its techniques in their own training and in working with client populations. Critics, however, suggest that this approach does not provide a normative stance or a theoretical approach toward a moral basis for prioritizing values (Barry, 1982).

The techniques employed in value clarification, in which people are taught how to identify what they value most and how this affects their decisions, can be adopted as important features both in the Deliberative and Invocation Models, because they can provide means to examine personal and collective priorities. Yet to meet the requirement of possessing a moral education, such activities need to include identification and discourse on moral issues and ways to resolve compelling but competing activities associated with cherished values. People may need to be made aware of, and learn to respect, values associated with other cultural systems. Furthermore, they should be provided with means to deal with situations in which certain values held by others seem fundamentally immoral and the extent to which they should or should not be tolerated. For example, these may include procedures labeled "female genital mutilation" practiced in certain populations, cultural beliefs that may result in withholding medical treatment from children, or certain attitudes regarding members of particular social groups that may result in discriminatory practices. Consequently, one's responsibility may be to actively oppose certain practices cherished by members of certain populations. In contrast to messages that specify the nature of responsible behavior (see the discussion about the Instrumental Model, which follows), the kind of messages that would be prioritized in the Deliberative Model would be those that focus on values and alternative conceptualizations of responsibility. These may include messages reflecting on the nature of health problems and what responsible solutions are, grounded in core values and shared moral frameworks. Messages and activities may also aim to facilitate the intervention population's awareness and skills to advocate potential options currently unavailable or less accessible.

Relationships

When responsibility is emphasized as a goal, particularly in the Deliberative Model[7] (characterized by high emphasis on responsibility as a goal and as a strategy), the relationship between the interventionists and the intervention population consists of ways to enhance relevant knowledge for decision making and training in moral reasoning, as well as discourse on values and priorities in which agreement may not easily take place. Interventionists may need to tread the fine line between presenting their points of view and using manipulative persuasion when they believe their population should prioritize a particular value over another. As Emanuel and Emanuel (1992) suggest in the context of the health provider-patient relationship, this underscores the need to engage in the moral development of the client rather than in sheer advice giving. The latter is more characteristic of the way the relationship is constructed in the Instrumental Model. The relationship between the interventionists and target population members in the Deliberative Model would thus be characterized by dialogue and mutual exchanges. The kind of activities prioritized would be those that emphasize self-reflexivity, specifically on what it means to make responsible choices based on values.

Developing critical consciousness as a way to advance a forward-looking notion of responsibility is exemplified in the Brazilian educator Paulo Freire's (1968a, 1968b) problem-posing participatory educational method. This method draws from a liberation philosophy originally developed in the context of literacy education. Freire's approach, linked with community development theories, has gained tremendous momentum in the public health literature (Wallerstein & Bernstein, 1994). This approach fosters processes of self-reflexivity that can lend a transformative capacity to the notions of accountability and obligation, by helping people see their situations as a reality they can and should transform (Freire, 1968b).[8] A Freirian approach implies that not only can people gain awareness and understanding of the social system but that they can gain confidence and learn how they can affect it to achieve what they think is important.[9]

Interventions represented by the Invocation Model—in which responsibility is emphasized as a goal but less as a strategy, although participants would develop critical thinking—would tend to employ strategies that resemble a values clarification approach. They would tend to emphasize the importance of values and norms in fostering or combating unhealthy practices, with limited emphasis on transformative capacities. These interventions, which do not emphasize responsibility as a strategy but only as a goal although they may succeed in raising awareness and discussions regarding obligations, would tend to offer limited training and resources for individuals or communities to change structural factors. The interventionists, therefore, would act less as catalysts and advocates than they would in situations in which responsibility is also highly valued as a strategy and serves as the mission of the intervention itself.

In the Deliberative Model, relationships between the interventionists and the intervention population would aim to enhance decisional processes regarding value priorities. The intervention population would thus be provided with messages on how to make decisions with an emphasis on dialogue and deliberation. When responsibility is emphasized both as a goal and strategy, this implies that the interventionists would need to be skilled in enhancing the process of moral discourse. Their training would need to include skills to foster ethical and moral deliberations, analyses of structural factors that contribute to the problem, and decision-making capacities to choose ways to address them. Clearly, this is a formidable challenge for which not many health interventionists may feel they have been adequately trained, or even for which they may have the personal disposition. Some interventionists may, in fact, feel they *know* what responsible behavior is or should entail and how to achieve it best. Some interventionists may believe that responsible behavior is refraining from sexual intercourse or insisting on the use of condoms or it may be taking medications according to the physician's directives. They may find it difficult to accept other alternatives.

Context

Institutional arrangements, or the types of structures and systems promoted or reproduced in the models that emphasize responsibility as a goal, can include forums that give opportunities for dialogue and discussions on moral priorities and forums such as public meetings, accessible information resources, and mass media that present comprehensive coverage of multiple perspectives on sociopolitical causes of health problems and how to address them. Also, to meet the prerequisite of agency, particularly in the Deliberative Model, there would be an emphasis on institutional practices that offer accessible options to adopt what are considered responsible health-promoting behaviors. Workplaces that enable employees to structure and control their work schedule or have facilities for physical activity available at convenient times would meet this criterion. Working within this model, employees' decisions to engage in health-promoting activities could be based on their assessments of their ability to adapt their work environment to meet their needs, as well as their obligations to their workplace. For example, they may coordinate work-related tasks and schedules with others and feel they can also meet moral commitments to themselves and significant others.[10]

Ethical Concerns

A major ethical concern associated with the models that emphasize personal responsibility as a goal is the issue of personal autonomy: specifically, the tension between one's accountability or obligations to others and the ethical principle and highly prized value in Western cultures of individual choice without being imposed on (see the discussion in Chapter 2). The tension between individual rights and the obligation to others becomes increasingly problematic as considerations of monetary cost become a central decisive issue in decisions about the allocation of health care services and funds. With growing emphasis on personal responsibility, individuals viewed as irresponsible may also be viewed as not deserving certain health care benefits or may be asked to pay more for particular services. A second concern revolves around the relationship between the interventionists and the intervention population: To what extent is the interventionist obliged to promote certain values and moral frameworks or to actively try to dissuade members of the intervention population from decisions the interventionist believes are irresponsible or immoral? The interventionist may suspect that the population, because of prejudice and fear, is discriminating against people with certain medical conditions or who persist in engaging in risky behaviors because of dangerous cultural beliefs. What is the role and what are the moral obligations of the interventionist whose values regarding what is responsible behavior differ from those of members of the intervention population?[11]

Emphasis on Personal Responsibility as a Strategy

Personal responsibility is treated in the Instrumental Model as a useful strategy for achieving the desired change, not treated as a goal on its own. The notion of responsibility, in this model, is used as an important persuasive appeal: individuals are reminded they are held accountable for and have an obligation to follow particular behavioral recommendations.[12]

Content

An appeal to personal responsibility is pervasive in many health communication campaigns. Messages are likely to stress that people need to take care of themselves for the sake of others who depend on them and that following certain recommendations is being responsible. These types of appeals were used in messages presented in posters and in television public service announcements produced for NHLBI's high-blood-pressure prevention campaign: Individuals were told they should be healthy so they could support their families; mothers needed to take care of themselves for the sake of their children. Another type of message was developed by the depression awareness, recognition, and treatment (D/ART) campaign, a public education intervention sponsored by the U.S. National Institute of Mental Health (Regier et al., 1988). One of the campaign's main themes has been, "People may need help to get help," and one of the messages developed was a public service announcement featuring a depressed young woman and how her sister helped her take the first step to get help.[13] On one hand, critics may point out that persuasive messages that appeal to people's sense of duty as breadwinners or caretakers may reproduce taken-for-granted institutional arrangements, such as giving priority to workplace demands over social activities and unequal gender roles. On the other hand, such messages may in fact foster altruistic and other-directed rather than self-directed orientations. This other-directed and caring orientation can be

THE FIRST STEP
IN GETTING HELP FOR DEPRESSION
IS THE HARDEST.

D/ART · DEPRESSION Awareness,
Recognition, and Treatment

Clinical **depression** is more than the "blues" or feeling "down." It's an illness that can affect a person's whole life . . . mood, mind, body, behavior . . . and severely disrupt work, family, and social life.

Often, people who are depressed don't seek the help they need. They think they can just "snap out of it" or "pull themselves together." The fact is people who are seriously depressed may need the support of family and friends to get help from caring professionals.

If someone you know is suffering from **depression**, help that person take the first step toward getting professional help. Learn more about **depression**. For a free brochure, call:

1-800-421-4211
EFFECTIVE TREATMENTS ARE AVAILABLE.

U.S. DEPARTMENT OF HEALTH AND HUMAN SERVICES · Public Health Service · National Institutes of Health · National Institute of Mental Health
DEPRESSION Awareness, Recognition and Treatment Campaign

Illustration 4.3

seen reinforced in other messages disseminated by D/ART, as displayed on the poster, *The first step in getting help for depression is the hardest:*

> Often, people who are depressed don't seek the help they need. They think they can just "snap out of it" or "pull themselves together." The fact is people who are seriously depressed may need the support of family and friends to get help from caring professionals. If someone you know is suffering from depression, help that person take the first step toward getting professional help. Learn more about depression.

The role of a caring person, willing to get involved and help another, is emphasized. The caring person can make a significant difference for the person in need. The person in need may not even recognize their need. The helping person needs to take the initiative, pursue pertinent information, and follow up with action, thus enabling the person in need.

Although the D/ART campaign messages that appeal to caring and encourage individuals to get involved and help may indeed facilitate a caring orientation and practice, the notion of responsibility they reinforce seems to focus on

Three Good Reasons To Control Your High Blood Pressure

"My dad died from a stroke at 49. I don't want that to happen to me, so I treat my high blood pressure."

"To take care of my three kids, I need to take care of myself. So I take my blood pressure medicine every day."

"Losing we and staying has helped lower my b pressure— my doctor even reduc my medicat

Illustration 4.4

the individual-level context. The messages of the campaign encourage and direct potential helpers to identify specific mental health problems for which the prescribed solution is a referral to particular health professionals. Referral to appropriate treatment and care, as explicated by the campaign messages, can literally save the life and affect the welfare of the depressed individual. Campaign messages tend to focus less on institutional aspects that also may be critical for the welfare of the person in need of mental health services. For example, limited insurance coverage for specific mental health services may prevent many people from seeking and obtaining adequate mental health treatment and professional care.

A different use of the notion of personal responsibility is illustrated in messages that suggest that people should be responsible and maintain their own good health to fulfill their obligations to others who depend on them. In a message disseminated by an NHLBI campaign on the prevention of high blood pressure, a woman is shown with the saying: "To take care of my three kids I need to take care of myself, so I take my blood pressure medicine every day." This message employs the notion of the personal responsibility of a mother's

Illustration 4.5

obligation to her children as an important motivational incentive. Similarly, one's children's future, reminds another message (see Illustration 4.5), is in the parents' hands. By implication, to be a responsible parent, one needs to protect one's health.

These messages, as noted regarding those in the D/ART campaign, reinforce important values: caring for others, being there and helping others. Yet when messages on responsibility are mainly used as a persuasive mechanism—as they typically are when interventions adapt a social-marketing approach—there seems to be little, if any, opportunity for discourse and deliberation on the nature of responsibility. What does it mean to be a responsible parent, a responsible worker, or a responsible citizen? Clearly, what it means to be "responsible" may differ according to cultural and ideological frame-

**It's your health,
it's your life,
it's your move!**

**Your next
appointment is on**

Date:

Time:

If you can't keep your appointment,
please call the office.

Illustration 4.6

works. Opportunities to deliberate people's obligation to self, others, and the community as a whole may be a prerequisite for developing a fuller moral sense of obligation.

Intervention messages are also likely to emphasize that lay persons should be told to follow particular regimens and to recommend that health providers employ particular persuasive techniques to increase compliance. Such messages and intervention practices may serve to further legitimize health professionals and their institutions as the main source of expert knowledge and the biomedical perspective as most relevant in the definition and solution of the health problem. In this context, therefore, institutional arrangements would potentially privilege those associated with medical services. This may be a conscious and officially formulated objective, as in the case of the campaign to reduce high blood pressure sponsored by the U.S. National Heart, Lung and Blood Institute (NHLBI), which used increased visits to doctors as an indicator of success.[14]

An example of a message that prioritizes medical institutions through messages on personal responsibility is, "It's your life, it's your move," featured as a major theme in an NHLBI campaign to reduce high blood pressure.[15] The move referred to in this message is that the person considered at risk should go to a doctor and follow a biomedical definition of what is wrong with his or her health. Other possible types of moves that involve personal responsibility, such as making changes in one's own or others' living or work conditions, are not likely to be mentioned or made explicit in this type of intervention because responsibility has been mainly used strategically to persuade the target population to follow a specific regimen rather than to change institutional arrangements.

An example of the strategic use of responsibility is a recommendation to appeal to people's fear of becoming a burden on others: "Hypertensives fear stroke because they would lose their independence and become a burden to their families. Messages should remind them of their potential to become a burden if their blood pressure is not controlled."[16]

Again, the notion of being responsible by not becoming a burden on others is a social value that can be associated with fairness (one does not want to unfairly burden others) as well as with the value of being physically and mentally independent, self-mobile, and a contributing member of society. Although it is difficult for most of us not to identify with these notions, they are also problematic: Are those who become dependent irresponsible? Should physical and mental independence be an absolute value?

Messages in the Instrumental Model also are likely to equate responsibility with specific actions and connote a particular notion of positive personal identity, for example, in the context of relational and social interaction. This is illustrated in the following messages taken out of the pamphlet *Better Sex: Healthy Sex* by the American Social Health Association, which stated: "Buying and using condoms says that you are a responsible person who wants to protect your sexual health." Not using a condom implies that one is *not a responsible person*. This raises ethical concerns regarding branding people with negative identity characteristics irrespective of the social context of their action, a topic further elaborated in the sections to follow.

A differential emphasis on responsibility as a goal or strategy in particular institutional contexts is likely to be associated with different approaches to defining the problem. The way the problem is defined can be influenced by the priorities and frameworks adopted by dominant stakeholders. More so, when personal responsibility is used instrumentally, the solution, as defined by the intervention sponsor, is likely to be taken as a given. In the Instrumental Model, where interventions' activities serve to disseminate messages defined by the sponsor, typically a health organization, problems defined by scientific criteria would tend to be the kind considered legitimate and important to address. Issues not supported by what intervention sponsors consider science-based evidence would not be readily sanctioned. This is illustrated in the way the issue of stress was framed as a problematic and "unofficial" risk factor for heart disease in the official documents of the National Cholesterol Education Program sponsored by NHLBI and in personal interviews with practitioners. On one hand, stress was recognized as a potentially important (risk) factor, based on the physiological responses of the body to stressful stimuli. On the other hand, the expert panels of this program concluded that the evidence to support stress as an official risk factor was inconclusive.[17] The type of scientific criteria used by these panels served as the main reason for their rejection of stress as a social-level risk. This can be explained by the composition of the program's experts and their strong orientation toward biomedical criteria[18] and may serve to illustrate how certain types of so-called risk factors or consideration of causes of the problem are likely to be less prioritized or legitimized because they are less valued by dominant stakeholders.[19]

In contrast, stress is viewed as a central determinant of illness and analyzed as an organizational and social-level construct in two areas of health. Both connect stress to power and sense of control. The first is in the area of work. Studies that took place mostly in Europe have pointed to a relationship between stress associated with institutional arrangements in the workplace to heart disease. These studies suggest that traditional stress management solutions did not address institutional factors, such as workload or the extent to which people feel they can control their tasks, which is likely to cause increased stress (Fox, Dwyer, & Ganster, 1993; Karasek & Theorell, 1990; Repetti, 1993).

McLeroy et al. (1987) provide a pertinent example of alternative definitions of the problem of stress in the workplace and stress-related interventions, which underscores the ideological as well as programmatic rifts between different stakeholders in addressing stress in the workplace, a critical issue that increasingly affects large segments of society. They compare divergent approaches as reflected in differential definitions of the problem of stress in the workplace, according to management and labor. The first model focuses on the person-environment fit and adopts a more psychological approach. The definition of the problem is thus on the individual level, and so is the solution. The second focuses on demands of the work situation as sources of stress and the range of control available to workers facing those demands. This approach is based on a structural perspective, and both the problem and solution are defined in structural rather than individual terms. They suggest that the choice of the research model, and by implication, the definition of the problem and solution to it, depends on the characteristics of the social system of the researchers and their ideological commitments. In an earlier example, the NHLBI expert panel, with its biomedical professional background, clearly adopted a biomedical model in its selection and interpretation of the notion of stress as a casual factor in heart disease.[20]

The second area in which the interrelationship between health, stress, and a feeling of mastery or control over one's life is seen as a critical factor is in the area of personal and community empowerment. Health is perceived as significantly affected by the extent to which people feel control or mastery over their life and living circumstances (Israel, Checkoway, Schulz, & Zimmerman, 1994; Wallerstein, 1992). Research findings cited by authors who advocate a community empowerment approach to health promotion point to a link between powerlessness and mental and physical health status, both on individual and community levels. The strategic approach they recommend "recognizes the interrelatedness of the role of stressors on health and quality of life at individual, organizational, and community levels" (Israel et al., p. 155).

Practitioners interviewed in community-based programs viewed stress from a more structural perspective (see Guttman, 1994). One practitioner described stress as a barrier to the acquisition of knowledge and sense of control:

> In the population that we're working with, maybe they have so many stresses because they're a lower income level that they don't equate, perhaps, nutrition with disease or the other problems that they may be having in their life. I've tried to bring it together to make them see that they can have more control over the quality of their life by changing certain behaviors.

Similarly, in a focus group report in which the participants were low-income urban residents (see Guttman, 1994), the interviewers concluded that

> Although most [focus group members] had correctly identified a variety of risk factors for hypertension, "stress" seemed to predominate their concern. "Life is too stressful" were examples of phrases that predominated the discussion of reducing risk for hypertension. The whole dialogue, in all groups always came back to stress as a major problem. People felt helpless or at least halfhearted in their abilities to manage stress. Most sought to escape it (through alcohol, dancing, television) rather than acknowledge it and cope with it.[21]

Major sources of stress mentioned by the participants in this group were work, a living environment perceived as unsafe, family, and money. Smoking was also related to stress, according to the focus group report. Smokers suggested that smoking is "a first-line coping strategy for stress management. When stressed they would reach for a cigarette." Similarly, in a large survey of residents in the Stanford Five-City Project, researchers reported that stress was mentioned by the respondents as a risk for heart disease about twice as much as saturated fat (Frank, Winkleby, Frotmann, & Farquhar, 1993). This brings us back to the topic of responsibility: Clearly, lay people, regardless of biomedical evidence, may view stressful life conditions as a central cause of risk behavior and illness. Yet if stress is viewed mainly as something a person can deal with by being more responsible on the individual level, they are likely to be viewed as having the obligation to successfully deal with stress by applying their willpower or other personal means. If we accept the view that stress is linked to structural factors, we risk casting blame on people who feel they cannot cope or have to resort to unhealthy stress-management strategies, such as smoking.[22]

Context

Messages given priority in the Instrumental Model also would tend to emphasize adaptation to current institutional arrangements and the virtue of making responsible uses of present resources. Resources offered by the intervention to help persons adopt its recommendations would be presented as a central feature. This is illustrated in one of the messages used in the materials of a county-level heart disease prevention intervention program, which was adapted from materials disseminated by NHLBI (see Guttman, 1994): "With the hectic schedules families have today it is often difficult to find the time to prepare a well balanced home cooked meal. Ordering-in, or picking up that quick lunch may be your only option at the time."

This message implies that the individual should be responsible and make the best of what could be considered a health-reducing situation. Clearly, the message did not frame the situation as problematic from a societal or structural perspective. Instead, it focused on a solution based on a consumer model: So-called responsible behaviors were couched in making the "right" consumption choices. Implied is that a hectic lifestyle in our social context is a given and needs to be coped with. No mention nor any exploration was made of the institutional conditions that create this hectic lifestyle, which leaves the individual with few of what are considered health-promoting options. The social and economic conditions (e.g., a workday daily schedule) that, according to the intervention, predispose individuals to unhealthy eating behaviors are presented as inevitable. Similarly, messages on how to infuse physical activity into one's daily schedule, typically perceived as dominated by one's work schedule, did not mention work-site-related constraints. Adaptation to current work schedules seemed to be presented as the optimal and, at this point, the only option.

Interventions in the Instrumental Model may therefore tend to have messages that underscore the embedded assumption that a responsible person learns to *adapt*. Intervention messages, in turn, would offer suggestions and tips on how to manage this adaptation and to squeeze in—despite personal as well as institutional obstacles—what they consider health-promoting behaviors. These types of messages would reproduce systems that are taken for granted, such as workplace schedules and salary structures. These, in turn, would reproduce social environments that promote antihealth practices. These include lack of opportunities for families to purchase nutritional foods or preventing them from eating together because of cost and work schedules. The latter, suggested researchers, tends to promote unhealthy eating habits in children and teenagers (National Cholesterol Education Program, 1990). Last, the strategic emphasis on personal responsibility may give preference to messages that prioritize and reproduce values that are dominant in U.S. culture that include individualism, a distrust of government intervention, a preference for private solutions to social problems, a standard of abundance as a normal state of affairs, and the power of technology (Bellah et al., 1991; Priester, 1992b).

Relationships

An intervention's intended populations are likely to be characterized as individuals who need to be provided with the right kind of motivational messages, information, and skills so that they can make what the interventionists consider responsible choices. They also are viewed as needing to have the necessary self-efficacy to do so. This constructs a particular mode of personal responsibility: following what health experts define as good and right. Practitioners would thus serve mainly as guides, trainers, and motivators.

Ethical Concerns

Bioethicists have raised ethical concerns associated with the notion of culpability: To what extent is the individual responsible for ill-health consequences that result from their own lifestyle-related behaviors? The answer to this question usually rests on whether the behavior is seen as voluntary or if it is seen as influenced by other factors, such as socioeconomic conditions or cultural influences. However, as bioethicists point out, this is not always easy to determine, and determining the extent to which a person is or is not culpable involves numerous ethical considerations (Veatch, 1980; Wikler, 1978). Regarding sexual activity, the implication that only those who use condoms are responsible and those who do not are irresponsible raises ethical concerns: Do people always have a real choice whether or not to use condoms? Sexual partners may not insist on using condoms even in situations considered high risk because they may fear it may harm the relationship, or they may actually risk personal, economic, physical, or social harm, or they may feel competing obligations (e.g., Chanda, Baggaiey, Phiri, & Kelly, 1994; Nyamathie, Flaskerud, Bennet, Leake, & Lewis, 1994: barriers associated with cultural norms; Lyman & Engstrom, 1992; Stein, 1994: gender issues; Orr, Celmentano, Santelli, & Burwell, 1994: depression, ethnicity, and social class). Messages that equate responsible behavior with condom use clearly risk blaming those who do not and may harm these individuals' self-concept or label them as irresponsible.

A related ethical concern is the implication that one's actions are sufficient to solve the pertinent health-related problem. As Callahan (1984) suggests, one of the critiques of health promotion approaches that overemphasize the responsibility of the individual is an implicit ideology regarding the production of health:

> The ideology of personal responsibility has implications for the way individuals organize their lifestyles in that it assumes not only that those individuals' responsibility for lifestyles will be sufficient to lead to a major improvement in their health but that the individual has the power and the autonomy to control their own lifestyle. (p. 85)

"Stopping AIDS is up to you, your family and your loved ones" is a message disseminated in a pamphlet from the Department of Health and Human Services titled *Understanding AIDS* (USDHHS, 1988, p. 1). Do individuals indeed have sufficient means to stop AIDS, even in their own communities or even in their own families? Is it really only up to them if their family members use drugs or engage in behaviors considered risky? Can they fully control circumstances even in their own interpersonal contexts that may put them at risk for AIDS?[23]

Findings from a study of African American women involved with physically abusive primary partners indicate that these women were less likely than other women in the study's sample to use condoms and were more likely to experience abuse when they discussed the use of condoms. They were also found to be more fearful about asking their partners to use condoms, more worried about acquiring HIV, and felt more isolated than women who were not in abusive situations (Wingood & DiClemente, 1997). Clearly, these women represent an extreme case of people who cannot be told it is totally up to them to prevent AIDS. Interventions can contribute by helping these women change their life circumstances and perhaps be less dependent on abusive relationships that put them at risk.

Emphasis on External Factors

In the Environmental Model, the emphasis is not on personal responsibility as either a goal or a strategy, but rather on regulation and engineering-type strategies. The purpose is to create a social and physical environment that channels target population members into health-promoting practices or helps protect them from hazards. For example, the intervention can influence the content and display of dishes offered in menus in restaurants, work site food services, or schools to reflect mostly, if not exclusively, so-called heart-healthy items; it could increase the likelihood that processed food products in the grocery store would all be low in fat and sodium content; or it could influence the production of automobiles so that passengers would not suffer from major injuries even when they collide.[24]

Relationships

On one hand, the types of relationships that develop within the intervention system can be characterized as paternalistic: an environment meant to advance health-promoting behavior created by those who believe they know what is best. Also, it privileges those whose products or services are determined to be beneficial. On the other hand, in a democratic state, this type of intervention could be a result of the responses of a responsible public who has gone through the deliberative stage. The controlled environment and the decisions regarding what is good and what is bad, or what should be regulated to provide a health-promoting environment in this context, can be a result of what are called *second-order choices* (Childress, 1990)[25] or *beneficent paternalism* or may reflect a communitarian approach (Beauchamp, 1988).

Context

Institutional factors or systems that this type of model of intervention would promote, sustain, or reproduce would depend on the process that brought them about. For example, if as a result of public deliberation on the merits and values involved, cigarettes are heavily taxed for the purpose of discouraging children from smoking, it could be argued that the process supports public debate and moral decisions regarding responsibility of the community toward members of the community: in this case, children, who are seen as particularly vulnerable.[26] A regulation that sanctions individuals for engaging in particular sexual acts because it may put them at higher risk for HIV infection may be seen as supporting constituents who disapprove of these practices for reasons other than health. One of the main concerns in this model is this: To what extent does it support respect for autonomy and how are possible tensions between autonomy and the public good reconciled?[27] The problem and solution would tend to be defined on several levels of intervention, ranging from assumptions that individual motivation is not sufficient to engage in certain health-promoting behaviors and that people need an environment that would help them carry out these behaviors or protect them from unhealthy temptations to assumptions that society has the mandate to protect people's health, even if this means interfering with individual and corporate interests.

Ethical Concerns

Serious concerns associated with enforcing social control and violating respect for people's autonomy are eminent: The engineering of one's environment not only restricts people's options but may be covert. People may not even be aware of the restrictions. On one hand, this would be precisely the purpose of an engineering approach: to get people to adopt health-promoting practices or avoid hazards in ways that are nearly automatic. On the other hand, this infringes on their right to choose among other options and to make decisions guided by what they believe is right for them. Two important related concerns are these: To what extent is the environment manipulated, which influences people's behavior, based on valid behavioral assumptions, and to what extent is the manipulation carried out to fulfill its promise? Behavioral models that underlie environmental design are, like other behavioral conceptual approaches, based on value-laden assumptions that support particular ideological frameworks of dominant stakeholders.

Table 4.2. summarizes factors associated with content, context, relationships, and ethical concerns associated with each model type.

Evolution and Adaptation

Because the models represent prototypes, an intervention may not fit exactly within one of them. Many health communication interventions are likely, however, to fit mainly into the Invocation and Instrumental Models due to their heavy use of a social-marketing approach and techniques of persuasive appeal that frame personal responsibility as an obligation to adopt recommended lifestyle behaviors. Furthermore, because most health communication interventions do not tend to employ a notion of agency that encompasses enabling moral education and skills to interpret what is happening (Harmon, 1995) in the sociopolitical context (Duncan & Cribb, 1996; Wallack, 1989), many are likely to be placed in the instrumental quadrant.

The models need not represent static situations. Promoting responsibility at the individual level may serve as one of the steps in enhancing awareness and reflexive and analytic skills to understand and act on societal issues that affect personal or local circumstances (Bernstein et al., 1994).[28] An illustration of how models of personal responsibility can transform from individual to societal domains (intermediary domains, such as organizational or community, can also be added), is shown in Figure 4.3. By increasing people's awareness and enhancing their capacities and skills to make responsible choices in personal matters, the intervention may serve to influence behaviors associated with personal lifestyle choices as well as the support of others and behavior in institutional contexts. People may become more aware and gain skills and capacities to influence structural conditions, for example, by forming advocacy organizations or pressure groups. Such advocacy activities and institutional changes may help change environmental conditions and enhance opportunities to adopt more health-promoting behaviors. These changes may contribute to an enhanced health status of individuals and healthier workplaces and living situations.

Besides personal responsibility, other values or justifications prominently featured in public health communication interventions can serve to create additional typologies that make distinctions among interventions. The next chapter presents a typology focusing on the value of community involvement, an increasingly dominant approach in health promotion that serves both as a

Table 4.2   Content, Context, Relationships, and Ethical Concerns in the Responsibility Models

Model	Relationship Between Practitioners and Intervention Population	Content: Prominent Messages	Context: Reproduced Institutional Practices or Arrangements	Ethical Concerns
Invocation (high goal, low strategy)	Provide guidance; generate discourse and discussions on the nature of responsibility	Personal and social norms and values believed to contribute to the prevalence of risk or foster health	Some current practices, schedules, and dominant caregiving systems reproduced	Infringement on respect for autonomy; questions regarding which moral frameworks prevail; concerns regarding victim blaming
Deliberative (high goal, high strategy)	Guidance and training in developing ethical deliberations; conflict acknowledged	Importance of moral decision making; nature of health problems; analysis of how to affect structural factors	Alternative practices and definitions fostered; changes take place in availability of resources to different constituency groups	Infringement on respect for autonomy; questions regarding which moral frameworks prevail
Environmental (low goal, low strategy)	Guidance through regulated options and opportunities (an earlier process of deliberation may have preceded their application)	Importance of environmental factors or behavioral approaches on health behavior	Social policy viewed as a means to affect behaviors; values associated with dominant behavior-change theories on which engineering solutions are based	Restricts free choice; limits options
Instrumental (high goal, low strategy)	Guidance, training; support; offer strategies and tips on how to adapt and implement recommended practices	Knowledge and skills acquisition to adopt recommended regimens; adaptation to and use of current social arrangements	Current practices, schedules, and dominant caregiving systems prioritized; values associated with individualism or personal gain prominent	Infringement on respect for autonomy; concerns regarding victim blaming

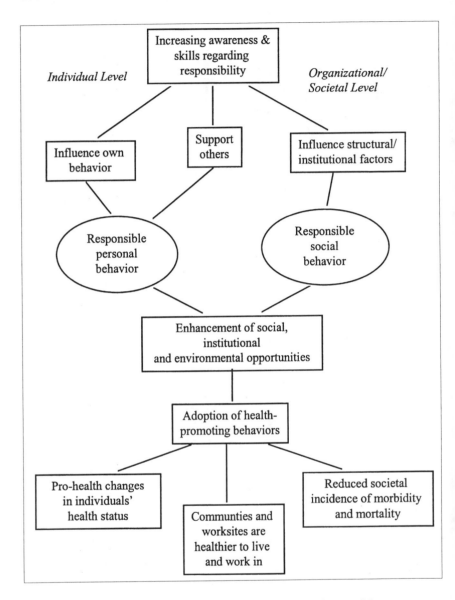

Figure 4.3. Evolution and Adaptation of Personal Responsibility Models

means to achieve particular health objectives and as a goal of enabling people to participate and control their own lives. The discussion of typologies concludes with suggestions on how they can be applied in an analysis that compares within and across interventions.

NOTES

1. This can correspond to distinctions made between values serving as means or ends (LaBonte, 1994).

2. Brickman et al. (1982) present a framework of four models created through a similar matrix, which they call *models of helping and coping*. It differentiates between a high and low emphasis on how much responsibility the patient bears for causing the health problem and the solution for it. An excellent discussion of these models and its application to the health care context appears in Northouse and Northouse (1992). This approach inspired the models presented in this chapter.

3. The way inactivity may privilege certain stakeholders is discussed in Chapter 1.

4. These dimensions draw from the distinctions between content and relationship made by Watzlawick et al. (1967); from bioethicist Daniel Callahan's (1990, p. 190) characterization of three levels of health promotion, which include cultural, entitlement, and institutional; and from Rothman and Tropman's (1987) typology of community organization practice models.

5. See Daniels's (1985) discussion of people who work in jobs that put them at high risk for disease or injury because they feel they have limited options for other sources of employment.

6. This is further elaborated in the final chapter.

7. Emanuel and Emanuel (1992) outline four models of the physician-patient interaction, which emphasize different understandings of its goals, the physician's obligations, and the role of patient values. Their approach and the title they gave the model, "the Deliberative Model," has been adopted here. In this model, the physician presents opportunities to the patient that can be considered through dialogue. This is presented as a process where although patients might be presented with the physician's preferences, they are also given the reasons for these preferences and possible alternative conceptualizations.

8. Meeting obligations through action and being able to act as autonomous agents correspond to the three components of responsibility stressed by Harmon (1995): that one should have received a moral education to be able to make moral choices, be able to actively interpret what is happening, and to exercise one's own will.

9. The latter, although it may sound as if it echoes self-efficacy models in health promotion (Maibach et al., 1991; Perry, Baranowski, & Parcel, 1990), is deeply grounded in a moral and educational approach that differentiates them from the behavioral strategies associated with self-efficacy-based interventions, which tend to be more strategic.

10. Parents in the workplace or people with needy parents may often feel their work obligations conflict with their commitment to others and that their work schedule overrides their personal commitments. Similarly, people may feel that although they would like to engage in activities that are good for their emotional, spiritual, or physical health, they cannot because of rigid work schedules or job demands.

11. This concern has been raised in the context of community empowerment (Robertson & Minkler, 1994) and will be further elaborated in the next chapter.

12. For example, in an interview I conducted with a practitioner in an intervention to prevent heart disease and stroke, the practitioner responded: "Whose else's responsibility [is it] if not the individual's?" indicating that it is taken for granted that responsibility for the health-related practices promoted by the intervention is mainly linked to personal motivation and behavior.

13. This was described on page 9 of the *D/ART Update,* Summer 1993, a publication of the program, published by U.S. National Institutes of Mental Health.

14. This refers to NHBPEP's report, *20 Years of Achievement* (see Guttman, 1994).

15. This message was found in an NHBPEP PSA. Other types of messages were "You can lower your blood cholesterol: It's up to you. All it takes are some simple diet changes" (*NHLBI Kit '90: The Right Moves,* p. 33, duplicated by the programs) or "You are in control" (*NHLBI Kit '90,* p. 36).

These messages imply that one's behavior change is necessary to influence one's health, which, as discussed, puts the main burden on the person (Guttman, 1994).

16. NHBPEP Communication Strategy, Draft, 1993, p. 24 (see Guttman, 1994).

17. NHBPEP *Working Group Report on the Primary Prevention of Hypertension*, 1992, p. 17. (see Guttman, 1994).

18. A detailed list of panel members and their affiliation can be found in Guttman (1994).

19. The same can be suggested regarding evaluation of outcomes, an issue raised in the assessment of large-scale health communication interventions that are mainly subjected to designs and evaluations based on biomedical standards of clinical trials (Hornik, 1997).

20. As indicated in the discussion on values and the definition of problems: a biomedical approach tends to view stress as an individual-level variable rather than one linked to institutional factors.

21. This quote is from an unpublished focus group report submitted to the Paterson Healthy Heart Program in New Jersey in 1992. This program is described in Guttman, 1994.

22. In a study that explored why mothers chose not to breast-feed their babies, one respondent explained that because she was living in such stressful conditions, she felt she had to smoke, and therefore she decided not to breast-feed, because she believed her smoking would contaminate the breast milk and harm the baby (Guttman & Zimmerman, in press).

23. This argument is further elaborated in the sixth chapter in the section on culpability dilemmas.

24. See also the discussion on engineering-type strategies in Chapter 3.

25. Childress (1990) cautions against a possible trend toward paternalism, which can deprive people of autonomy. However, he also suggests that there are situations of autonomous choice, where people can choose to have choices made for them: "It is important for the moral life that people be competent, be informed, and act voluntarily. But they may choose, for example, to yield their first-order decisions" (p. 13).

26. Dan Beauchamp (1987, 1988) suggests that principles of health and safety are shared purposes of the community and should not be subordinated to those of the market, property, and individual liberty. In an interview in 1993, Beauchamp explained that although health promoters support public policies that place restrictions or make particular products more expensive to protect a particular population, they do not like to acknowledge the fact that they are also imposing a burden on many thousands of others who are not likely to engage in harmful behaviors. He explains that the underlying justification for this approach is a collective value, often made invisible by creating an image that the potential harm affects more individuals than it actually does or presenting it as an important risk factor. Wikler (1978) discusses arguments for and against paternalistic measures adopted for the purpose of influencing individuals' lifestyles. Utility and personal responsibility were included in his analysis among the problematic issues involved. He outlines types of cases that might be used to support these measures but concludes that when intrusive, manipulative, or coercive measures are taken to promote health, the moral justifications needed are typically complex, and the principles used in making a case for them would require numerous exceptions and qualifications.

27. See McLeroy et al. (1987) regarding ethical issues related to health promotion in the workplace.

28. Bellah et al. (1991) discuss the importance of making choices in the context of what is good not only for one's self but good for society.

5

Analyses of Intervention Types

Community Involvement

> Indeed, the great classic criteria of a good society—peace, prosperity, freedom, justice—all depend today on a new experiment in democracy, a newly extended and enhanced set of democratic institutions, within which we citizens can better discern what we really want and what we ought to want to sustain a good life on this planet for ourselves and the generations to come.
>
> —*Bellah et al. (1991, p. 9)*

From grassroots initiatives to large-scale government campaigns, more and more public health communication interventions hail community participation and involvement as an underlying justification for their goals or as the key to their strategic approaches. Community involvement is also accorded a central part of the World Health Organization's strategy of "Health for All by the Year 2000" (Robertson & Minkler, 1994). Clearly, differences between the numerous interventions that emphasize community involvement can be substantive: "Citizen involvement in health promotion can run the gamut from manipulation and tokenism to actual control" (Bracht & Gleason, 1990, p. 115). The previous chapter described typologies constructed to help discern socially significant differences between interventions according to the way they emphasize personal responsibility. The typology presented in this chapter focuses on one of the most cherished values of democratic societies: participation, referred to here as *involvement* and discussed in the context of the involvement of community members as it relates to the health-promotion undertaking.

The value of involving the community—even in large-scale public health communication interventions that aim to reach large populations and use mass media strategies—may rest on several premises. For some, the major impetus is a belief that people's behavior is profoundly affected by the community context:

> Behavior is formed and influenced by the dominant culture as experienced in myriad social relations in the context of the community. Communities shape individuals' behavior both symbolically and tangibly, transmitting values and norms. As systems of exchange and influence, communities establish opportunities for people to behave in some ways but not in others. (Thompson & Kinne, 1990, p. 45)

Interventions in the community context are conducted not only because the community is viewed as a crucial site to reach people but because it is believed the community itself can serve as a change agent. According to this perspective, participation is valued because it is believed communities themselves may be mobilized to further public health objectives, and participation is the best way to ensure that the effects of the intervention would be sustained over time (Bracht, 1990b, p. 20). Last, not only does community involvement have a strategic advantage; its intrinsic value and moral imperative rests in the belief that it is "perhaps the best antidote to that most pernicious of modern political ills, the fragmentation, disempowerment, and alienation of the ordinary citizen" (Green, 1989, p. 44). Community involvement or participation is viewed as essential to the fulfillment of democratic ideals (McNight, 1987). These views are reflected in the World Health Organization's 1986 Ottawa Charter, which calls for programs that will help people control their own destinies (Robertson & Minkler, 1994). In addition, in the development of public health communication intervention messages, researchers and practitioners have increasingly noted the importance of involving target audience members in the design of messages, whether through focus group methods or involving them as actual producers of messages (e.g., Freimuth & Mettger, 1990; Duke & Omi, 1991). What are the underlying values of this type of involvement? Is it for strategic purposes, to produce messages that are more persuasive, or is it to elicit the issues target audiences find important?

MODELS OF COMMUNITY INVOLVEMENT

The four models in the typology of community involvement presented in the discussion to follow are constructed similarly to the models in the previous chapter and are illustrated in Figure 5.1. The models are created by differentiating whether the value of community involvement is used as a goal or as a strategy or both. The analysis applies the same analytic dimensions used in the previous typology: (a) *content:* meanings prioritized in messages and privileged stakeholders; (b) *relationship:* relationships between the interventionists and targeted population members; and (c) *context:* institutional arrangements or social structures changed or reproduced by the intervention's activities.

| | | GOAL | |
		Low	High
STRATEGY	*Low*	*Service:* Community involvement low both as goal and as strategy	*Augmentation:* Community involvement high as goal but low as strategy
	High	*Use, Collaboration:* Community involvement low as goal but high as strategy	*Mobilization:* Community involvement high as both goal and as strategy

Figure 5.1.   Models of Community Involvement as Strategy or Goal

The models of community involvement are labeled, for the sake of facilitating the discussion, as follows: *Service* (low emphasis on community involvement as either goal or strategy), characterized by the intervention mainly providing specific health-related services, such as screening for risk factors or providing educational activities to meet specific health objectives; *Augmentation* (high emphasis on community involvement as a goal but low in strategy), characterized by interventions that emphasize involvement as a goal but do not employ strategies that enhance the capacities of community-based organizations, particularly of those constituencies not connected to established organizations; *Use-Collaboration* (high emphasis on community involvement as goal but lower emphasis on strategy), characterized by interventions that rely heavily on involving community-based organizations to implement the health objectives of the intervention; and *Mobilization* (high in emphasis on both goal and strategy), in which intervention activities help facilitate involvement of community-based groups and individuals both in determining which problems to address and how to accomplish this. As in the previous typology, the purpose of the distinction between models is to help describe different types of relationships that can develop in the intervention context as well as activities and messages that may tend to support particular institutional practices or societal structures.

Emphasis on Community Involvement as a Goal

Values associated with autonomy and self-determination serve as the basis for community involvement when emphasized as a *goal* in health promotion endeavors: Community members should be able to determine what issues in their community need to be defined as problems and addressed and how to address them. In the community development and health promotion literature, this kind of involvement is typically referred to as *empowerment,* defined as "the process by which people, organizations and communities gain mastery over their lives" (Rappaport, 1981, p. 3). Empowerment, however, has also become a buzzword appropriated for strategic use by politicians and corporate management (Wallerstein & Bernstein, 1994).

Emphasis on community involvement both as a goal and a strategy would entail an intervention that would be a "social-action process in which individuals and groups act to gain mastery over their lives in the context of changing their social and political environment" (Wallerstein & Bernstein, 1994, p. 142). This would call for strategies that could enable people to gain such mastery and facilitate social changes. Strategies could include means to increase grassroots organizations' capacities or the development of resources and a power base to gain political power and mobilize diverse constituencies. Skills-building strategies would also be included, for example, negotiation, collaboration and conflict resolution, public relations, and advocacy skills.

When emphasized mainly as a goal but not as a strategy, as in the Augmentation Model, the goal of involvement would be prominent, but the intervention would tend not to offer strategies that enhance involvement skills. In this model, intervention programs may provide funds to community groups or organizations to develop their own activities in order to achieve self-defined goals. Relatively little support, however, would be offered on how to develop capacities of diverse constituencies within and outside these organizations to define health-related problems. Because the interventionists would not engage in strategies that mobilize constituencies who do not belong to well-established groups, only constituencies already connected to the system would be likely to be given opportunities for capacity building.

Content

Messages in the models that emphasize community involvement as a goal would prominently resonate values associated with autonomy, participation, empowerment, and self-determination. Participation, political action, advocacy, ownership, and community involvement in decisions regarding allocation of resources—also associated with these values—would be emphasized in messages and prominent activities. Biomedical solutions would be likely to be less emphasized. Messages with transformative capacity would be prominently featured and may include information about how to analyze social conditions, how political and bureaucratic structures function, and how to analyze and create policy documents (LaBonte, 1994). Messages may also be developed and produced by community members themselves as part of a problem-solving educational experience, following a Freirian model, and as means for stimulating discussion among the peers of those who produced them (Rudd & Comings, 1994).

Because mobilization is often energized by controversy, the tone of some of the messages may be combative and may emphasize controversial rather than presumably neutral positions. For example, messages may refer to tactics used by alcohol and tobacco industries to target minorities or children; messages may tell about companies that neglect to control environmental pollution from manufacturing plants located in sites near low-income residences; messages may stress corporate labor and compensation practices that discriminate against unprotected laborers and deny them health and other benefits. These types of messages, though, may be suppressed when dominant stakeholders promote a consensus approach, as noted in the discussion to follow (Janes & Corbet, 1996).

Current institutional practices and resource allocation would be scrutinized or challenged when involvement is emphasized as a goal. The intervention's population would be encouraged to define problems from their own perspectives (Rappaport, 1981). Community building, explain McKnight and

Kretzmann (1984), is likely to involve "taking a thorough look at the public dollars already being spent in the neighborhood and devising strategies aimed at shifting their uses away from traditional transfer and maintenance functions toward [economic] investment approaches" (p. 17). In both models that emphasize involvement as a goal, the need to identify and develop community resources and the importance of mobilizing individuals and groups would be featured as an important message. In the Augmentation Model, however, relatively little emphasis would be given on how to actually carry out this type of mission or how to deal with conflict, which may occur when different priorities among constituencies become apparent (Janes & Corbet, 1996). Also, there would be less of a tendency to seek out, identify, foster, and include marginal individuals or groups in the intervention discourse.

In the Mobilization Model,[1] characterized by a high emphasis on community involvement both as a goal and a strategy, predetermined health-related objectives of the intervention program are less likely. Individuals or groups in the community may choose to focus on issues not directly related to specific health objectives. They may prefer to postpone screening programs for elevated blood pressure or cholesterol and work on developing economic opportunities in their community or changing grocery store practices. Activities would aim to generate discussion on what health-related issues should be prioritized. This model draws from community action and community development models, which aim to address the most pressing issues related to the well-being of the residents.[2] E. R. Brown (1991) describes such a case: Community members chose to focus on crime in a community project whose goal was to promote low-income elderly residents' health. With the adoption of community development and social action strategies and by addressing the problem as identified by the residents, the intervention enabled the residents to overcome their social isolation and increased their political power as well as their physical health.

Health promotion approaches that emphasize community involvement as a goal invariably view health as inextricably related to social conditions, such as economic opportunities, safety, and housing. Community involvement interventions, therefore, would tend to extend a biomedical definition of health. The World Health Organization's prescriptions for health promotion at the community level exemplify this perspective (Whitehead, 1992). It firmly poses a causal link between health and social, political, and economic factors and defines health as a resource for everyday life (Robertson & Minkler, 1994). This approach would be reflected in messages that include an emphasis on advancing public policy initiatives or the enforcement of regulations whose purpose is to affect the physical and social environment of the involved communities (Wallack et al., 1993).

Context

The literature on planning and public participation lists several important features for conducting public involvement in planning community programs (Forester, 1985; Syme & Eaton, 1989) that can provide appropriate contextual prerequisites for community involvement in interventions corresponding to the Mobilization Model. These include strategies to generate agreement on the process of participation among all stakeholders,[3] public participation early in the planning process, public awareness of the power involved, and availability of information to all participants. From the outset of the intervention, before specific goals and objectives are articulated, formal and informal forums for identifying people's concerns, community resources, and potential solutions would take place in the community and involve diverse community constituencies (Fawcett et al., 1996). In the Augmentation Model, such forums may not be created or reinforced. Instead, current institutional arrangements offering certain forms of participation would be sustained and reproduced. Organizations that received support from the intervention sponsors may nevertheless gain additional resources and their power and influence would potentially grow as well.[4]

Lorraine Gutierrez (quoted and cited in Bernstein et al., 1994), in a discussion on community empowerment for health promotion published in a special *Health Education Quarterly* issue on this topic, laments that one of the problems of empowerment theory as it is practiced in health promotion contexts is "its focus on individually based, incremental, social change" (p. 289). Gutierrez explains that the change strategy used is typically based

> on personal and collective transformation, rather than on changes in policy or other societal forces. It assumes that by changing the consciousness and capacity of those with less power, that the social order can be transformed. It does not look to ways in which conflict is necessary for social change, nor does it focus on changing the consciousness of those in power. (p. 289)

This critique makes two important points: First, structural factors and well-entrenched economically based institutional arrangements are clearly difficult to influence, even by a well-meaning, well-designed public health communication intervention that aims to facilitate empowerment among those with limited power. Ronald LaBonte (1994) eloquently phrases this concern:

> Health promotion and empowerment nonetheless exist between two perils: That of co-opting or neutralizing social struggle and conflict within the conservative ethos of institutions, and that of naively proclaiming the community as the solution to all sociopolitical and economic health problems. (p. 255)

Janes and Corbet (1996) elaborate on this critique and propose that an overemphasis on self-help, self-determination, and empowerment ignores risks that are beyond local control. They further argue that "the failure of such efforts, doomed from the start, may be blamed on the communities themselves" (p. 11).

The second point is that conflict, as Gutierrez suggests, may be obscured in efforts to mobilize communities, particularly in efforts in which a consensus model is adopted for furthering what are believed to be community interests. Conflict with forces outside the community may be acknowledged but suppressed in order to "work with the system," thus losing its transformative capacities as a powerful drive for change (Janes & Corbet, 1996; LaBonte, 1994). But even more troubling may be suppression of conflict within the community itself. In the name of consensus, situations may be created in which, as Janes and Corbet (1996) suggest,

> Disaffected groups are persuaded to drop demands or "leave the table." The resulting plans are watered down so as not to offend a vocal minority, and in the end, one has to wonder whether the real needs of the multiple interests groups in a locality have been served at all. (p. 6)

To illustrate this phenomenon, Janes and Corbet describe a case that occurred in Colorado, where consensus was achieved only after a demand to address the health and welfare of youth was dropped and services for the elderly were prioritized instead.

Whereas conflict may arise in all community involvement models, it would be mainly valued in the Mobilization Model. In this model, stakeholders are more likely to recognize the importance of acknowledging that individuals and groups—particularly those who have not been in the mainstream—may have competing definitions of what is important and what should be done and that there are competing claims on limited resources. Relationships between intervention constituencies may thus be adversarial as well as collaborative. Consensus, therefore, may not be highly prioritized, and intervention constituencies may seek alternative ways to negotiate ways to accomplish their goals. Compromise, negotiation, and accommodation may be more characteristic of the relationship development process that evolves between constituency groups and the intervention professionals. By implication, the notion of consensus challenges us to unpack the values embedded in consensus and explore why it is so highly valued in certain social contexts and suppressed or problematic in others.

Relationships

As implied by the word *mobilization,* the interventionists presumably have, at least initially, a certain amount of power to move people or organizations. They are responsible, therefore, for transferring this power into what Rappaport (as quoted in Lugo, 1996) describes as "the conditions and language and beliefs that make it possible to be taken by those who are in need of it" (p. 282). The professionals' role in this model would include finding ways to enhance target population members' skills, particularly those who have less organizational resources. These efforts can include helping them gain access to information and support of indigenous community leadership (Robertson & Minkler, 1994).

In addition to mobilization, relationships within the intervention system in this model are likely to include partnerships or alliances, following Rothman and Tropman's (1987) framework. Rothman and Tropman present models of community organization practice, described as prototypes representing three orientations in social planning. Locality Development, their first model, is characterized by consensus: The practitioner takes the role of an enabler-catalyst and teacher of problem-solving skills. The second model, the Social Planning Model, is characterized by an emphasis on task goals and problem solving. The practitioners serve as implementors and facilitators, typically sponsored by the dominant power structure. These two models correspond to variations of the Augmentation and the Use-Collaboration models described in this chapter, in which interventionists guide or facilitate activities among community-based organizations toward achieving the health-related goals of the intervention sponsors. Rothman and Tropman's third model, the Social Action Model, is characterized by goals that aim to shift power and institutional relationships. Practitioners typically act as activists-advocates and are more likely to think of their constituents as fellow "partisans" rather than "clients." The medium of change is a political process, and the intervention's goals can be either task or process goals. The latter are goals regarding building a constituency with the ability to acquire and exercise power. This model corresponds in part to the Mobilization Model. Rothman and Tropman's three models can help contextualize health promotion intervention activities in a broader social-planning perspective, as indicated in the health promotion literature on community empowerment (Israel et al., 1994), and can inform the distinctions made in the typology developed here of community involvement models.

Evaluation activities also entail different types of relationships and may achieve different outcomes across intervention types. As noted by Fawcett et al. (1996), evaluation

> may enhance (or reduce) capacity to influence the environment, and to varying degrees. On one end of a continuum of evaluation, nonparticipatory evaluation can be completely coercive and proscribed, without input from those whose efforts are being appraised. At the other extreme, fully participatory (or participation-controlled) evaluation can be completely initiated, designed, and administered by the community initiative. (p. 163)

The latter would represent the relationship between the evaluators and the intervention population in the Mobilization Model; the former would be more typical of relationships in the Service and Use-Collaboration Models.

Relationships in the Mobilization Model may also consist of consultation, mentoring, and training in skills, particularly in earlier stages of the intervention. These may be similar to relations that develop in the Use-Collaboration Model, where the emphasis on involvement is mainly as strategy. The difference would be that because involvement per se is the goal (or guiding value) of the mobilization, the dynamics of the relationships would change in the direction of comradeship. In contrast, in the Use-Collaboration Model, interventionists would not strive to reframe the definitions of the problems or strategic approaches to address them. The main difference between the relationships in the Augmentation Model and Mobilization Model is that in the former, the professionals would not reach out to or serve as catalysts for constituencies who are outside the mainstream; in the latter, they would.

The role of professionals as facilitators or as those who can presumably empower others is inherently problematic. As LaBonte (1994) explains, "Professionals, as the empowering agent, the subject of the relationship, remain the controlling actor, defining the terms of the interaction. Relatively disempowered individuals or groups remain the objects, the recipients of professional actions" (p. 255). Wallerstein and Bernstein (1994) have also noted the habit or the temptation of professionals to define problems for the community. Even those with a strong community-oriented predisposition admit that as professionals, they may inadvertently find themselves naming the problem for others and that they need to critically assess their relationship with people in communities:

> Even in community settings, the language we use may reinforce a professionally driven solution to the problems. To our surprise, we often hear ourselves say in our work or personal lives: "Don't drink and drive," "Give up those cigarettes before you get cancer," or "This community needs to recognize that drugs and violence are killing its people." (Wallerstein & Bernstein, 1994, p. 141)

Ethical Concerns

Promoting community involvement as a goal raises several concerns regarding unintended outcomes. One important concern, associated with ethical principles of justice and fairness, is that groups that are more influential or vocal or that manage to mobilize particularly powerful constituencies may obtain more influence in the decision process and allocation of resources. The notion of community itself is problematic and also raises concerns regarding ethical principles of justice and autonomy. Some argue that it is an overromanticized ideal, and loyalties within communities are diverse. Leaders that emerge may not necessarily represent the community, and public forums may be manipulated by specific interest groups (Janes & Corbet, 1996). A related concern is that problems identified by communities may not seem the most pressing issues that warrant the use of scarce resources, according to the intervention professionals.

> In such contexts, public health workers are very much on the horns of a dilemma: on the one hand, paternalism and power rear their ugly heads—should we just tell people what's wrong; on the other, "empowered" communities may come to the

table with a set of needs and demands that are, in an objective epidemiologic sense, insignificant. (Janes & Corbet, 1996, p. 9)

Fawcett et al. (1996) add a similar concern in the context of evaluation: The rigor and mission of the evaluation activity to provide a valuable assessment may be compromised as competing interests of different constituencies enter as decision makers and participants in the evaluation process.

A third related and vexing ethical concern is associated with pitting values associated with a community's overall desire to decide on what they believe is right against values associated with ethical principles of justice and the public good: Definitions of problems and solutions that emerge from community settings may not be compatible with those of other communities or society as a whole. Communities may in fact use professionals to advance what others may consider exclusionary agendas. Dominant community groups, as Robertson and Minkler (1994) explain, citing examples of anti-gay-rights groups in Colorado and Oregon, may "assess social problems and propose solutions that reflect racism, sexism, ageism, or other problematic and divisive approaches" (p. 307). Similarly, communities may want to divert limited societal resources to areas that would not likely benefit from the intervention or may even harm society as a whole. For example, they may want to promote industrial enterprises that would provide employment for local residents but that, in the long run, would irreversibly deplete natural resources. A fourth concern, elaborated previously, is that a focus on the community as the main responsible entity for social change may serve to put the burden of responsibly onto the community rather than on state or other agencies.

Last, the actual effectiveness of the emerging or newly created community-based structures raises important concerns. Mobilizing and recruiting membership and getting people involved and sustaining their involvement pose formidable challenges. A critical issue, therefore, is to what extent or how can the community groups sustain themselves? These developing entities may lack long-standing visibility and a structural tradition and are likely to have limited financial backing, which may adversely affect their effectiveness and persistence (Bracht & Gleason, 1990). Last, the promise of citizen participation is not easily achieved. Getting people involved is not an easy task. Studies indicate that in many cases, participation may be limited in terms of members of the population and time. An intervention that aims to go beyond the involvement of chosen constituencies thus requires extensive preparatory effort and facilitation capacities (Bracht & Gleason, 1990).

Emphasis on Community
Involvement as Strategy

Public health communication interventions, even when conducted through federal government initiatives or national organizations, increasingly rely on collaborative efforts with professional, local, business, and community-based organizations (Bracht, 1990a; Giesbrecht et al., 1990). For example, the D/ART campaign was "supporting organizational networks that comprise a nationwide outreach mechanism" (USDHHS, 1991). Participation of different constituencies would be greatly valued by intervention sponsors, because it both supports democratic ideals and is believed to be strategically efficient and effective: Existing resources, networks, and ties can be used to disseminate messages to, and recruit and engage, target populations in intervention activities. Furthermore, theoretical approaches and applied studies provide evidence that community-based forums may be the best and perhaps the only way to reach many constituencies. As Bracht (1990b) concludes, "The active involvement of the community, its leaders, and its organizations is generally assumed to be a necessary ingredient for successful population wide strategies" (p. 19).

Participatory models can differ. In some, a hierarchical order is dominant: A lead organization or group convenes other groups to collaborate but continues to maintain leadership and control regarding the distribution of resources and decision making. In other instances, several groups may form consortia or coalitions while maintaining equal amounts of official power. In other instances, participation of diverse constituencies is mainly exercised through board memberships or advisory committees, whereas in others, constituencies may become an integral part of the intervention's staff or its management.[5] Differences may also occur according to the types of groups or organizations invited to join or participate in the intervention, whom they represent—for example, their professional or vocational affiliations, geographic location, ethnicity, and political power, and which groups are excluded—and whether groups or organizations are created specifically for the intervention's purpose. The latter may occur when stipulations by funding organizations indicate that only particular types of organizations would be eligible for funds.[6]

What is shared across interventions that belong to the Use-Collaboration Model, and what differentiates them from those that belong more to the Mobilization Model, is that a relatively well-defined health goal is pursued, and participation of organizations and community groups is greatly valued as a means to accomplish the chosen objectives. Consensus, important not only for reaching large target audiences through their affiliated organizations but also for having organizations become involved and for legitimizing their messages, is likely to be emphasized.[7]

Thus, the Use-Collaboration Model is similar to the Augmentation and Mobilization Models in the emphasis it places on working with community groups and organizations to achieve intervention goals. It mainly differs in that it does not emphasize involvement, participation, or empowerment as an overriding goal. Because the focus is on accomplishing predetermined goals, the intervention staff may contact and work mainly with those who are accessible or who can give them access to the intended population. An important goal of interventions in this model would be the goal of institutionalization: having collaborating community-based organizations "take over" the health-related objectives of the sponsors of the intervention (Lefebvre, 1990).[8] Although this goal may serve to both improve services and provide a sense of ownership[9] to the community groups, it can also be problematic: Critics fear that it may deplete scarce resources and divert the responsibility for service delivery from the public to the voluntary sector (Green, 1989).

With the focus on problems that have already been defined, unless participating organizations make a strong case for the relevance of other problems, only issues within current definitions of the intervention's problems would be addressed in the Use-Collaboration Model. Capacities for analyzing the conditions of social problems would be less emphasized. The interventionists, though, would heavily engage in capacity building in order to help participating organizations or groups advance program objectives by providing them with training and resources. The collaboration strategy adopted by the National Institutes of Health in its campaign to reduce the risk of high blood pressure, which it described as Shared Service and Community Resource Models, tends to correspond to the Use-Collaboration Model approach and illustrates the collaborative strategy.[10]

Content

The types of messages mainly emphasized would be those that advance the specific health promotion goals. In many cases, the content of messages is likely be developed by experts and produced by the sponsoring organizations. The health issue defined by the intervention would be framed as prominent and important, and messages may include incentives, persuasive appeals and advice on how to address the problems associated with it. For example, on the topic of substance-abuse prevention, parents may be given work sheets to complete with their children on how to resist peer pressure, or a community-based organization would be given ready-made templates to reproduce and disseminate among their populations (e.g., Perry et al., 1996; NHLBI Kit '90: Manual A[11]). Catalogs that display a wide array of promotional and educational materials produced by government, not-for-profit, and for-profit organizations can be obtained by institutions, groups, and individuals. Illustration 5.1 shows examples of templates produced by a U.S. national public health communication campaign and provided as resources for local initiatives.

Consensus is likely to be highly valued and emphasized as an important means for achieving programmatic goals in the Use-Collaboration Model. Emphasis is also likely to be put on so-called win-win relationships where, from the perspective of the intervention and the stakeholders it collaborates with, each party, and the intended population as well, benefit from the collaborative effort. Consequently, only issues that potentially benefit all those who are involved are likely to be on the agenda.[12]

Context

In terms of the broader social context, unless the purpose of the collaborative effort is to make specific institutional changes, current structural or institutional arrangements would be reproduced. Although the intervention program may attempt to engage individuals and groups from a wide spectrum, the constituencies who are given priority or privilege are most likely to be established agencies and groups. These are likely to have considerable resources and networks. This may contribute to strengthening their power bases and resources. Fringe or unaffiliated groups are less likely to be included and would be less likely to benefit. This may result in not addressing the needs and concerns of the unaffiliated or those who are less predisposed toward the topic of the intervention.[13]

Relationships

The types of relationships that develop among the professionals and the population in the Use-Collaboration Model would be—as the model's name indicates—collaboration on mutual objectives. As it may occur also in the

The results of your blood cholesterol test are ready.

These are the cutpoints:
- **less than 200 mg/dL is desirable**
- **200-239 mg/dL is borderline high**
- **240 mg/dL and over is high blood cholesterol**

Remember

☞ limit salt
☞ limit alcohol
☞ watch your weight
☞ take your blood pressure pills
☞ get your blood pressure
   checked

Your next appointment is: _____

When you feel an urge to smoke. . .

Say Stop! ➡ **Think:**   ➡ **Act:**

- Of why I want to quit.   • Sip, eat, chew
- I can wait out the urge.   • Keep hands busy
                                  • Move/get up
                                  • Talk to a friend
                                  • Sigh, yawn, or
                                    breathe deeply

Illustration 5.1

Mix and Match Postcards
Purpose: multiple risk factors—a selection of postcards reinforce important health messages for awareness and treatment/control.
Audience: general public, patients. Ideas for use: mix and match the information on the fronts and backs of these postcards. Physicians' offices can use the cards as reminders for ongoing patient contact. Health promotion or smoking cessation programs can use them to promote upcoming programs. Production notes: Reproduce on a

The results of your
blood cholesterol
test are ready.

Remember Your Next Appointment!

Say Stop!
Think
Act

Illustration 5.1 Continued

photocopying machine on index or cover weight paper. Copy on both sides and then cut them apart. Add your organization's name, address, and logo.

Service Model, intervention programs would use community organizations' activities or sites to conduct their activities (e.g., screening or educational activities), or they may sponsor activities that serve to support their objectives. Agencies and groups in the community would also work together to achieve mutual or overlapping goals or to resolve competition over scarce resources. There would be likely to be an emphasis on consensus building for the purpose of collaboration, and the staff of the sponsors of the intervention would tend to act as facilitators and try to get various organizations and their constituencies involved. Various collaborative structures may be applied; they may consist of coalitions, partnerships, or formal or informal collaborative agreements in which funds may be officially allocated through grants for participating organizations, or resources may be shared through participation in joint projects.

Ethical Concerns

Several ethical concerns are associated with interventions that correspond to the Use-Collaboration Model. The goal of getting community groups to address social problems on their own in their community can clearly promote important values associated with autonomy and self-sufficiency and help develop these organizations. But the objective of institutionalization, prominent in such interventions, as Green (1989) cautions,

> should not have to function as a permanent substitute for federal agencies, particularly because their tax dollars fund the regulatory structure. They themselves do not have the financial means to sustain such an effort, and their involvement in competition for scarce funds is frequently disempowering. (p. 44)[14]

Community resources may be diverted to specific activities that should be provided by public services. For example, an intervention can channel community groups to devote their limited resources to screenings. But this could be done by health insurance plans or government agencies. These local organizations could use their resources to address other urgent needs of their members for which no alternative services are provided or are low on the public's agenda.

Because community organizations may be the intervention sponsor's only link to many community residents, the benefit of reaching these residents may prevail over concerns regarding possible depletion of these organizations' resources, particularly when the intervention personnel would be cognizant of this possibility and careful to ensure that such depletion would be avoided.

Furthermore, a stronger sense of community may emerge as groups, coalitions, boards, and voluntary associations work together even if the collaborative effort is a result of incentives or directives from official agencies or funding organizations. However, this beneficial outcome raises another set of concerns (Janes & Corbet, 1996): Alliances created as a response to and along the definitions of dominant or official agencies may not represent truly autonomous entities that can define the health-related problems from their own perspective. Instead, this may represent "vertical communities" (a concept introduced by Roland Warren as cited by Janes and Corbet, 1996), which may serve as a "mechanism by which such power is deployed at the local level" (p. 4). The resources obtained by such vertical communities may turn out to mainly serve the interest of the sponsoring organization or result in leading those in power to assume that the collaborative efforts genuinely represent the community, which they may not. Furthermore, those who participate as community representatives tend to be from more privileged social groups (Bracht & Gleason, 1990). Attempts to gain a more representative group often fail because of a lack of time and interest by others and difficulties in deciding who is really representative. Another problem is that public participation can be used by political groups and administrators for their own ends. They may say that "we had community participation; they chose to do it this way," or "it's up to the community to show that they want this program to work; it's not our fault if it doesn't" (Janes & Corbet, 1996, p. 7).

Emphasis on Service

The Service Delivery Model does not emphasize involvement as either a goal or a strategy, though clearly, even interventions that correspond to this model involve individuals and community groups in various forums and activities. The intervention would tend to offer its activities to groups or organizations believed to be in special need or who seek out its services.[15] The intervention may have special outreach initiatives to reach specific members of the population viewed as having special needs for the services it offers. This may be done through neighborhood organizations or facilities, such as senior centers, local media, churches, township events, or work sites. Service-focused interventions, although they may not have the transformative mission of those that focus on empowerment, LaBonte (1994) cautions, should not be labeled as disempowering. Services can be offered in a supportive, noncontrolling way by caring professionals and provide the population services they need and want.

Content

The types of messages emphasized relate to following recommended health regimens, consulting health providers, and using existing resources to support behavior change. The intervention's activities would tend to support current institutional practices by providing services that may enhance access to or complement current health care practices. This may be accomplished by focusing on referrals and the expertise of health providers and also by pointing to current problems in the system that have necessitated the initiation of the program. For example, these may include issues such as lack of access to health care providers in particular neighborhoods, the high cost of prescribed medication, food selections in school food programs or workplaces considered nonnutritious, work conditions considered unsafe or stress producing, and lack of facilities for physical activities. The staff of the programs may work to address these issues as well, by contacting particular organizations, such as specific work sites, and offering suggestions or activities for health-promoting changes. In contrast to the Augmentation, Collaboration, or Mobilization Models, there is less emphasis on involving the community members in the process of articulating the problem and the selection of the types of solutions that should be adopted. The programs tend to prescribe activities deemed most suited, whether they design and promote the use of walking trails, launch contests among youth on antismoking slogans, or implement specific types of smoking-cessation programs.

Context

Because many of the services that promote prevention or treatment of health risks are likely to offer services that draw from a biomedical perspective, institutions and constituencies associated with biomedicine would tend to be privileged. Few changes would be made in structural and institutional arrangement, but those who receive the services would be provided help and assistance according to the intervention's service mission.

Relationships

The practitioners would relate to community members mostly as providers who have expertise related to the topic of the intervention, which would tend to be framed from a biomedical perspective. Practitioners would also develop and market educational programs to increase target population's awareness and skills and modify its beliefs related to lifestyle changes. Guidance and training relationships may develop, as well, in interventions that would aim to foster self-care and support groups, and representatives of the population may be involved in helping in service delivery as peer educators or advisers.

Ethical Concerns

Service-oriented intervention types, by not contributing to empowerment, may use opportunity cost and thus, by default, disempower the populations they serve.[16] The population misses out on an opportunity to engage in empowering activities. Another related concern is that a service orientation of an intervention, which typically would be expert dominated, may address an issue that is not a top priority to the community. Although the intervention may invest resources and aim to energize residents and practitioners about a particular health topic, for example, child immunization, problems of severe pollution or nonhygienic living conditions may be more urgent and critical to the population. By focusing on the intervention's specific health objective, it may shift community attention and resources to areas that may be less critical to the community, deplete scarce human and monetary resources, and distract from core social values and substantial problems challenging the community or society as a whole.[17]

Table 5.1 summarizes examples of the types of relationships, prominent constituents or messages, and institutional practices likely to be emphasized in the four types of community involvement. Table 5.2 provides examples of ethical concerns that can be associated with each model.

Change and Adaptation

Although the community involvement models have been presented in polar quadrants, participation can take different forms, both in the way an intervention program itself is structured and in the way it relates to its target audience. The models that represent ideal types cannot reflect the dynamics that take place in the intervention's social context and changes occurring over time. Even in the models in which involvement is mainly used strategically, community organizations may benefit from collaborating with other organizations and from access to and use of the intervention program's resources. This can occur across all types of models. Similarly, the outcomes of service-type interventions may be considerable and critical to individuals who need them, and

Table 5.1 Examples of Relationships Between the Practitioners and the Targeted Population, Privileged Stakeholders and Messages, and Reproduced Institutional Practices in the Community Involvement Models

Model Type	Relationships	Privileged Stakeholders and Messages	Reproduced Institutional Practices
Augmentation (Community involvement high as goal, low as strategy)	Guidance and facilitation of target populations	Emphasis on values associated with autonomy, participation, and self-determination	Established organizations or groups, institutional arrangements that offer some forum of participation; groups currently affiliated with official sources of power tend to gain power and resources
Mobilization (Community involvement high as goal and as strategy)	Interventionists aim: to serve as catalysts, facilitate or empower target populations; to enhance skills and capacities of population members and to eventually work as partners	Emphasis on values associated with autonomy, participation, and self-determination; messages on political causes with transformative capacity produced by the population; controversy; scrutiny of institutional practices; less emphasis on predetermined health issue as a goal	Strategies to generate participation; development of forums to identify people's concerns, community resources, and potential solutions involving diverse constituencies; aim: to shift in power relationships and resources
Use-Collaboration (Community involvement low as goal/ high as strategy)	Interventionists offer guidance, support; teach skills; among the constituencies, collaboration on mutual objectives	Specific health goal emphasized; experts and biomedical institutions; definition of problem tends to adopt that of sponsoring agencies; consensus highly valued; conflict avoided or suppressed	Collaborative structures, current practices; conflict suppressed and attempts made to work within the system; sponsors' goals and definition of the problem prevail
Service (Community involvement low as goal and as strategy)	Interventionists serve as service providers or experts, offer guidance, training, help, and assistance and provide resources	Emphasis on following recommended medical regimens and use of current resources; programs chosen according to what seems most suited, usually related to biomedical approaches	Support of current institutional practices by providing services that may facilitate access to or complement them; little change in structural or institutional arrangements

Table 5.2   Examples of Ethical Concerns Associated With Each Type of Model

Model Type	Examples of Ethical Concerns
Augmentation (high goal, low strategy)	The more influential or vocal groups would obtain more power and resources and manipulate public forums. Constituencies acting as leaders may not represent the population as a whole or parts of it. The intervention may burden and deplete community resources. How can the intervention sustain itself when it may lack a structural tradition? It would be assumed that the community needs to solve its own problems using its own resources.
Mobilization (high goal, high strategy)	An overromanticized notion of communities may prevail, whereas loyalties among constituencies may be diverse. There may be competing interests among population groups that may not be reconciled. Community priorities may conflict with or even harm the public good. It would be assumed that the community needs to solve its own problems using its own resources.
Use-Collaboration (low goal, high strategy)	The intervention may burden and deplete community resources. There may be competition among community groups to gain resources, which may adversely affect their relationships. Community entities may form to meet the demands of the funding organizations thus creating pseudorepresentation. Well-established and connected groups will gain, whereas marginal groups will be deprived of opportunities. A presumed community identity would be formed, which would lead those in power to believe particular groups represent the whole community. It would be assumed that the community needs to solve its own problems using its own resources.
Service (low goal, low strategy)	Loss of opportunity cost may occur by not contributing to enhancement of community development in terms of self-determination or empowerment. Issues that may not be top priorities to the community may be emphasized, and important issues may not be addressed or may be deemphasized. Certain constituencies may be benefit more than others. Scarce community resources may be diverted or depleted.

they may also serve the community as a whole. These types of interventions cannot therefore be dismissed as unimportant (LaBonte, 1994). Furthermore, lessons learned from previous accomplishments, even in less participatory models, can be applied to more participatory approaches.[18] Involvement in the health-promotion activities of the intervention can help community organizations gain recognition, widen their influence, and develop their leadership and needs-assessment skills. Collaboration activities can serve to further mobilize the community and help forge alliances to address issues that extend the original collaborative venture.[19] The process of empowerment, from the personal to more macro entities, is also seen as an important function of participatory activities; even if they do not embody institutional change participation, they can lead to the development of local skills and competencies that could be used for future community development and could be extended to other aspects of people's lives (Bracht & Gleason, 1990). Figure 5.2 illustrates how community involvement models can be seen as a dynamic process, and how they may evolve and move over time from one type to another, particularly as practitioners gain experience and establish deeper ties within the community, as community members join groups and organizations they feel best represent them, and as a transformation of power relations within and outside the community takes place (Rothman & Tropman, 1987).

APPLICATIONS: ANALYSES OF INTERVENTION TYPES

The framework of models that describe different types of interventions can serve to provide an analytic tool to help differentiate between interventions that appear to emphasize the same prominent value. Many interventions in health promotion are likely to correspond to the Service and Use-Collaboration Models, because they focus on predetermined health objectives, and involvement of the community serves more as strategy than as a goal, though some may strive to be more of a Mobilization Model type (Lugo, 1996). Such interventions typically have predetermined definitions of the medical conditions that need to be addressed, and their main strategy is working through a coalition to reach their objectives. Many national or state-initiated interventions may also fall into the Augmentation quadrant because they emphasize support of local initiatives and provide resources to select community organization or projects.[20] Application of the models to intervention programs can help identify what model is implicit in the program's intervention approach, what type of training or predisposition is important for their staff, and what type of resources are important.[21] Each type of model illustrates different types

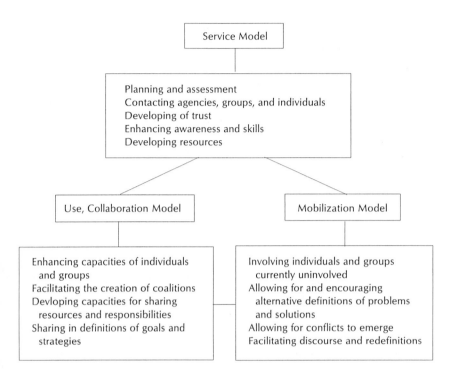

Figure 5.2. Dynamics of Community Involvement Models: Examples of Adaptation

of purposes or intervention approaches. As indicated in the models, different types of skills and training on the part of the practitioners and program resources are necessary to effectively achieve these types of goals. Application of the models can also help describe how values, when emphasized as strategies but not as goals, may be taken for granted as effective strategic appeals, but less attention may be accorded to other value-laden implications. The analysis can also help examine the extent to which the intervention provides selective access to information, resources, expertise, and decision making to its various stakeholders.

How can the typology of models be applied toward an analysis of actual public health communication interventions? Following are examples of two types of analyses, each drawing on a series of questions that can be used as a guide on how to apply the typologies to an analysis of interventions. The first analysis compares different interventions that appear to rely on the same values or justifications but that represent distinct types of interventions. The analysis would examine what differentiates between the interventions, what values are dominant in each one, and what conditions may be necessary for one intervention to become more similar to another. The second analysis applies the framework to analyze a how a particular intervention stands in terms of its consistency with the values it presumably aims to adhere to. It examines the intervention by comparing the prototype to which it actually corresponds to its intended ideal type. The analysis would examine why the intervention may have failed to achieve the ideal type, what values have been emphasized, and what conditions may be necessary to achieve the desired type.

Analysis 1: Comparison Between Interventions That Appear to Rely on the Same Value

The models can be used to differentiate between intervention programs that emphasize the same value but that nevertheless may represent very different intervention approaches. This analysis can indicate the extent to which particular values play a role in shaping interventions and how interventions that appear to uphold the same values may differ. The analysis can be guided by the following description of the process, and it can use the description and work sheets in Resource C. The following four-step procedure can guide the analysis:

1. *Determine what model each intervention corresponds to:* (a) What kind of model best represents what occurs in each intervention? (b) What is the relationship between practitioners and target population members? (c) What kinds of messages does each intervention emphasize? (d) What values are dominant in each intervention?

2. *Identify additional embedded values:* (a) What other dominant values are associated with each intervention? (b) What values are not emphasized in the interventions?

3. *Compare the interventions and identify similarities and differences:* (a) In what ways are the interventions similar? (b) What values were emphasized in certain interventions but not in the others? (c) What factors explain the similarities between the interventions? (d) What factors explain the differences between the interventions?

4. *Draw implications for design, evaluation, and ethical concerns:* (a) What different strategic approaches may be used to achieve shared goals? (b) What sociopolitical conditions may help reach a more desired model? (c) What sociopolitical conditions may impede the implementation of an intervention according to a desired model?

The comparison between several interventions that emphasize the same value but nevertheless may represent very different intervention approaches can show in what important ways these interventions differ: the extent to which they develop different relationships with their constituencies or to which their messages emphasize and privilege certain stakeholders or institutional arrangements. By examining the social context and the values embedded in each intervention, the comparison may also serve to point out specific social conditions in a particular context that need to be addressed to implement an intervention that would achieve desired outcomes. The comparison can also serve for theory development: What social conditions are associated with the development of different types of interventions, what social conditions serve to make significant differences among them, and what conditions are needed to achieve desired intervention types?

Analysis 2: Comparison Between Ideal and Actual Intervention Models

The models can be used to examine the extent to which a specific intervention achieves desired outcomes by comparing how it compares to one of the prototypes. The analysis can serve to describe in what way the actual intervention may differ from the ideal type it strove for, what may explain this discrepancy, and what conditions may be necessary to achieve the desired type. In this type of analysis, we first need to determine the ideal prototype and the actual model adapted by the intervention. Then, we can compare them to each other and examine why the intervention deviated from the ideal type, what values or sociopolitical factors may have contributed to this process, and what the practical and ethical implications are in terms of relationships, privileged messages, stakeholders, and institutional arrangements of the intervention; each may be associated with one type of model and not with another.

A case study reported by Lugo (1996) on a project that aimed to provide services to women, as well as to foster empowerment and community development, illustrates how this analysis can be accomplished. Lugo outlined how factors associated with conflicting mandates of the program's funding and limitations of staff skills played important roles in not achieving the ideal empowerment model. The actual intervention she described corresponded to the Use-Collaboration Model and to some extent, the Service Model. A new phase of the intervention, gaining from the lessons learned in its first implementation, aimed to move the intervention from one type of involvement to another. Lugo also outlined social conditions believed to be needed to enable the intervention to achieve the broader mission of empowerment. This, she suggested, can be done by placing empowerment and community development "as core functions, with full support of funders and staff" and not as an "extra" (p. 288).

The analysis can be guided by the following four-step description of the process, and the description and worksheets in the Resource sections (this volume) can be used.

The process consists of these four steps:

1. *Determine the ideal model:* Determine what type of model the intervention belongs to according to normative expectations and prominent social values; specify the ideal relationships between practitioners and target stakeholders and the kinds of capacities or skills the professionals and targeted populations need to accomplish the intervention goals;

2. *Determine the actual model:* Determine what kind of model best represents what actually occurs in the intervention, including the relationships between intervention practitioners and target population members. Determine what capacities or skills the intervention professionals have and what capacities or skills the intervention's targeted population has acquired. Identify what kind of message is emphasized by the intervention.

3. *Compare the ideal and actual models:* Examine in what ways the actual model corresponds to the intended model and what values have been prioritized or deemphasized.

4. *Draw implications for evaluation and planning for future initiatives:* Determine what goals or strategies need to be modified or changed to move the intervention from its current state to its ideal model, including train-

ing of practitioners and necessary resources. Determine whether the ideal model can be implemented within current institutional arrangements and dominant social values.

This comparison can help identify necessary resources needed to get the intervention to correspond to the ideal model or what social conditions may impede it from achieving desired outcomes. It can also serve for theory development by describing significant differences between an actual intervention and its ideal type; it may help explain the discrepancy and point out what conditions may be necessary to achieve the desired type, thus contributing to theory and practice (Freudenberg et al., 1995).

NOTES

1. The term *empowerment* has been used to describe different types of intervention approaches (Fahlberg, Poulin, Girdano, & Dusek, 1991) and therefore was not used to label these models.

2. A large body of literature about this topic can be found under community organization (e.g., McKnight, 1992; McKnight & Kretzmann, 1984), participation (Price, 1990), community action (E. R. Brown, 1991), empowerment or mobilization (e.g., Hatch & Derthick, 1992; Weston et al., 1992), and advocacy (Thomas, 1990). Two special issues of *Health Education Quarterly* in 1994 were devoted to this topic (Issue 2 [Summer] and Issue 3 [Fall]).

3. In an evaluation with Paul Speer, conducted in New Jersey in 1996, of community coalitions for the prevention of substance abuse, one respondent explained that grassroots groups that were part of the coalition were dissatisfied because they were not able to be on its board because only one person served as the representative of all grassroots groups. This respondent felt his organization was not given the opportunity to participate in decision making.

4. Though, in this model, only selected organizations are likely to benefit; as indicated in the discussion on adaptation and change, this can lead to increased involvement of constituencies that previously had little power.

5. See Bracht and Gleason's (1990) discussion of involvement types and examples of the evolutionary process.

6. Janes and Corbet (1996) critique the creation of such entities, which they suggest result in

> vertical communities [which] in fact represent the interests of the State.... They do this by providing money, which in turn creates organizations to accept and spend it, and a relationship of dominance as the bureaucracy or foundation insists on auditing and controlling how the money is spent. Soon, unexamined, the bureaucracy, even the people for whom the money is being spent, particularly those receiving it directly or being employed by an organization, begin to see themselves as a "community." In a case of mistaken identity, such groups achieve significant, ill-placed, external legitimacy. (pp. 4-5)

Others strongly support these types of structures (e.g., Henry, 1996), as indicated in the conditions for grant funding by W. K. Kellogg.

7. For example, in an interview with a practitioner who worked with one of NHLBI's educational programs, the issue of consensus was presented as very important both for the messages' credibility and for dissemination purposes:

> (Consensus is) really important. It's not just the government saying it. It's the whole medical care establishment that is dealing with these issues and have the opportunity to agree or not to agree. . . . It's all well and good to have the recommendations come out, then to put them into practice you need these organizations to help you get the word out to their constituents. . . . (The consensus) better assures that once these organizations buy in.

Similarly, consensus was presented as an important process for achieving the best solution:

> When the process brings together diverse expertise, and the experts are willing to learn from each other, the thoroughness of the problem and solution examination, as well as the quality of the consensus can far exceed that produced by the same experts acting independently. (Roccella & Ward, 1984, p. 240)

But as coordinators of educational programs at NHLBI noted, the utility of consensus has its limitations.

> The compromise of views inherent in most consensus exercises nearly inevitably leads to an outcome that falls short of what the present state of the art would indicate to be planning and may hasten adoption of its result; its result may deviate far from the technically possible optimum. (p. 240).

8. Lefebvre (1990) described the goal of federally funded programs—to outlive their original programs by becoming institutionalized in the community—as a daunting task, still in its learning stages. He presents a strategic plan to implement this process that draws heavily on a social-marketing perspective.

9. Ownership is an important construct in community development and means that local people need to have a sense of responsibility for and control over the change-promoting activities in their community so that they will continue to support them after the initial organizing efforts (Thompson & Kinne, 1990).

10. See NHLBI's *Churches as an Avenue to High Blood Pressure Control*.

11. *NHLBI Kit '90: The Right Moves* is a folder that contains two manuals, one for program planners and the other on information for consumers that can be reproduced. The manuals are produced by the National Heart, Lung, and Blood Institute, U.S. Department of Health and Human Services.

12. The theme of "win-win" was brought up several times in the materials of one of the community interventions for the prevention of heart disease I studied that heavily uses social-marketing techniques and organizes collaborative ventures among several work and commercial organizations (see Guttman, 1994).

13. Marginalized groups and unaffiliated individuals may be least likely to be given opportunities to get involved in policy-making processes related to health or other topics (Capek, 1992; Wallace-Brodeur, 1990). In an interview in 1993, Wallack suggested that "you define the problem the way the person with the money defines the problem, so that problems are defined in ways to be noncontroversial, to fit with the methods of interventions that are acceptable." Community agencies that get involved are usually those that adopt the same understanding of the problem so that getting community agencies involved that are used as surrogates for the community as a whole is likely to end up reinforcing a conservative view of the problem.

14. Green, in a personal interview in 1993, commented that when grant-funding agencies incorporate an "institutionalization" expectation of their grants, they may lock the community into a commitment of carrying out something that might not be in its best interest.

15. An example from one of the interventions I studied illustrates a strategy that emphasizes serving mainly those who seek the program:

> Much of what we do is who wants a program. Because I came, [we did] not have to reach out whatsoever. Prior to me coming, their whole push was "okay, we want to reach out. Let's try this and this and this and let's call this and this." When I came, they were throwing lots of different names at me. "Why don't you talk to her about a program? This church organization, community leaders." A couple of months after I was here, something happened, last January, last December—the phone started ringing. I'll tell you. None of us had to reach out. . . . People are calling us left and right. Our calendar is filling up. (Guttman, 1994)

16. This is a variation of the argument LaBonte (1994) cited in his discussion of the critique of personal care. LaBonte suggested that services do not necessarily have to be disempowering and cautioned against polarization. Similarly, Lawrence Green, in a personal interview in 1993, cautioned against villainizing service-type interventions. He argued that many have contributed significantly to promote the health of the public and individuals and created a base for more participatory types of intervention. He added, though, that the intervention should only address issues that are viewed as pertinent and important to the community.

17. The concern regarding depletion was discussed earlier in the context of the Use-Collaboration Model. The next two chapters further elaborate the notions of distractions and distortions.

18. Lawrence Green, in an interview in 1993, expressed concerns regarding strong critiques cast at service-type interventions:

> I guess the one thing I worry about most is the tendency to polarize the perspectives in the [health promotion] field. We've come to some agreement in this discussion that there are problems with the way the federal programs come down. On the other hand, without them, a lot wouldn't be happening, a lot wouldn't be getting done. We have, in fact . . . a very dramatic reduction in heart disease and stroke in this country. It is spectacular, it is a public health success story that rivals earlier decades' success with immunizations. So it's no good to dismiss the way the programs have been done in the past. The question now is "How can we extend this success so it can reach the populations who haven't benefited as much from it?" And then the answers begin to move in the way that you and I have been discussing, ways of empowering communities to take greater control of themselves, ways to help them bring out their own experience, the relevance of health programs and heart health programs to their own definition of what they need, in terms of quality of life and social programs. Otherwise heart health is going to be low on their agenda and it should be, if it can't be shown to be relevant. If it can't be made relevant, then it shouldn't be pushed.

19. A discussion on this topic, although framed somewhat differently, can be found in Neil Bracht's (1990a) book, *Health Promotion at the Community Level*.

20. For example, an intervention intended to mobilize a community in Westchester County, New York, in a cholesterol education program used community advisory boards to assist in the development and implementation of the program. Although it aimed to adapt its activities to the needs of the community, its main focus was cholesterol (Weston et al., 1992).

21. Some of the practitioners I interviewed who were working in programs to prevent heart disease in community contexts said they felt they needed much more training and resources in community development. This can explain their heavier emphasis on service delivery than on collaboration and development (Guttman, 1994).

6

Ethical Dilemmas and Practice-Oriented Questions

The fundamental value of studying and understanding ethical thought is not that we thereby have definitive guides to moral conduct. Rather, the value lies in becoming aware of the moral options available to us, of the general paradigm within which moral inquiry can take place as concrete human beings grapple with real-life issues. Individual moral choices are frequently not between obvious right and wrong, good and bad, but between actions and values that contain elements of both. The challenge, then, is not so much finding an ethical standard to use but applying a defensible standard in specific instances.

—Barry (1982, p. 89)

W ork for health is a moral endeavor," exclaims Seedhouse (1988). But it is not, he clarifies, "a moral endeavor in the sense of a crusade" (p. xiv). Yet messages of public health communication interventions often carry connotations of righteousness and virtue. Their rhetoric is often composed of images of "wars" and "attacks" on diseases or substances, which may vilify particular behaviors, sanctify others, or inadvertently stigmatize certain members of society. Furthermore, an intervention's goal to promote people's health may infringe on their privacy, personal preferences, or autonomous decisions (Levin, 1987). The design and implementation of public health campaigns thus invariably raises ethical dilemmas, dilemmas that cannot be neatly solved by applying specific ethical principles. "Ethics," Seedhouse explains, "is always a question of degree, a question of deliberating about which interventions in other people's lives will produce the highest possible degree of morality" (p. xv). Because people hold different values and beliefs, he continues, there are no clear-cut solutions to what we may consider a good intervention in someone else's life. Whatever solutions are adopted, they depend in one way or another on values: "Even advice about diet and exercise is never based wholly on fact. At some stage a value judgment of some kind will be made" (p. xv). Seedhouse's words echo the main thesis of this book: Value judgments are performed in all facets of the intervention. Inherently, they involve ethical considerations[1] and raise ethical dilemmas. The latter are often invisible, especially when it is taken for granted that interventions inherently aim to promote the health of the public.

Health care is a context replete with ethical issues. Medical care providers are often acutely aware of ethical dilemmas in their daily practice and the practice of medicine in general. Modern technologies that allow for procedures to prolong people's lives also force people to make painful decisions: when to use sophisticated technologies and when to refrain from using them, and who should decide? Who should be chosen to benefit when resources are scarce? Public health communication interventions, although they may not involve immediate life-and-death issues, are also rife with ethical concerns similar to those raised in biomedical contexts.[2] The interventionists also face the dilemmas of when to apply the most effective communication techniques and when to refrain from using them, how to achieve the most effective persuasive message that is ethically derived and delivered (Ratzan, 1994), and what resources should be allocated to this effort. Although they presumably aim to promote the good of intended populations (Rogers, 1994), benefits from their outcomes may not be equally distributed. In addition, because more and more public health interventions adopt sophisticated social-marketing techniques, the enhanced ability to persuade raises concerns regarding the extent to which they may engage in unethical manipulation (Faden, 1987): "[A] preventive health campaign is a marketing effort, subject to all the risks of motivational marketing—hyperbole, demagoguery, or praying upon fears and prejudices" (Goodman & Goodman, 1986, p. 29).

The 14 ethical dilemmas presented in this chapter address four major areas: (a) the use of particular intervention strategies, (b) the possibility of causing inadvertent harm, (c) issues related to power and control, and (d) issues related to social values. The chapter concludes with a series of practice-oriented questions presented in summary tables. Brown and Singhal's (1990) thought-provoking discussion of ethical dilemmas in the use of television programs to promote social issues inspired the development of this framework and provided some of its core constructs.[3] Brown and Singhal underscore dilemmas regarding the content of messages and the promotion of equality among viewers, here included in the area of intervention strategies; dilemmas related to unintended effects, here also referred to as unintended effects but expanded to include a discussion of social values and power and control; and dilemmas related to the use of the media for development, here incorporated in the discussion of strategies.[4] The ethical concerns raised in this chapter also draw on Forester's (1989, 1993) adaptation of Habermas's (1979) work in the context of planning. Because public health communication interventions are clearly a communicative process, their potential impact raises concerns regarding claims made by the intervention that may influence people to adopt healthier behaviors but may also result in what can be viewed as communicative distortions. These may influence the way people think and interpret the social phenomenon in ways that misrepresent important social processes that actually take place or that may serve the interests of dominant social groups.[5]

Four precepts are singled out for discussion: *truth, consent, identity,* and *framing.*

Truth: The truthfulness of the messages can affect people's beliefs, for example, about what illness is, what activities are health promoting, who is responsible for the health problem, and how important it is to attend to the problem as it has been defined by the intervention, as well as beliefs in the effectiveness of the recommendations. This can be related to ethical concerns about intervention strategies, including their persuasive messages, and regarding values or cultural reproduction.

Consent: The legitimacy of the norms invoked may affect people's willingness to consent to presumed authority and can be related to ethical concerns about power and control.

Identity: People's senses of identity may be influenced as a result of exposure to certain types of messages—for example, those that may label them as deviant or bad—or the development of particular relationships in the health-promotion context. These activities can be related to ethical concerns about inadvertent outcomes.

Framing: The selection or prioritization of issues may affect people's comprehension or perceptions of priorities and can be related to ethical concerns associated with social values and ideologies. For example, one way of framing the issue is that certain health conditions should be pursued mainly through education rather than through institutional or structural changes.

The bioethics literature discussed in the previous chapters also provides us with constructs to examine ethical concerns. These include ethical principles of avoiding doing harm, respect for personal autonomy and freedom to make one's own decisions, utility, concern for justice and fairness in distribution of resources, and adherence to the obligation to care for those with whom one has a special relationship or toward whom one has particular commitments. The first eight dilemmas apply what Duncan and Cribb (1996) describe as *analytic health care ethics,* which rely on ethical principles. The last six dilemmas raise more structural-level issues and are concerned with how public health communication interventions may (inadvertently) serve to reproduce power relations or institutional systems or practices.

DILEMMAS CONCERNING CAMPAIGN STRATEGIES

1. The Persuasion Dilemma

The persuasion dilemma incorporates two concerns, which represent the flip side of each. The first raises concerns regarding the persuasive capacities that may infringe on people's autonomy. The second is concerned with whether the intervention fulfills the ethical imperative of doing the utmost to promote the good of its intended audience by applying the most persuasive tactics to help people adopt its recommended health-promoting messages.

To what extent is it justified to use persuasive strategies to reach the intended health-promoting effects of the intervention?

The dilemma regarding the ethics of the manipulative potential of persuasion is often shared, though less often acknowledged, by many if not all public communication interventions (Witte, 1994). Because public health interventions' goals typically aim to influence target populations' beliefs or behaviors, persuasive and social-marketing strategies are often employed.[6] The ultimate goal of these intervention strategies, as Witte (1994) points out, is to get people to practice what the interventionists believe are health-promoting behaviors. Efforts to do good and convince the public of the benefits of adopting particular behaviors or of avoiding others thus often include persuasive strategies to arouse anxieties or fears and facilitate persuasion. Witte (1994) maintains that public health communication researchers and practitioners are adept at using persuasive strategies (e.g., how much and what type of information to use about a certain topic, how to order it) to manipulate people's perceptions. This raises concerns regarding the use of manipulative or persuasive tactics, which by definition infringe on individuals' rights for autonomy or self-determination. Similarly, it raises concerns regarding paternalism or the belief that certain experts or professionals know what is best for particular members of society or the public as a whole. Whereas these concerns traditionally are raised in the practitioner-patient context (e.g., Bok, 1978; Childress, 1982; Veatch, 1980), they are also highly relevant in the public health communication intervention context because such interventions are purposeful efforts to get people to adopt health-related practices perceived as beneficial to them or as helping them avoid potential harm (Beauchamp, 1988; Campbell, 1990; Faden, 1987; Pinet, 1987; Doxiadis, 1987). According to the principle of respect for autonomy, health promoters should honor the self-respect and dignity of each individual as an autonomous, free actor.

The use of persuasive appeals also raises concerns regarding the extent to which such appeals distort or manipulate information (as elaborated by Forester, 1993) or the extent to which such manipulative strategies can undermine the development of connectedness, responsiveness, and a sense of genuine care, which are important components in an ethic of care (Baier, 1993). Similarly, the use of persuasion raises concerns regarding legitimacy and control: Persuasive messages that aim to affect attitude change and the adoption of the recommended behaviors succeed essentially by controlling people's perceptions and thus limiting their choices from a wider range of options (Faden & Faden, 1982). As Salmon (1989) reminds us, "At the center of this conflict is the fundamental tension between social control and individual freedoms.

Social-marketing efforts, by definition, employ mechanisms of social control" (p. 19).[7] Inherent in the design and implementation of public health communication interventions, therefore, is a tension between competing values of autonomy and of doing good.

To what extent should health promoters model their persuasive messages on advertising or marketing techniques—even when these tactics are viewed as the most promising venues for affecting attitudes and behaviors?[8] Highly persuasive messages that use emotionally charged fear-raising and guilt-raising appeals can be justified by communicators on the basis of utility, especially if they draw on research that used target audience members' perceptions.[9] When audience members are asked what types of messages would work for them or would help modify people's behavior and get them to adopt the recommended activity, respondents often suggest that interventionists should use scare tactics or fear appeals.[10] But does this mean that these messages are the optimal and ethical ones? The use of persuasive strategies in the context of advertising has been criticized as being potentially unethical because they may use manipulative, misleading, or deceptive messages: concerns compounded because advertising campaigns tend to target populations particularly vulnerable to their messages. This critique can be applied to public communication campaigns as well (Pollay, 1989). The American Cancer Society, according to critics, used inflated statistics in its efforts to persuade women to engage in preventive cancer detection behaviors. The persuasive messages they used may have unduly terrified some women, argue the critics. The American Cancer Society justified its use of these statistics by saying they believed they could serve as effective means to get women to adopt preventive measures and seek early detection (Blakeslee, 1992). In contrast, Salmon and Kroger (1992) report that practitioners in the U.S. National AIDS Information and Education Programs, a government-sponsored health agency, decided to give prominence to the principle of what they considered *do no harm* and to avoid messages that could potentially frighten target populations.[11] A different approach was revealed in a surprising announcement made by an advisory panel to the National Cancer Institute. This panel recommended that the Institute should only provide scientific data and should not engage in persuasive appeals to get women to get mammograms at a particular age. Instead, it suggested the Institute should let the public draw its own conclusions (Kolata, 1993). This approach raises ethical concerns as well: To what extent are health promoters *obligated* to use persuasive strategies if they believe these strategies to be the most effective method to achieve the goals of the campaign and to fulfill their mandate of maximizing the health of the target population? This concern relates to the second persuasion dilemma: the extent to which the intervention employs the most effective tactics to deliver messages that will help people or organizations adopt the recommendation of the intervention addresses several key concerns. The first is, to what extent do the interventionists have the knowledge, expertise, and resources to develop appropriate messages, and second, what are the best strategies to develop such messages: Do the interventionists have the resources to develop messages and strategies that can indeed be effective? Should the interventionists employ current marketing techniques and work mainly with professionals or adopt approaches in which intended audience members act as equal partners in message development?

2. The Coercion Dilemma

Is it justified to promote restrictive regulations or policies regarding individuals' behavior to achieve the health goals of the campaign?

The use of coercion poses the same types of concerns raised regarding persuasion:

> Questions about the morality of coercion, manipulation, deception, persuasion, and other methods of inducing change typically involve a conflict between the values of individual freedom and self-determination, on one hand, and such values as social welfare, economic progress, or equal opportunity on the other hand. (Warwick & Kelman, 1973, p. 380)

One of the arguments in support of strategies that restrict or regulate people's or organizations' activities or control their environment is that they are relatively effective in promoting the desired health-related outcome.[12] As McKinlay (1975) states, "One stroke of effective health legislation is equal to many separate health intervention endeavors and the cumulative efforts of innumerable health workers over long periods of time" (p. 13). For example, legislation for smoke-free environments is viewed as a strategy that can have a larger impact on smoking behavior of large numbers of people than educational programs (Glantz, 1996). Similarly, engineering-type solutions can also be seen as relatively effective (Schwartz, Goodman, & Steckler, 1995). Redesigning roadways and improving the safety engineering of cars have been shown to significantly reduce automobile accidents and fatalities, independent of the actions of the drivers. Similarly, changing lunch menus of schools or work organizations has been shown to affect the food consumption of the students or workers in these organizations (Ellison et al., 1989; Glanz & Mullis, 1988). On a more macro level, regulation of the food industry and restrictions on food production could increase the likelihood that consumers would buy foods relatively low in saturated fats and free of contaminants, making their food consumption healthier. This type of reasoning can be seen as applying the principle of utility or the obligation to maximize the greatest utility from the health promotion efforts to the greatest number of people (Hiller, 1987). However, it raises concerns regarding the ethical principle of individual autonomy or the right people have not to be restricted in their personal choices. Notwithstanding concerns for autonomy, in addition to its potential utility, an important justification for the use of restrictive strategies is based on the assumption that individuals' choices are in fact not autonomous but influenced by powerful social and market circumstances. People in our society, explain proponents of regulative strategies, are surrounded by persuasive antihealth messages and antihealth environments, and therefore, they do not freely choose unhealthy behaviors. This justifies the use of prohealth persuasive or coercive strategies or of policies to restrict the freedom of groups, including marketers of certain products (Pinet, 1987). One example of this approach is efforts to restrict the placement of cigarette vending machines, a strategy shown as effective in curtailing cigarette sales, especially among children and adolescents (Feighery et al., 1991). Another example of policies to promote health through restrictions on public access to a product is the Japanese government's ban of birth control pills,[13] which was adopted in part to promote the use of condoms and justified partially by being perceived as a way to curb the spread of HIV infection (Jitsukawa & Djerassi, 1994; Weisman, 1992).

Coercive approaches are fraught with ethical concerns, including the infringement on individuals' free choice and free-marketplace enterprise, which are particularly prominent values in Western society. Market autonomy, according to its proponents, is the optimal method for the distribution of goods and for balancing economic contribution and economic rewards. Restricting it would impose restrictions on choices to individuals and thus impinge on individual autonomy as well (Garret et al., 1989). But the marketplace, maintain critics, does not provide free choices for individuals or communities because other socioeconomic factors influence the distribution of goods, services, and wealth (Beauchamp, 1987; Bellah et al., 1985, 1991). Dan Beauchamp (1987) argues that, relative to other intervention approaches, enforcement strategies enhance the public good on the societal level while minimally intruding on individuals because they mainly place controls on the marketplace. Instead of placing restrictions on personal liberty, he explains, by controlling potential hazards through a collective action and sharing the burdens of protection, intervention policies can foster a sense of community responsibility for the welfare of its members. Even if we adopt this perspective, we are still left with questions regarding the extent to which individuals should be restricted from engaging in practices perceived as risky from a health-promotion perspective but nevertheless desired by some. What are the boundaries? When should society intervene? Does society have an obligation to intervene when the individual's well-being is threatened by his or her own action (Pinet, 1987; Wikler, 1987), or should it intervene only when a person presents a danger to others, as in the case of communicable diseases?

Regulative strategies may also be applied to the channels that disseminate intervention messages. Because broadcast media, although they may be considered a public good, are licensed to commercial or not-for-profit organizations, does this imply that interventions should be able to use these media as dissemination channels? Or more specifically, should commercial media be regulated to support messages of health interventions (Packer & Kauffman, 1990), or should the interventions pay for the broadcasting of their ads through the use of excise taxes?[14]

3. The Reliability Dilemma

Are the recommendations proffered by the public health communication intervention accurate and reliable? Should the interventionists disseminate what they believe is the best information they currently have, even if it may prove to be inaccurate?

To what extent are the recommendations proffered by the intervention based on reliable and accurate information? Inconsistency and inaccuracies were found in the information given to callers responding to public health communication interventions and provided by telephone hot lines among 33 agencies that served as part of an AIDS intervention (Baxter & Gluckman, 1994). People were not getting information that was reliable and consistent with current guidelines. The situation may be further complicated when there are no consistent or agreed-on guidelines, as when recommendations based on certain scientific studies may be refuted by others (Payer, 1993). For example, the reliability of evidence regarding certain recommendations about salt, cholesterol, or dietary fiber consumption is disputed by some experts who either reach different conclusions regarding their preventive capacities or argue that one cannot generalize from large-scale population studies to individuals (Marshall, 1995; Riis, 1990). Do we need, therefore, to wait for what would be considered more reliable scientific information? But this, as Riis suggests, "could lead to a kind of defeatism in which any initiative could be postponed because 'we still do not know enough' " (p. 189).

The reliability dilemma becomes even more complex because of the observation that people—even when provided with in-depth information—may feel they know too little to make an informed choice, even when they actually know more than they did before. Providing people with more information, as illustrated in studies from the risk perception literature, may result in less confidence in the information and consequently in diminishing people's abilities to make informed choices (Hughes & Brecht, 1975). Should public health communication interventions therefore provide a great amount of information but risk saturating people with an overload of messages? Should they risk making people feel they are unable to resolve the contradictions?[15] Or should the intervention provide the intended public with less detailed information to avoid confusion or so-called information overload? But then, how would the intervention serve to repudiate competing misconceptions and misinformation (for example, those presented in the media) that the interventionists believe mislead the public and should be refuted?

A second dilemma associated with reliability concerns language style. Some fear that if recommendations are stated in tentative language, they may be confusing or not effective (Barr, Waring, & Warshaw, 1992; Kolata, 1995; Miller, 1990). On the other hand, if recommendations are made using very strong language and leave no room for doubt, some fear they may be inaccurate or may backfire. "With the proliferation of guidelines and advice," commented a physician, "we are grotesquely overselling to the American people. The danger of that is that they will not believe the stuff we have that's documented" (Kolata, 1995, p. C12). Providing more health information is not necessarily health promoting and may, in fact, bring opposite outcomes: a public on one hand saturated with health messages and on the other, confused and distrusting. A marketing consultant suggests that we can end up with people who are distrustful of the health information they hear and "throwing up their hands and eating everything they want in quantity"—with a vengeance (Dullea, 1989, p. 72). This dilemma is illustrated in the case of the controversial advice provided by an advisory panel to the National Cancer Institute in 1993. To avoid waiting for a definitive scientific prescription and in light of conflicting views of medical experts, the panel had recommended that the Institute should only disseminate scientific data to the public but not engage in persuasive appeals to get women to get mammograms at a certain age. Some of its members suggested that they just tell people what the state of the art is, rather than offer specific recommendations (Kolata, 1993). The Institute, after adopting the recommendation, found that this approach could backfire, when that decision "set off a firestorm of criticism." One group wanted the Cancer Institute to take a clear stand against younger women taking mammograms; others wanted it to uphold its previous recommendations that younger women should take the test (Kolata, 1995). Four years later, the Institute had decided to officially endorse the recommendation of routine mammograms for all women in their 40s, despite continuing uncertainties among scientists. The new recommendation was influenced, suggested journalists, by political considerations and the adoption of a patient advocacy perspective, rather than by pure science because "uncertain advice is not received kindly" by either patients or physicians ("More Obese Adults," 1994).

Last, is it justified to embark on interventions with messages and strategies that are not fully tested in situations where the problem is defined as urgent and needing immediate action? Should an intervention be implemented even if it is based on limited resources, time, and expertise but justified by a caring perspective or that whatever will be done is better than nothing?

4. The Targeting Dilemmas

Who should be targeted by the public health communication intervention? Should the intervention devote its resources to target populations believed to be particularly needy or to those who are more likely to adopt its recommendations?

Who is targeted by the intervention generates a host of ethical concerns. These include concerns of equitable reach: Should the intervention attempt to reach all segments of the population, or should it target only specific population groups? This concern corresponds to consideration of entitlement: Who should be eligible to receive the potential benefits of the intervention? Should the entitlement be universal or selective (Turshen, 1989)? A second concern is whether interventions may in fact serve to widen the gap between those who have more opportunities and those who have less (Farley, Haddad, & Brown, 1996)[16] and whether the issues they emphasize are more relevant to certain cultural groups than to others. Similarly, concerns can be raised regarding the extent to which interventions address issues that are important to groups with special needs and the extent to which interventions provide a forum for diverse perspectives on how the problem and solutions to address it are perceived and implemented. These concerns represent tensions between principles of justice and utility. According to the latter, one is obliged to maximize the greatest utility from the health promotion efforts (Hiller, 1987). However, when intervention resources are limited, should only those who are most likely to adopt the recommended practices be targeted, or should the intervention target those who are viewed as having the greatest need but are least likely to adopt its recommendations (Des Jarlais et al., 1994; Kahn, 1996; Marin & Marin, 1990; White & Maloney, 1990)?

Many health interventions aim to target populations considered underserved. The problem with this approach, suggest critics, is that to address inequalities in health care, one must face inequalities in other areas of life as well. Thus, despite sincere efforts, if interventions do not address structural or socioeconomic factors, disadvantaged target groups who may not have sufficient opportunities to adopt their health-related recommendations are not likely to do so. Consequently, the messages and activities are likely to have only a minimum of the desired effects, and the intervention approaches used can be deemed ineffective or a waste of precious public resources.[17] Considerations of overall efficiency and effectiveness may also play an important role in the decision of whom to target. One approach, typically referred to as a population approach, targets relatively large segments of the population.[18] Its premise is that modest changes (e.g., in blood cholesterol levels or systolic blood pressure) in large populations produce relatively substantial changes in overall morbidity and mortality. This serves as the main rationale for many community-based interventions. The populationwide net impact, however, may not affect certain subgroups who may be particularly in need of an intervention or who may in fact benefit most from a targeted intervention (Fisher, 1995). As Geoffrey Rose

(1985)—a noted epidemiologist and proponent of the population approach—suggests, this tension illustrates the *prevention paradox:* an intervention strategy that "brings much benefit to the population [but] offers little (at least on the short term) to each participating individual" (p. 38).[19]

An alternative targeting approach is to focus on those at high risk and aim to make significant changes in the health-related behavior of a relatively small number of individuals. The dilemma is whether the intervention should target those who seem to be most in need but are relatively few in number or devote its limited resources to reaching as many people as possible, thus resulting in increasing the health of the population as a whole.[20] Furthermore, certain groups may particularly benefit from an intervention, though others may not (Andreasen, 1995). After reviewing the results of a demonstration project to reduce smoking (the COMMIT Trial), Fisher (1995) concludes, "organizing programs to address relatively small pockets of heightened risk may be viewed as inefficient." Fisher proposes it would be best to target pockets of light-to-moderate smokers with no formal education beyond high school because this "may be the most efficient approach to accomplishing a substantial impact over the whole community" (p. 160). Yet this particular effort would exclude the heavy smokers, the primary target of the intervention.

Health interventions often serve as social experiments for policymakers or researchers. Policymakers want to know what works, what types of interventions can be considered effective. This leads to another ethical concern: Because such interventions are designed as clinical trials, they use designs in which some populations are not targeted and are not provided with resources or activities believed to benefit them. This raises the same kind of ethical concerns raised in the context of clinical trials: Is it ethical to deny certain people a "treatment" that may benefit them for the sake of proving its efficacy in a so-called scientific way?[21]

5. The Harm Reduction Dilemma

Should an intervention engage in strategies or support behaviors that are not socially approved or viewed by some as immoral, to prevent further harm to certain people?

On what grounds is it justified to provide new syringes to people who use injection drugs or to train them on how to clean injection needles, for the purpose of avoiding HIV infection? Should adolescents be provided with contraceptive devices and education on sexual practices that are less likely to transmit infections even if their parents or their community believes premarital sexual activity is immoral? Should interventions promote a message that an effective way to avoid automobile accidents is to have designated drivers that take turns at refraining from excessive alcohol consumption?[22] Interventions that adopt strategies that would answer these questions in the affirmative often justify it (though not always explicitly or consciously) on a harm reduction approach. The harm reduction perspective was articulated in England in the mid-1980s and has gained momentum in Europe and Australia as a response to the urgency of preventing the spread of HIV infection in the area of injection drug use. Its proponents say that although it raises ethical concerns, such as sanctioning behaviors viewed as immoral or harmful to the individual, harm reduction strategies can in fact be justified on both moral and practical grounds. Syringe exchange programs, for example, can be justified on the basis of several ethical approaches that for the purpose here are characterized as the following: (a) doing good, because they protect individuals from the adverse effects of HIV infection; (b) utility, as findings on the reduction of HIV infection among users of injection drugs who participate in syringe exchange programs indicate they are also more likely to enroll in drug rehabilitation programs; (c) justice, because there are limited rehabilitation programs and opportunities for those who use injection drugs; (d) public good, because the users of drugs are an integral part of the community, and protecting the health of the community requires protecting the health of drug users (Des Jarlais, 1995); and (e) caring, because those who use injection drugs should be seen as people who need help and connectedness. Critics of harm reduction strategies, however, may believe their use reinforces immoral or harmful behaviors (e.g., sexual behavior or drug abuse). These views are contested by others who propose that such programs do not increase and may actually decrease the risk-promoting behavior. Some opponents may object in principle to supporting a practice they perceive as immoral, regardless of potential beneficial consequences.

DILEMMAS CONCERNING INADVERTENT HARM

Although well-meaning, and usually with distinct health-promoting objectives (Rogers, 1994), health interventions may contribute to unintended outcomes that can be considered detrimental for individuals or society. The dilemmas specified in the following discussion concern three types of outcomes that may contribute to potential harm: (a) labeling or stigmatizing individuals, (b) denying the less privileged of pleasures they can afford, and (c) unfairly placing responsibility and blame on individuals or groups.

6. The Labeling Dilemma

By telling people they have a certain medical condition that puts them at risk, does the intervention label them as ill? Does the intervention stigmatize certain individuals or affect their sense of identity by portraying the health-related conditions they have as undesirable or bad?

The labeling dilemma evokes two interrelated concerns regarding causing potential harm to direct and indirect target populations.[23] The principle of do no harm, or nonmaleficence, is the obligation to bring no harm to one's client (Hiller, 1987). The first concern is whether people's level of anxiety or worry is increased by assigning them to the role of persons who are ill (Barsky, 1988). On one hand, interventions' goals are often to encourage target populations to participate in screening activities and to identify those who are considered to be at risk for a particular disease to manage or prevent it. On the other hand, these interventions serve to frame particular medical conditions, such as high blood pressure or high levels of blood cholesterol, as diseases and to label individuals as patients (Guttmacher, Teitelman, Chapin, Garbowski, & Schnall, 1981; Moore, 1989; Shickle & Chadwick, 1994). This labeling may actually cause them harm (Barsky, 1988; Bloom & Monterossa, 1981). Individuals identified as possessing certain symptoms considered as risk factors find themselves in a peculiar variation of the Parsonian sick role (Parsons, 1958): They officially become patients but they are not truly sick at the present; only at risk and needing help. This represents a new variation of the "at-risk" appellation (McLeroy et al., 1987), which obligates them to accept help from those considered experts and to actively cooperate with the agency or professional that offers the helping service. Labeled individuals are thus placed in the role of being obliged to follow a therapeutic regimen and to be in a state of continuous worry about their health. This raises ethical concerns not only about increased medical control over people's lives (e.g., concerns about consent; Forester, 1993) but also the extent to which social interventions affect people's senses of identity (Forester, 1993). Barsky (1988), a physician, observed high levels of anxiety among many of his patients, whom he labels the *worried well*. The dilemma is how to advise individuals that they may be at risk for potentially detrimental health complications without labeling them or contributing to their anxiety, which may adversely affect their well-being or senses of identity (MacDonald, Sackett, Haynes, & Taylor, 1984). The second concern associated with inadvertent harm is whether the intervention contributes to the stigmatization of people. The use of messages that employ fear-raising appeals may potentially stigmatize populations who are in that situation already and who possess the medical condition or attributes alluded to by the intervention as something that should be avoided or is greatly socially undesirable. This can spoil their identity or stigmatize them, as exemplified in the cases of individuals who have been infected with HIV (e.g., Herek & Capitanio, 1993) or people with disabilities (Wang, 1992). Wang reports that messages against drunk driving or aimed to promote the use of seat belts, which depicted the horror of being confined to a wheelchair, were perceived by individuals with mobility disabilities as devaluing them and attacking their self-esteem and dignity.

How does one reconcile the use of persuasive appeals that on one hand serve to scare people about potential hazards and thus raise their motivation to avoid it but on the other hand may present a negative image of, label, and adversely affect the identity of others? One suggestion is that instead of using individual-level fear appeals, persuasive messages could appeal to people's altruistic motives, their sense of community, and willingness to help others. For example, as Wang (1992) suggests, messages that aim to prevent handgun injuries can focus on the incidence of injuries among children. In addition, messages can focus on the institutional factors that cause or contribute to the problem, such as particular corporate interests. For example, messages can focus on the interests of gun manufacturers and the influence strategies of pro-handgun lobbying organizations.

7. The Depriving Dilemma

Does an intervention that urges people to avoid practices associated with certain health risks serve to deprive certain populations of pleasures they may find hard to replace?

Health interventions that aim to change certain practices believed to put people at risk for disease or injury may inadvertently deprive them of behaviors or products that have important significance in their lives or senses of identity. Typically, many behaviors associated with risky pleasures (Shaw, 1996) are consumption of foods or tobacco (or even risky driving) that are inexpensive in money and mental or physical effort and are relatively accessible to people from lower social strata. Increasingly, it is argued, and this is supported by evidence on discrepancies in the adoption of health-promotion behaviors, individuals with greater means and socioeconomic resources find it easier to refrain from practices considered risky. The quality of life of the latter may in fact suffer from what critics have labeled "forceful, evangelistic health propaganda" (Strasser et al., 1987, p. 190). Denying people inexpensive pleasures without providing them with alternative ones thus poses an ethical dilemma, because the health intervention, although trying to do good, may actually harm those who cannot avail themselves of more costly alternatives.

Certain practices, such as smoking, although deemed unhealthy, may serve people in disadvantaged situations as their only means of perceived control. For example, bans on smoking in hospitals have raised an outcry among advocates of individuals with mental health problems. They argue that expecting mental health patients "to kick the habit when they're going into the hospital, which is an awful event to begin with, is really cruelty to the n'th degree" and "having a cigarette is a patient's one pleasure, the one opportunity for personal autonomy" (Foderaro, 1994, p. 44). Similarly, interventions characterizing certain foods or practices as unhealthy may deprive members of particular cultural communities of activities that have special cultural significance. Also similarly, certain practices (e.g., sexual relations with many partners, use of public baths, unprotected sexual intercourse) that may be viewed by certain people as an important part of their identity may be harshly condemned by intervention messages, which may be viewed by some people as an assault on their fragile personae (Odets, 1994). Practitioners or researchers engaged in the design and implementation of public health communication interventions should therefore carefully examine whether the implications of their call to relinquish certain practices, foods, substances, or products may deny those who are particularly vulnerable from important rewards that they cannot easily substitute. Those who are particularly vulnerable may not be able to adopt the recommendations because of socioeconomic circumstances, special cultural meanings, or because the undesired practice serves as a means for coping in a hostile social environment.

The dilemma of what to say to people in disadvantaged circumstances represents the tensions between principles of doing good, promoting the public good, refraining from doing harm, and allowing for autonomous choices, as well as values associated with justice and caring. The messages developed in 1995 by the Gay Men's Health Center in a series called "Staying Negative—It's not automatic" represent an attempt to balance these competing values (Illustration 6.1).

8. The Culpability Dilemmas

The emphasis on personal responsibility in interventions elicits several dilemmas:

> *By suggesting that people modify their behavior, and implying that they may be responsible for ill-health outcomes associated with it, are people unfairly blamed?*
>
> *Is it fair to condone certain behaviors that entail considerable risk as socially approved and even socially desired while disapproving of others that are considered irresponsible?*
>
> *Should the intervention allude to the notion that individuals are responsible for the behavior of others, or does this cast an unfair burden on them?*

With growing emphasis on individuals' lifestyle behaviors as prominent risk factors for ill health, personal responsibility has become a highly visible and prominent theme in many health interventions (McLeroy et al., 1987).[24] Their messages often urge individuals to take responsibility for their own health and to adopt health-promoting behaviors. The emphasis on individual responsibility presumably is based on the assumption that particular health-related behaviors are freely chosen or at least under the voluntary control of the individual. Those who fail to adopt practices promoted as health protective can be characterized as irresponsible by implication. The intervention's intended populations, however, may not adopt recommended practices because of the constraints imposed by economic or sociocultural circumstances and therefore should not be held accountable for not adopting the health-promoting practices.

The issue of accountability or personal responsibility, when raised in the context of health promotion efforts, underscores a highly contested moral issue in social interventions—victim blaming (e.g., Beauchamp, 1987; Crawford, 1977; Eisenberg, 1987; Faden, 1987; Marantz, 1990; Ryan, 1976). It refers to locating the causes of social problems within the individual rather

"When I'm feeling good is when the condoms get clumsy."

"I like sex with someone I don't know. It makes me feel most alive, but a lot of times it happens after I've been out drinking. When I'm feeling good is when the condoms get clumsy. I just tell him to not bother. I don't want to stop drinking but I spend days panicking wondering if I'm going to get infected when I'm too wasted to care."

staying negative – it's not automatic

We have free workshops that can help you stay uninfected. By talking about the sex you are having, what you like about it and what you don't, you can make partying — and sex — safer. **Call today.**

SUCE — 212 337-3343
Substance Use Counseling and Education
GMHC

© 1995
photo: allen frame/frank franca
This campaign is sponsored in part by

Illustration 6.1 © 1995 Gay Men's Health Crisis, photos by Allen Frank/Frank Frame

than in social and environmental forces. On one hand, because individuals are viewed as autonomous and able to make voluntary decisions regarding their behaviors—especially those characterized as related to lifestyle—the responsibility for modifying their behavior is viewed as primarily their own. On the other hand, many who do not adopt health-promoting behaviors because of their social or economic circumstances are viewed as particularly vulnerable to antihealth influences. This argument adds complexity to the issue of personal responsibility or culpability: When are we to consider that the person's behavior is voluntary and when is it to be viewed as affected by powerful cultural or institutional factors (McLeroy et al., 1987)?

The question of how to determine what is voluntary leads us to another dilemma associated with responsibility: Should one be free to choose whether or not to adopt practices that may lead to illness or disability? Furthermore, who should be responsible for adverse outcomes that result from people taking risks with their health? Some claim that people who take risks with their health impose burdens on others and society as a whole, especially when the public needs to take care of them or pay for their health care or disability (McLachlan, 1995; McLeroy et al., 1987; Veatch, 1980). This points to tensions between ethical principles of personal autonomy and the public good, and it raises the following questions: Should health interventions promote messages that suggest that individuals should be liable for increased costs they may place on the medical care system, under the assumption that their voluntary acts may cause injury to others? Should people who do not adopt what are considered responsible practices be charged with higher health insurance premiums or denied all or part of their insurance claims if they do not, for example, use seat belts (Beauchamp, 1987)? What behaviors can be characterized as truly voluntary, and when do we not hold the person culpable (Veatch, 1982)? This dilemma leads to the dilemma of certain risk-taking and injury-prone behaviors being socially sanctioned and even approved of as socially desirable (e.g., sports or dangerous occupations), whereas others are not. What are the moral criteria for making such distinctions? Should individuals who engage in socially nonapproved health-related risks be held accountable for their injuries or diseases while those whose socially sanctioned behaviors may lead to the same kind of consequences are seen as heroes (Keeney, 1994)?

The third dilemma concerns the extent to which one is responsible for the behavior of others. Interventions often disseminate messages that appeal to significant others to ensure that the person who is seen as being at risk will adopt the recommended practices.[25] Although these interventions intend to do good by using what they consider effective persuasive messages or to emphasize the importance of caring (Noddings, 1984), they may do harm by implicitly blaming significant others. This may occur when the person who is believed to be at risk does not adopt the recommendations or when the significant other feels they are not capable of influencing the person at risk. Thus, when persuasive appeals turn to significant others as a means to influence health outcomes, we need to closely examine the ethical implications.[26]

Another ethical concern regarding blame and responsibility is whether an intervention makes a claim that one's actions are necessary or sufficient to cause or prevent the ill-health problem. If the messages frame the individual's behavior as a *sufficient* condition for causing the potential harmful outcome, that raises serious ethical concerns because this insinuates that it is the individual's behavior that is the only cause for ill health.[27] Although most intervention messages do not explicitly make such allegations, people who are increasingly bombarded with messages about personal responsibility may interpret them as such.[28] For example, in a series of "Health Notes" included in a kit for professionals produced by the NHLBI and reproduced by local public health communication intervention programs, messages were prevalent that stated "It's up to you: High blood pressure can be controlled, but you are the *only* person who can control it" [italics added].[29] The means to control it, according to the printed material, were weight control, limited salt intake, avoidance of alcohol, engaging in exercise, and complying with a medication regimen. By implication, if one did *not* adopt these practices, this neglect would be a likely reason to get a stroke. On the other hand, this can be considered an empowering message that lets people feel they are in control. A television PSA aimed to encourage individuals with elevated blood pressure to stay on treatment, produced by the same organization, elicits the same dilemma: It shows stark scenes of homes without their inhabitants and the voice-over solemnly tells viewers that particular individuals who did not take their high blood pressure medication appropriately, indeed died, leaving their loving family members behind: "Meet the people who didn't take care of their blood pressure. . . . Mr. Remos left a beautiful family." Clearly, the implication is that these people were not responsible in taking care of their blood pressure; therefore, their family now suffers. These messages imply that the persons' nonadherence caused their deaths and that they neglected their fundamental responsibility. The person who did take care—is still alive. Thus, persuasive messages may inherently involve the potential inducement of guilt feelings or obligation (Faden, 1987).

An emphasis on responsibility, as discussed in the labeling dilemma, can lead to distortions in attribution of blame. In a report on findings from a focus group conducted in a community fraught with socioeconomic problems, respondents tended to blame themselves or their "weak characters" for not adopting the recommended medical regimens to control high blood pressure.[30] These respondents did not consider the possibility that socioeconomic and institutional factors may serve as significant barriers, irrespective of their personal dispositions. Similarly, Jeffery et al. (1990) describe findings from a study of a hypertension prevention program in which the participants proffered different attributions of causes for their failures to adopt recommended preventive behaviors. Participants who were experimentally assigned to the weight-loss groups were significantly more likely to blame themselves for their problems with adherence than were those assigned to the non-weight-loss groups. They tended to internalize the blame and attribute it more to their personal characters rather than to external or situational attributions (e.g., lack of support or environmental conditions). It is interesting that the differences in the types of attributions did not predict weight loss or other medical outcomes. This phenomenon of self-blame echoes critics' concerns regarding blaming the victim[31] and justice or fairness, because health promoters have the obligation to treat their target population fairly in terms of burdens (e.g., risks, costs) and benefits (Hiller, 1987).[32]

Ethical concerns associated with justice thus raise the issue of whether the intervention provides all members of the population with reasonable opportunities to pursue the goals emphasized in the intervention (Daniels, 1985), what should be considered as reasonable opportunities, and who should decide on the definition. The issue of equal opportunity was raised by focus group members in a community program studied by the author (Guttman, 1994). Intervention messages that emphasized choice and responsibility to prevent heart disease (originally produced by the NHLBI) were contested by members of the focus group. The messages state that one's "choice begins at the grocery store," but the members felt that what people in the community could actually consume was very limited because they were restricted by the relatively high prices and low-quality produce available to them at the only grocery store in walking distance. The intended population would mainly use the store because it did not have easy access to other food outlet options.[33]

Justice is providing equitable opportunity to those who are more restricted in their current options. Daniels (1985) explains that providing an opportunity to the less advantaged does not necessarily mean that individuals can
purchase what they would *like* to, but it does mean that they should be provided with equal opportunity to purchase nutritious foods viewed as necessary
to maintain good health. This raises concerns regarding principles of justice, as
indicated by epidemiologic studies: *Decreases* in morbidity and mortality from
heart disease are usually more prevalent in the more affluent population, because they are more apt to adopt healthier lifestyle behavioral modifications
(e.g., Blane, 1995; Thomas, 1990; Whitehead, 1992; Williams, 1990;
Winkleby, 1994).[34] An additional concern associated with using the notion of
personal responsibility as a persuasive strategy for health promotion is the extent to which the emphasis on an individualistically oriented conception of
personal responsibility raises people's expectations of the health care system as
a whole. This issue is discussed in the dilemma concerning the promise of good
health, elaborated in the discussion to follow.

DILEMMAS CONCERNING POWER AND CONTROL

Power and control can be maintained through indirect means, including ideologies and implicit coercion (Mumby, 1988). Concerns associated with power
and control thus need to identify existing or potential patterns of control and
privilege in public health communication interventions (see Duncan & Cribb,
1996; Salmon, 1989, in the adaptation of a Faucauldian perspective). The following three dilemmas focus on potential manifestations of power and control
in three types of instances.

9. The Privileging Dilemma

*By focusing on specific health problems or particular ways to address them,
does the intervention privilege certain stakeholders or dominant ideologies?*

By focusing on particular medical conditions, interventions, by definition,
prioritize these conditions and privilege certain individuals or social institutions over others. First, framing the issue in medical terms serves to privilege

the health and medical institutions that have framed it as such, including, more specifically, agencies and professionals who specialize in treating the condition and pharmaceutical companies whose products have been developed to treat it. This raises ethical concerns regarding who is privileged (both purposefully and inadvertently) by a certain intervention and what the implications are for society as a whole. Many commercial enterprises can profit from intervention efforts by increasing markets for their products or services (Freimuth et al., 1988; Wang, 1992), and often, as illustrated in the case of the National High Blood Pressure Education Programs and the National Cholesterol Education Programs, interventions may specifically act to support the authority of biomedical professionals by urging the public to see their doctors. In fact, one of the criteria for the success of these interventions is the increase in the number of visits to physicians.

According to Zola (1975), labeling a particular physical condition as a medical condition or disease has serious political, economic, and social consequences and privileges the medical establishment. Once a condition or behavior is defined as a matter of health and disease, the medical profession is thereby licensed to diagnose, treat, control, or intervene. The mere act of characterizing a certain level of blood cholesterol as an important medical condition, and having the detection and treatment of this condition promoted through an intervention, potentially results in placing a large number of individuals in the social position of patients and in the creation or enhancement of a whole industry of screening and monitoring paraphernalia. It may also privilege manufacturers of particular food products. This raises ethical concerns regarding the extent to which one condition should be prioritized over others and the extent to which particular stakeholders' perspectives and interests are given more prominence over those of others. A related concern is, to what extent does an intervention prioritize particular social values and beliefs over others? Values related to individual responsibility, individual-level solutions, and market autonomy are often emphasized in health interventions. This emphasis is likely to reproduce values dominant in American culture that include individualism (Bellah et al., 1991), a distrust of government intervention, a preference for private solutions to social problems, a standard of abundance as a normal state of affairs, and the power of technology (Priester, 1992a). To what extent does a public health communication intervention contribute to sustaining or reproducing certain beliefs and social and cultural institutions that support them, intentionally or not?

Another concern is, to what extent do interventions privilege particular agencies or groups by collaborating with them or providing them with resources or legitimacy? Interventions tend to work with groups in the target community that are established and already have resources, thus emphasizing principles of utility. Critics maintain that this can help perpetuate the power of these groups while depriving less-established or non-mainstream organizations of potential resources and legitimization. Although interventions may attempt to involve individuals and groups from a wide spectrum, constituencies who are given priority are most likely to be established agencies and groups that already have considerable resources and networks or are predisposed to the topic of the intervention. Consequently, they are less likely to address the needs and concerns of those who are unaffiliated and who are relatively marginalized. As a result, the latter are least likely to be given the opportunities to get involved in policy-making processes related to an intervention that aims to affect their lives (Wallace-Brodeur, 1990). Last, an additional concern is the extent to which certain groups or organizations are more privileged by being able to produce (persuasive) information and get it disseminated (Rakow, 1989). To what extent do particular organizations or groups have more access to information that will support their claims regarding what health issues should be focused on or what strategies should be adopted?

10. The Exploitation Dilemma

May involving community-based or voluntary organizations in a health intervention serve to inadvertently exploit these organizations, although such involvement may support values of participation and empowerment?

More and more interventions, including those sponsored by the federal government, follow a model of using local agencies or organizations to implement much of the intervention process. This raises ethical concerns regarding the extent to which interventions create expectations that voluntary groups will carry out functions that should be served through public services. For example, national and state-level initiatives rely on local screening activities that take place through the collaboration of local agencies and voluntary groups to achieve the programs' official goals. These programs' long-term goals are to institutionalize these types of activities so that local organizations can continue them in the future without sponsorship or funding. Capek (1992) and Green

(1989) note that there is a potentially problematic aspect related to the goal of institutionalization, of having community organizations eventually take over the mission of the (funded) intervention program, especially if that mission entails service delivery. As Green has explained earlier, community organizations should not be expected to take over as permanent substitutes for federal agencies; trying to do so can disempower them and divert scarce resources from their primary goals. On one hand, local involvement promotes democratic goals. On the other hand, concerns can be raised regarding the extent to which the involvement of the group or agency in the intervention serves this group or the community it represents in the long run. Are organizations that become involved being exploited by the program because it may not serve their interests in the long run? In addition, are its constituents given the opportunity to decide on the goals and priorities of the intervention? This also raises concerns regarding the extent to which particular organizations should be obligated to participate and whether certain organizations are viewed as having obligations for community members' health. Similarly, should organizations that choose not to be involved be sanctioned? Last, in what ways does the intervention enterprise itself serve as a means of control and subjugation of individual or local framing of social and health-related issues? The latter is further developed in the control dilemma, described in the following discussion.

11. The Control Dilemma

May implementing certain health-promoting interventions serve to increase state, corporate, or organizational control over population or organization members?

States and organizations increasingly engage in surveillance activities to identify, quantify, and monitor health intervention activities. In what ways does such surveillance—often a primary condition for obtaining the support of dominant social institutions—constitute a structure to control or regulate people's behaviors? Surveillance has become a prominent feature of modern life (Duncan & Cribb, 1996) that enables dominant institutions to learn about what people do or do not do, including their purchasing patterns, their medical states, and their cultural beliefs. More so, the sites and means to monitor people have become increasingly ubiquitous, ranging from the ability to obtain detailed information from individuals' credit card purchases, phone and electronic media uses, to genetic screenings. Concerns about implications of surveillance as they relate to the notion of control have already surfaced in the context of work organizations and can be applied to municipal, state, and national contexts as well. Work organizations increasingly offer what are called wellness and disease prevention or health promotion programs. The mere provision of such programs in work organizational contexts often indicates the success of health interventions. Obviously, work site disease prevention activities, as part of a health intervention, have numerous advantages. Work site interventions can provide interventionists with access to particular groups and present workers with opportunities or even tangible incentives to participate in health-promoting activities.[35] Justifications for these activities relate mostly to principles of doing good (for the employees) and utility (e.g., increasing productivity, decreasing absenteeism, and enhancing the organization's image). Nevertheless, numerous ethical concerns have been raised regarding the work site as a place to promote health (e.g., Hollander & Hale, 1987; Roman & Blum, 1987).

One of the major concerns is the extent to which involvement with employee health gives the work organization a mandate to literally pry into what until now had been considered employees' private affairs. With health linked to lifestyle, organizations can engage in activities to find out what their employees do on and off the job—in the name of concern for their employees' health. They can use this information to justify managerial decisions not necessarily in the interest of the employees. Similarly, management can make presumably health-related demands on employees that are not directly linked to their work (Conrad & Walsh, 1992; Feingold, 1994). The so-called "new health ethic" may serve as a new vehicle for enhancing worker discipline, screening for undesired workers, or fostering uncritical loyalty to the company, say these critics. Ethical concerns related to autonomy and privacy and justice can be raised in this context. Specifically, to what extent are individuals discriminated against because they are characterized as potential liabilities to the organization (Feingold, 1994)? Furthermore, surveillance activities, by framing what is good and bad or normal, become on their own a mechanism of control and can thus serve to "shape the public domain and thereby the self-consciousness of the governed" (Duncan & Cribb, 1996, p. 345). Critics have suggested that wellness and health promotion programs, especially in work organizational contexts, typically construct disease etiology in terms of individual behavior and individual responsibility for being healthy, and they adopt a biomedical framework for assessing risk and risk factors (Alexander,

1988). Alternative conceptualization of risk factors for illness include social and institutional factors, such as the extent to which workers have latitude for decision making in their jobs (e.g., Karasek & Theorell, 1990). This raises concerns regarding the extent to which it is justified for health interventions to mainly emphasize one particular version of health-risk etiology, an issue raised in Chapters 1 and 3 regarding the way problems are defined and further examined in the dilemmas related to social values, which follow.

DILEMMAS CONCERNING SOCIAL VALUES

Do public health communication interventions turn "good health" into an ideal? Do they contribute to making health a "super value" that should be vigorously pursued? Is it implied that "good health" is what "good people" are rewarded with? These are some of the concerns associated with the growing emphasis on health as a value in widely disseminated public health communication interventions. Intervention planners need to consider how their interventions contribute to cultural changes that include the reinforcement or transformation of specific values or ideologies. Over time, interventions as an aggregate produce cultural changes, even if they do not change individuals' behaviors (Pollay, 1989). The three dilemmas presented in the following discussion reflect these concerns by focusing on issues characterized as distraction, promises, and health as a value.

12. The Distraction Dilemma

By emphasizing health-related issues in personal, organizational, and societal agendas, does this emphasis serve to distract people from important social issues?

Having health-related issues capture such a prominent position on personal and public agendas serves, suggest critics, to distract individuals and society from other, more significant problems, such as economic equity or environmental hazards.[36] As communicative action, health interventions can be viewed as framing issues and selectively drawing attention to them while deemphasizing others, thus making the issues promoted by the intervention seem more important. Communicative practice, argues Forester (1993), cannot be viewed simply as an enactment of goals but as the "practical communicative organizing (or dis-organizing) of others' attention to relevant and significant issues at hand" (p. 5). Pollay (1989) reiterates this argument:

> Interventions also serve to set agendas, direct people's attention and order people's priorities. Public health communication programs aimed at making individuals more responsible for their diets may also direct attention away from government and industry policies putting pollutants, toxic waste and carcinogens into the ecology and food chain. (p. 190)

These assertions are supported by research findings from the agenda-setting perspective according to which campaigns to prevent drug abuse were found to influence public perceptions on the importance of these issues (Shoemaker, 1989). Public health communication interventions can serve to prioritize or frame certain issues as important and thus may serve to distract attention from others that do not get government support. Taking this claim a step further, as discussed in Chapter 4, educational messages on how to adapt to current schedules or to limited resources can serve to distract people from institutional or structural conditions that limit their activities or in fact produce conditions that pose a risk to their health. They can also serve as a vehicle to advance people's adaptation to situations that are not favorable to them. Turshen (1989) offered an example in the area of nutrition education: "Nutrition education too often shows people how to adjust to intolerable situations; in an extreme example, South African nutrition education programs teach Blacks how not to starve on starvation wages" (p. 196). Bellah et al. (1986, 1991) also express their concerns about distraction, but their discussion moves us more to a macro sociopolitical arena; they described social institutions as forms of *paying attention* to particular issues, on one hand, but on the other hand, as *socially organized forms of distractions*. The process of distraction is significant, they explain, because of its impact on the functioning of a democratic society: "One way of defining democracy would be to call it a political system in which people actively attend to what is significant" (Bellah et al., 1991, p. 273).

Public health communication interventions, particularly those that employ social-marketing approaches, tend to emphasize and affirm mainly individual-level solutions. As such, they raise the following concerns: To what extent do interventions affect public perceptions and emphasize individual-level solutions as the main course of action, at the expense of other approaches (e.g., organizational or societal)? To what extent does the intervention promote only a lifestyle-modification agenda and not present the public with alternative perspectives (Farrant & Russell, 1987)?[37] These may include messages on how health risks of the public are intricately vested in competing interests of powerful organizations, such as the food and tobacco industries, government interests, or the medical profession.[38] Green and Kreuter (1991) distinguish between reductionist and expansionist approaches to health interventions. In the former, health is identified from broader social issues; in the latter, the specific health issue of the intervention, which is often assigned to the practitioner as its sole mission, can serve as a basis for consideration of a broader range of social issues. But this is not easily accomplished. As a staff member working on a federally funded intervention explained in an interview I conducted in 1992, he did not see his role as a social-change agent in the sense of trying to change structural factors. "If I would have wanted to do that [social changes], I would have gone to be a social worker," he emphatically said. In an interview connected with another initiative, also in 1992, a practitioner lamented to me that neither she nor the other staff members in their health promotion program were trained in community development. They lacked skills, she said, to develop programs to address community-level or structural factors, and therefore their program focused on increasing public awareness of the topic and promoting personal behavior changes. Certainly, the issue of affirming multiple types of causation of health and illness poses challenges to researchers and practitioners: What is the ethical mandate of the researchers or practitioners? Are they mandated to emphasize only the types of messages directly related to the specific domain of behavior change of the intervention, thus possibility distracting attention from other causes? Are they obligated to provide messages on sociocultural or other factors and ways to assess and address them?

13. The Promises Dilemma

Do health interventions that urge people to adopt particular practices and suggest that by doing so, they will be healthier, make promises that may not be beneficial to the public?

Interventions tend to emphasize good health as a reward for adopting what is considered a responsible lifestyle. Their messages may promise people that if they adopt recommended regimes, they will be rewarded with good health. This, maintain critics, reinforces the notion of individual needs as the basis for health care and is problematic not only from a practical perspective but a moral one as well. Callahan (1990) and others (e.g., Barsky, 1988) argue that a major challenge facing the health care system is the escalating expectations of the public for medicine and health care. Two related premises and promises that underlie the current health care system are flawed, suggests Callahan (1990). The first is that health care should emphasize meeting individual needs, and the second is that this can be done economically and in an efficient manner. From a practical perspective, it is argued, the more individuals' expectations are raised, the more they will increase their demands from the health care system, which in turn will increase demands for expensive procedures and services for an ever-increasing range of what can be considered medically related (Gaylin, 1993). According to Callahan (1990), there is a direct conflict between preferences of the individual, whom he suggests, given the choice, will tend to demand the most expensive and comprehensive health care possible, and the depleted limited resources of society.

The ethical concerns raised in this context mainly relate to doing harm, by raising expectations that cannot be met, and the public good, by increasing demands on an overtaxed and costly health care system. Also, the emphasis on personal rewards may serve to deemphasize caring and connectedness to others and the value of relationships (Noddings, 1984). Another concern relates to justice. There is a growing gap in the use of health care between those who have easy access to medical services and those who do not (Gold & Franks, 1990; Mandelblatt, Andrews, Kao, Wallace, & Kerner, 1996; Thomas, 1990). On one hand, individuals who have the opportunities to adopt recommended health-promoting regimens have raised expectations and will increasingly see medicine as an unlimited social good. On the other hand, those who have fewer opportunities to adopt health-promoting regimens may be made to feel inadequate, guilty, or hopeless. In addition, with more and more personal and social issues (e.g., infertility) viewed as potentially solved by medical technology—and therefore within the domain of medical care—it can be argued that those who have more opportunities will be tempted to demand even more medical services. These demands, argues Gaylin (1993), will increase the cost of the health care system to society beyond any cost-saving measures proposed by health insurance reform policies. Those who have fewer opportunities will be less likely to use current resources, which can adversely affect their health status (Gold & Franks, 1990; Thomas, 1990). This corresponds to the phenomenon of the knowledge gap (Dervin, 1980; Olien et al., 1983; Rakow,

1989) and raises ethical concerns regarding justice and fairness. The promises that cannot be fulfilled lead to the final dilemma presented in this paper: the implications of emphasizing health to such an extent that it becomes cast as an ultimate value.

14. The Dilemma of Health as a Value

By making health an important social value that should be pursued by the public, does the intervention promote a certain moralism that may clash with other important social values?

Broadening the definition of the role of medicine in disease and health and raising people's expectations accordingly raises additional concerns: Do public health communication interventions, by emphasizing the importance of health and a healthy lifestyle, contribute to health becoming an ultimate value? (Gillick, 1984).[39] Preoccupation with health and turning it into an important value may distract people from other areas of human existence. As Callahan (1990) warns,

> Health sought for its own sake, or because of the jobs or profits it produces, leads to a kind of personal and social madness. One can never get enough or be too safe. We will spend too much on health, be in a state of constant anxiety about mortality, and be endlessly distracted from thinking about more important purposes and goals of life. (p. 113)

Promoting health as a value may also have implications for people's perception of self and others or their senses of identity. An emphasis on health, argue critics, may serve to promote values of individualism at the expense of values of connectedness and caring. For example, slogans such as "It won't happen to me," "It's your health," "Take care of yourself," reflect an emphasis on individualism and a separation between those who value health and those who do not (Burns, 1992):[40]

> "Take care of yourself"—"assume responsibility for your own health"—"assess your own risk"—"personal wellness"—These are all slogans of a perspective on health that is essentially individualistic. It's what you'd expect in a culture that sees the self as separate and looks at human relationships as market transactions. It is self-centered and body-centered. . . . Prevention programs that over value the self have the benefit of helping individuals stay well, but they allow the precise separa-

> tion of self from others: health vs. sickness, we versus them. They promote a concentration on the self, neglecting the possibility that although illness may be embodied, health is something we share with others. (pp. 10-11)

Interventions for AIDS prevention tend to emphasize the use of so-called negotiation skills for achieving sexual partners' compliance in adopting safer sex practices (e.g., Fisher & Misovich, 1990; Franzini, Sideman, Dexter, & Elder, 1990). The word *negotiations,* though, can connote an interchange that emphasizes personal interests, similar to marketplace transactions (Burns, 1992), one of which is personal health, rather than values that emphasize relationships or caring. This critique does not suggest that we should not help people enhance their communication skills with sexual partners to prevent potential harm. Rather, it raises the concern that this type of emphasis can put women and members of particular cultures, who tend to greatly value caring and relationships, in a double bind (Lyman & Engstrom, 1992; Scott & Mercer, 1994).

A related concern is, To what extent does the promotion of health as a value by interventions contribute to the medicalization of life (Fox, 1977) or, using Habermas's terms, the colonization of human experience (Habermas, 1979)? Callahan (1990) argues that with health increasingly being viewed as an important value, definitions of what is a "good life" become dependent on medical criteria. Barsky (1988), a physician who became concerned with people's growing obsession with health when he saw many of his patients become what he calls the worried well, makes a similar point:

> The point is that the pursuit of health can be paradoxical. Secure well-being and self-confident vitality grows out of an acceptance of our frailties and our limits and our mortality as much as they can result from our trying to cure every affliction, to evade every disease and to relieve every symptom. (pp. xi-xii)

Callahan (1990) emphatically adds that this can result in too much of an "obsessive . . . quest for health" (p. 37).

Broadening (or distorting) the definition of health into a construct of all-inclusive wellness that encompasses physiological, psychological, and social factors, including character traits, personal appearance, criminal activities, moods, and desires, may serve to medicalize human existence. Increasingly, human experiences of life, birth, pain, death, coping, and joy are defined as health related, and people, it is suggested, tend to lose the capacity to live and cope without medical definitions (Fitzgerald, 1994).[41] Ethical concerns, in other words, focus on the extent to which health interventions serve to colonize or medicalize human experiences, foster dependency on medical institutions, or deemphasize people's cultural and spiritual well-being. To this, Marshall Becker (1986), in an article titled "The Tyranny of Health," adds a warning that health has become a "New Morality"[42] and that

> health promotion, as currently practiced, fosters a dehumanizing self-concern that substitutes personal health goals for more important, humane, societal goals. It is a new religion, in which we worship ourselves, attribute good health to our devoutness, and view illness as just punishment for those who have not yet seen the Way. (p. 20)

Health thus becomes a metaphor for self-control, self-discipline, self-denial, and will power. It becomes a moral discourse and "an opportunity to reaffirm the values by which self is distinguished from other" (Crawford, 1994, p. 1353). Viewing health as an ultimate value may harm those who, according to these criteria, are portrayed as not being healthy by making them feel they have been punished or are unworthy.

The dilemma of treating health as a value may be addressed by adopting a social rather than "a distinctive biological view of health" (Levine, Feldman, & Elinson, 1983, p. 400). A social view of health does not focus on the absence of organic and mental disease but on the way it influences individuals' quality of life, their ability to function, perform, and do what they want to do (Levine et al., 1983), and the extent to which one can enable their self-actualization. A social view of health reminds us that health is likely to be conceived and valued differently across cultural and social groups whose needs and social conditions may differ. Robertson and Minkler (1994) cautioned, however, that even the adoption of a social conceptualization of health, and having health valued as a resource rather than a commodity, risks the commodification of health. The definition of health may again be "conferred by a new set of experts with new knowledge bases and new skills" (p. 299).

PRACTICE-ORIENTED QUESTIONS

This chapter concludes with a series of practice-oriented questions presented in four tables. They provide examples of how dilemmas associated with ethical concerns can be applied to the design and implementation of interventions, the assessment of their goals, and the evaluation of their outcomes. Such questions can be used for both analytic purposes and as a basis for empirical and design work. For example, questions associated with dilemmas regarding the use of policies that place restrictions on people's behavior can help formulate the development of designs that take into consideration the considerable ambivalence, resistance to, and often lack of enforcement of such policies.[43] Intervention designs may thus incorporate methods to study and understand the intervention population's values, beliefs, and preferences regarding policy restrictions as well as methods to develop opportunities to enable and facilitate discourse among various intervention constituencies on the pertinent issue. In the area of targeting, articulating questions about the extent to which the intervention indeed reaches different segments of the population may help compel intervention designers to closely examine the strategies they use to reach various audiences and to test the extent to which the intervention efforts may not reach certain individuals or populations. Such questions may also prompt them to closely consider what populations they may decide to exclude and how to justify such an exclusion. For example, they may decide to exclude populations that can afford to pay for services provided by the intervention. These questions may need to be addressed through advocacy, public policy, and considerations of entitlement and resource allocation.

Questions about labeling may help interventionists reconsider what types of persuasive messages should be used in the intervention. Labeling concerns may influence the way focus group interviews are conducted because these often serve campaign designers as a basis for the development and selection of persuasive appeals. Consideration of labeling may encourage designers, in their formative research, to explore messages and persuasive approaches that specifically avoid the potential of labeling and stigmatization. Perhaps, they may choose to explore ways to involve and engage intended audiences in the health-promotion effort through values associated with social responsibility and the public good instead of focusing mainly on appeals to personal vulnerability.

If the intervention employs participation or involvement as its strategy or goal (as discussed in Chapter 5), questions about potential exploitation of local voluntary organizations may contribute to (a) the specification of the expectations of the intervention from each organization that participates in the intervention and (b) the analysis of potential short-term and long-term costs that may be associated with this participation. Design implications might be the provision of criteria for choosing long-term strategies that will ensure that the organization's resources will not be depleted or that if the intervention provides services that should be provided by public agencies, public policy will ensure that service provision will not rely on community voluntary efforts (e.g., by incorporating public policy goals associated with resource allocation). Tables 6.1 through 6.4 present examples of practice-oriented questions, one table for each major area of general concern. The dilemmas described in this chapter are identified in the first column. The second column presents examples of questions, the third, examples of design implications, the fourth, justifications for why the activity may be pursued by the intervention, and the fifth column lists potential ethical concerns that may need to be balanced with these justifications. The questions can be further adapted to the specific context of the interventions and can be used in their assessment and the design of evaluation criteria. Because the enterprise of health interventions includes diverse health promotion and disease prevention efforts, these dilemmas and questions can also be applied and adopted to other contexts. For example, ethical concerns associated with targeting, persuasion, or distraction are applicable to all interventions that aim to reach particular populations, regardless of the strategies they employ and whether they aim to curtail illicit drugs or cigarette sales through stricter enforcement or to educate workers on the importance of adopting safety precautions.

Table 6.1   Questions Drawn From the Strategies Dilemmas

Dilemmas	Questions	Design Implications	Justifications	Ethical Concerns
Persuasion	Is it justified to use highly persuasive tactics to achieve intervention goals? Is it justified *not* to use highly persuasive tactics, even if they might effectively achieve intervention goals?	Choice of strategies Evaluation of effectiveness	Doing good Not doing harm	Autonomy Belief Consent Doing good Utility
Coercion	Is it justified to promote policies that regulate or place restrictions on individual's behaviors even if they may be effective? Is it justified *not* to promote policies that place restrictions on individual's behavior but might be effective? Is it justified to promote policies that place restrictions on the marketplace which in turn restrict individual choice? Would restrictions on the marketplace or the social environment help distribute the responsibility for people's well-being across the community or would these restrictions penalize particular individuals? Would regulation such as an excise tax pose relative hardship on those who are less economically advantaged?	Choice of strategies Evaluation of effectiveness	Doing good Protecting others Autonomy Market autonomy Public good Justice	Autonomy Consent Doing good Utility Justice

Targeting	Should the intervention's resources be devoted to populations believed to be particularly needy but hard to reach or to those who are more likely to adopt its recommendations? Does the intervention widen the gap between those who have more socioeconomic advantages and those who have less in social and health-related outcomes? Does the intervention reach all segments of the population to the same extent? Are issues that are more salient to the more dominant cultural groups given more priority in the intervention? Does the intervention address issues that are important to groups with special needs?	Choice of strategies Targeting Evaluation of effectiveness	Doing good Justice Care	Justice Care Utility
Harm reduction	Should the intervention engage in strategies which support behaviors that are not socially approved or are seen by some as immoral, in order to prevent further harm to certain populations? Should the interventions promote messages that may reduce people's exposure to immediate harm but may serve to maintain practices that can cause ill health in the long run?	Choice of strategies Evaluation of effectiveness	Doing good Utility	Support of immoral activities Doing harm

Table 6.2   Questions Drawn From the Inadvertent Harm Dilemmas

Dilemmas	Questions	Design Implications	Justifications	Ethical Concerns
Labeling	What are the implications of labeling a person as a "patient," "at risk," or "having a disease" after getting them to be screened for a particular symptom? Does the intervention raise the level of anxiety, fear, or guilt among target populations? Does the intervention stigmatize certain people by characterizing them as having a particular undesired medical condition?	Choice of strategies Choice of types of messages or appeals	Doing good	Identity Doing harm
Depriving	Might the intervention serve to deprive disadvantaged people of accessible pleasures without providing them with alternative options when decreeing that practices or behaviors associated with certain risks should be avoided? Does the campaign deprive people of cultural activities that are of particular significance to them?	Choice of strategies and appeals Evaluation of intended and unintended outcomes	Doing good	Doing harm Justice Autonomy Caring

Culpability	Choice of strategies	Autonomy	Autonomy
	Choice of types of messages	Doing good	Framing
	or appeals	Utility	Distraction
	Targeting	Justice	Beliefs
	Evaluation of intended and		Justice
	unintended outcomes		Doing harm
			Consent

To what extent should one be free *not* to adopt practices that might put them at risk?

Does the intervention claim that adopting its recommendation is a necessary or even a sufficient condition for what is characterized as good health?

To what extent does the intervention imply that one person is responsible for the health-related behaviors of others (e.g., spouse, friend, employee) and to what extent should they be held responsible?

Should the intervention promote messages that individuals should be liable for the societal costs of their risk-taking voluntary activities, and what are considered hazardous or antihealth behaviors?

Which behaviors are truly voluntary, for which a person can be held culpable, and which are not voluntary, thus exempting the person from full responsibility?

What behaviors with high injury potential should be seen as socially desirable, which are not, and what are the moral criteria for making these distinctions?

Are individuals inadvertently blamed or stigmatized by the campaign if they do not adopt its recommendations?

Does the intervention rely on personal responsibility messages as its main strategy for getting target audience members to adopt the recommended practices?

Do all target populations have reasonable opportunities to adopt the recommended practices?

Who decides what is reasonable or unreasonable risk-taking behavior?

Table 6.3   Questions Drawn From the Power and Control Dilemmas

Dilemmas	Questions	Design Implications	Justifications	Ethical Concerns
Privileging	When focusing on specific health problems or particular ways to address them, does the intervention privilege certain stakeholders or ideologies? Should specific health-related conditions be prioritized over others? Should the perspectives and interests of particular stakeholders be given priority over those of others? Does the intervention legitimize, prioritize, or privilege particular agencies or groups compared to others? Are certain social values or ideologies emphasized compared to others? Do the intervention practitioners have special access to information or other resources in producing (persuasive) information and getting it disseminated? Do particular organizations or groups have more access to information to support their claims regarding the intervention's priorities? Do particular organizations or groups have relatively more resources to access sociodemographic characteristics of target audiences, which would enable them to develop more persuasive messages?	Choice of goals Choice of strategies Choice of partners Choice of types of messages or appeals Choice of evaluation outcomes	Utility	Justice Truth Utility

Exploitation	When involving community or other voluntary organizations in the campaigns, which presumably aim to advance values of participation and empowerment, to what extent does this in fact serve to exploit these organizations? Are particular organizations made to feel obligated to participate in the intervention's activities? What is the basis of this obligation? Should organizations that choose not to be involved in the intervention be sanctioned? Are organizations that participate in the intervention exploited by it since diverting their resources toward the intervention's activities might not serve their constituencies or organizational interests in the long run?	Choice of strategies Choice of allocation of resources Choice of goals and level of intervention	Autonomy Utility	Justice Framing Autonomy Doing harm
Control	When providing health-promoting services, to what extent might their use serve to control organizational members? To what extent does the intervention promote a topic that can serve as a means for social or organizational control?	Choice of goals Evaluation of unintended consequences	Utility Doing good	Autonomy Consent Belief

Table 6.4   Questions Drawn From the Social Values Dilemmas

Dilemmas	Questions Related to the Dilemmas	Design Implications	Justifications	Ethical Concerns
Distraction	Does the intervention focus on specific health topics, thus possibly distracting people from other important health-related issues? Does the intervention promote a lifestyle-modification agenda and not present the target audience with alternative perspectives on etiology and behavior change?	Choice of goals and level of intervention Choice of strategies	Doing good	Framing Belief
Promises	By urging people to adopt particular practices and behaviors and claiming that these will help promote their health, does the intervention make promises that might not benefit all people? Does the intervention contribute to increased demands on the health care system that cannot be met? Does the intervention increase the gap of health care use between those who are more privileged and those who are less so?	Choice of strategies Evaluation of unintended consequences	Doing good Utility	Identity Doing harm Framing Utility Justice
Health as a value	By making health an important value that should be vigorously pursued, does the intervention promote a certain moralism? Does the intervention contribute to the notion that "good health" should be a reward for "good people"? Does the intervention contribute to making health an ideal or a super value that people need to vigorously pursue? Does the intervention contribute to the medicalization of life?	Choice of goals and level of intervention Choice of strategies Evaluation of unintended consequences	Doing good Utility	Truth Identity Justice Framing Doing harm

NOTES

1. Interest in ethical issues in the health care context is increasing, which is evident in the inclusion of ethics in health professionals' training, in the growth of the number of books on bioethics, the creation of ethics committees in hospitals, and in recent editions of health communication books (e.g., Kreps & Thornton, 1992; Thornton & Kreps, 1993; Northouse & Northouse, 1992).

2. See Burdine, McLeroy, and Gottlieb, 1987; Duncan and Cribb, 1996; Eisenberg, 1987; Faden, 1987; Faden and Faden, 1982; Gillon, 1990; Gruning, 1989; Morgan and Lave, 1990; Parrot, Kahl, and Maibach, 1995; Salmon, 1989; Winett et al., 1989; Witte, 1994.

3. This is previously discussed in Chapter 3, which presents an alternative framework regarding ethical concerns in health communication interventions or campaigns.

4. See an excellent review by Cambridge, McLaughlin, and Rota (1995). Nagel (1983) presents ethical dilemmas in policy evaluation. Some of these share the same concerns raised in this chapter. The nine dilemmas he discusses concern policy optimization, sensitivity analysis, partisanship, unforeseen consequences, equity, efficient research, research sharing, research validity, and handling official wrongdoing.

5. Duncan and Cribb (1996) present on a similar critique but offered less of a detailed analytic approach, drawing on the work of Faucault (1975, 1977).

6. See Elder, Hovell, Lasater, Wells, and Carleton, 1985; Evans, 1988; Fine, 1981; Lefebvre and Flora, 1998; Jaccard et al., 1990; Manoff, 1985; Manuel et al., 1991; Rogers and Storey, 1987; Scherer and Juanillo, 1992. For example, the National Cholesterol Education Program's (NCEP) 1992 Communication Strategy document states that it

> is not enough to create messages based on scientific consensus—it is critical to provide messages that the audience will understand, that they will care about, and that they can act on. To accomplish this, the NHLBI's public education efforts have successfully employed the principles of social marketing. (p. 8)

7. See also a discussion by Laczniak et al. (1979) on ethical issues in social marketing.

8. Not all health promoters believe these to be the most effective techniques. See Wallack's (1989) critique.

9. A popular approach is the use of focus groups.

10. The National High Blood Pressure Education Program followed this approach when it used messages intended to arouse fear of stroke in its public service messages based on findings from focus group interviews. Reported in *Analysis of High Blood Pressure and Cholesterol Target Audience and Message Test Reports, 1978-1991,* prepared by E. B. Arkin, August 1992, for NHLBI.

11. In this case, though, the planners might have also assumed that fear appeals might be ineffective, according to the authors. The use of fear appeals has been endorsed as effective, for example by the National Heart, Lung and Blood Institute's National High Blood Pressure Education Program in its 1993 communication strategy plans.

12. An additional discussion is presented in Chapter 3 in the discussion of strategies.

13. This was discussed in Chapter 3.

14. For a recent treatment of the ethical issues regarding the use of "sin taxes," see Kahn (1994).

15. This is discussed as one of the health promotion paradoxes in Guttman, Kegler, and McLeroy (1996).

16. For example, bicycle helmet promoters in Quebec found that the benefits of their program were unequally distributed and that the program was one third as effective in poorer municipalities. This concern further developed in the dilemmas concerning inadvertent outcomes.

17. In fact, it might even cause inadvertent harm, as discussed in the Culpability Dilemmas section

18. This approach is mentioned in most, if not all, the official documents of NCEP and NHBPEP reviewed by the author. It is detailed in NCEP (1990). For an in-depth epidemiological rationale, see Geoffrey Rose (1981, 1985).

19. Kenneth McLeroy presented this paradox in the Society for Public Health Education's Scientific conference in North Carolina in 1994. It is described in Guttman et al. (1996).

20. Nagel (1983), in the context of policy analysis, describes a similar dilemma he calls the Equity Dilemma, which refers to a frequent conflict between policy goals of efficiency and equity.

21. Everett Rogers gave an example, at the 1993 conference of the International Communication Association in Washington, DC, of how practitioners and researchers decided to forego an experimental design of interventions for smoking prevention among children and youth after they got requests to implement their program in communities that were supposed to provide a "control."

22. The Designated Driver campaign typically has not been framed as following a harm reduction approach, but it can be seen as such because its messages essentially condone, or at least do not aim to change, excessive alcohol consumption (by those who are not designated to drive) to prevent alcohol-related auto accidents. An implicit underlying assumption is that because interventions cannot change people's alcohol consumption behavior, at least, health promoters can try to prevent accidents. This approach raises additional concerns regarding the framing of the issue of alcohol consumption to be discussed in the Distractions Dilemma.

23. A third concern is raised in a practice-oriented manual produced by the U.S. Center for Substance Abuse Prevention (1994) regarding the labeling of some young people as at high risk. Even with the intention of furthering their best interests, there may be unintended negative consequences: the label may stigmatize them and may serve as a negative self-fulfilling prophecy. It is suggested instead to refer to "youth in high-risk environments," which emphasizes the critical role environmental factors play in substance abuse.

24. The issue of personal responsibility was discussed in Chapter 2.

25. NHBPEP Communication Strategy (Draft, 1993, p. 24). See "Husband: Darling, did you take your high blood pressure medicine today? Daughter: Mom, I made Dad's favorite dish for dinner: macaroni and cheese. Mother: Did you remember to use the skim milk and low-fat cheese? Daughter: I sure did." (NHLBI Kit '90, pp. 19-20).

26. We may need to develop ways to determine and make distinctions between formal duties and obligations that may stem from legal relationships, and moral obligations of benevolence or care that stem from special personal ties. This has been discussed in Chapter 3.

27. This was suggested by bioethicist Dan Wikler (personal communication, 1993).

28. As mentioned earlier, NHLBI PSAs presented individuals who did not follow their medical regimen, had strokes, and consequently were dependent on others or ruined their retirement plans. This can be seen as falling within the category of people's (irresponsible) behavior being a necessary cause for their condition, as well as the implication that they were not behaving responsibly toward their loved ones.

29. These are found in NHLBI Kit '90. A typical message in this type of campaign is "It's your life, it's your move." This message is from NHBPEP's PSAs. Other types of messages are "You can lower your blood cholesterol: It's up to you. All it takes are some simple diet changes," or "You are in control." These messages imply that one's behavior change is sufficient to influence one's health, which as will be discussed, puts the main burden on the person.

30. This is described in Guttman (1994).

31. For example, in a report of a focus group in a local heart disease prevention program whose members were from a from a lower socioeconomic background, the participants described themselves as being "weak" (of character) or having "lack of willpower" to explain why they did not consume only low-fat foods to prevent potential health complications. The report concludes that in general, "these people didn't perceive themselves as mentally tough or competent to put up

with sacrifice, pain, and suffering. Their discussion was peppered with negative self-statements and statements of (low) self-worth" (Guttman, 1994). This observation suggests that they blamed themselves for not adopting the recommended health-promoting behaviors and felt guilty about it.

32. There are different theories and interpretations of justice and several perspectives on how costs and benefits should be distributed. One perspective emphasizes the notion of giving equal availability of the health promotion resources to everyone while others allocate resources according to those who are perceived as bearing the greatest need, in an attempt to balance the principle of equity with people's inequalities regarding personal abilities and circumstances (Garret et al., 1989).

33. The National Cholesterol Education Program's (1990) report on *Population Strategies for Blood Cholesterol Reduction* cites findings that foods that are particularly sensitive to income level are meats, fresh fruit, and vegetables. The latter are seen as important to a nutritious diet. It also reports that the consumption of low-fat milk and whole-grain bread is positively related to income, possibly reflecting the growing concern regarding health in the higher socioeconomic groups. In addition, according to this report, research findings indicate that the use of fresh vegetables, fresh fruits, and juices decreases as household size increases, and intakes of vitamins C and B6 are inversely related to household size, as expected from lower income elasticity for fresh fruits and vegetables in larger households. Educational levels are also found to influence food consumption, where higher educational level is associated with consumption of fruits and milk and lower consumption of so-called convenience foods, and these families are reported to eat more meals together.

34. Daniels (1985) provides a framework often cited in the bioethics literature for the analysis of justice in the context of health care. See also Chapter 2. He argues that justice is based on providing access or opportunity to resources that allow individuals to provide for their necessary needs but not necessarily their preferences. Once individuals have access or opportunities, they can make their own choices regarding the types of risks they want to take. Some people, though, may have special needs that are not merely preferences, and these need to be addressed in a special way. Daniels also argues that for a prevention activity to meet claims of justice, it needs to provide equal opportunities to prevent individuals from being exposed to risks. Prevention efforts that provide opportunities only for people with greater socioeconomic status, such as the promotion of nutritious foods that are only available at higher prices, can be seen as not meeting this criterion of justice.

35. Incentives such as competition and prizes have been the cornerstone of several demonstration interventions in Finland and the United States and adopted in local efforts (see Guttman, 1994). Feingold (1994) reports of "disincentives" posed by Hershey Foods Corporation on its employees: They have to pay an extra $30 a month if they have high blood pressure and $10 if they do not exercise.

36. Pollay (1989) makes a similar point in his discussion of distractions in the context of advertising: "Promoting the trivial is criticized as wasteful or indulgent, distracting resources from more substantial needs" (p. 187). He suggests, though, that in the case of public information campaigns, "the criticism of triviality is less germane than in the case of product advertising" (p. 187). The authors cited in this chapter (e.g., Forester, Bellah et al., Barsky) are likely to disagree with this comment.

37. See Milio (1981) for a detailed discussion. Farrant and Russell (1987) describe in detail how health promotion materials developed in Great Britain for the prevention of heart disease excluded the discussion of how social factors can contribute to this disease. See also Duncan and Crib (1996).

38. See Waitzkin (1989, 1991) for a discussion of the social-political-economic factors of the etiology of illnesses and arguments for why it should be raised in the context of the medical practitioner-patient encounter. This critique has been aimed also at the campaigns that promote the designated driver, a topic discussed in the dilemma of harm reduction. They can be seen as

framing the issue of drunk driving as logistical—people need to make sure that the person who is supposed to drive is not intoxicated. The issue is not framed as a cultural and normative issue. Thus, the norms, values, and practices related to alcohol consumption and the economic interests in maintaining current high levels of consumption are not addressed in the campaign.

39. This rather than as a means to another end or as an instrumental value, as explained by Green and Kreuter (1991).

40. See Tesh (1988).

41. See Fox (1977), Illich (1975), and Zola (1975) for critiques of medicalization.

42. See also Fitzgerald (1994) and Gillick (1984).

43. For example, for discussions on public perception of restrictive policies, see Bull, Pederson, and Ashley 1994; Casswell, 1994; Forster, McBride, Jeffrey, Schmid, and Pirie, 1991; Gostin and Brandt, 1993; Hilton and Kaskutas, 1991; Jones-Webb, Greenfield, and Graves, 1994; Schmid et al., 1990.

SOURCE: Collage by Oren Kramek.

7

Toward a Normative Approach

In recognizing the role of his own value preferences, the change agent does not abandon his values or attempt to neutralize them. It is neither possible nor desirable to do so. Rather, awareness of his own value perspective allows him to bring other perspectives to bear on the choice of goals and to reduce the likelihood of imposing his own values on the population whose lives he is intervening.

—*Warwick and Kelman (1973, p. 391)*

In a book that explores values in U.S. society, Bellah et al. (1985) describe one of their informants as a person who "lacks the language to explain what seem to be the real commitments that define his life, and to that extent the commitments themselves are precarious" (p. 8). People committed to public health promotion endeavors, observes Kenneth McLeroy, have traditionally rarely been involved because of any prospects of financial gain or personal glory. Their commitment stems from a sincere desire to be of service, to help, and from a moral commitment to do good (Guttman et al., 1996; see also Rogers, 1994). The foundation of these commitments, however, may be precarious, because the conceptual and moral frameworks that are typically applied in public health communication intervention do not capture the subtlety of the value-laden aspects of the intervention phenomenon. Furthermore, the ethical concerns that are usually acknowledged tend to address a relatively narrow range of strategic applications. The primary purpose of the analytic approaches described in this book has been to advance the development of conceptual tools to help make value-laden assumptions more explicit and to identify ethical concerns in all facets of public communication interventions. The conceptual tools—although discussed in terms that may apply particularly to health interventions that incorporate health communication aspects—can be applied to the wide gamut of planned health promotion and disease prevention efforts, including the development and implementation of social policy. This chapter has two main purposes: First, a reminder that the application of conceptual tools is also inherently value-laden,[1] because analytic constructs are selected according to what is viewed as important. Second, to encourage the adoption of a self-conscious normative approach in program design and evaluation.

VALUE-LADEN, VALUE-CENTERED ANALYSES

The mere choice of each construct in an analytic framework is value laden: Constructs are articulated and chosen according to what the analysts have framed as potentially significant or what they believe should be valued. Four major constructs serve as the core of the analytic framework, as was described in the third chapter: (a) the way the problem is defined or the goal of the intervention, (b) the way the solution is defined or the locus of the solution, (c) the strategic approach chosen, and (d) the way the outcomes of the intervention are assessed. One of the functions of these constructs is to draw our attention to value-laden choices embedded in each of these facets. The choice of locus of intervention as a major analytic facet of the intervention phenomenon denotes a normative perspective: It presumes that intervening in one level significantly differs from intervening in another and that this difference is important. Furthermore, it implies that intervening at one level at the presumed expense of another carries moral implications. In other words, the analytic framework cannot be conceived as value neutral.[2] An acknowledgment of the value-laden premises that underlie the analysis should not diminish its contribution. The fact that values are embedded in the health promotion enterprise is not problematic per se, as Tesh (1988) maintains. The phenomenon of social interventions—including their analysis—is inherently value-laden and should be recognized as such. Furthermore, the moral responsibility of the analysts and scholars should be recognized as well. Because values in health promotion are typically hidden or taken for granted, this poses an analytic, political, and moral challenge. "I argue," asserts Tesh, "not that values be excised from science and from policy but that their inevitable presence be revealed, and their worth be publicly discussed" (p. 3). The challenge, therefore, is to identify embedded values, not only in the interventions, but in the analysis itself. Embedded values should not only be made explicit but perhaps even contested. Thus, rather than allowing values to be hidden or taken for granted, they should become part of a discursive process.

The frameworks presented in this book have been drawn mainly from a Western approach to values and ethics, which places a strong emphasis on personal freedom combined with a somewhat ambivalent view of the role and responsibility of government in shaping and curtailing individual behavior. The analytic constructs applied in the framework also draw from a Western public health approach. This approach treats distinctions between particular levels of interventions, such as individual, organizational, and larger social entities, as analytically and politically significant. The definitions of particular levels or loci of intervention draw from a normative perception of the nature of society and how to accomplish desired social changes. The challenge of the analysis is twofold. First, it requires the application of constructs that can help make meaningful observations and distinctions among values viewed as pertinent in the context of the intervention phenomenon. This requires that making decisions about social values should be included in the analysis as well as ways to identify them to determine what values have been emphasized or deemphasized in the intervention. The more difficult challenge, though, is the *normative:* to identify and choose what values *should* be emphasized in the intervention and find a way to indicate when value conflicts raise substantial ethical dilemmas. This calls for an analysis based on a normative or ideological commitment.

The major values used in the frameworks presented in this book have been identified through an adaptation of prominent ethical principles as they are discussed in the bioethics literature, drawn primarily from the literature on health promotion. The ethical principles associated with these values include the moral duty to do good and refrain from doing harm. The underlying purpose of such interventions is thus to improve the health of the target population. This may be attempted through the dissemination of messages that aim to persuade people to adopt health-promoting practices and avoid hazardous ones. Associated with the commitment to do good is the value of caring, which implies that a person's commitments may depend on particular circumstances or personal relationships and not necessarily on abstract or absolute principles. Furthermore, the intervention may be based on what are considered societal core values, such as respecting and promoting personal and collective freedom or autonomy. Related values include respecting people's privacy and promoting personal and collective growth or self-actualization, as well as maintaining responsibility to one's self and others. Values associated with justice and fairness, and the prerogative of promoting the good of the public, have been noted as prominent as well. The latter is also associated with utility or efficiency and the recognition that social organizations often have to operate within limited resources. Rewarding personal initiatives and leaving it up to the free marketplace to distribute rewards and resources is an important value among certain constituencies; it certainly represents a strong ideological orientation.

Inasmuch as these values and justifications do not encompass all possible types of moral reasoning, their use as core analytic constructs can serve to illustrate the application of an analytic approach that examines embedded values in intervention facets. The core ethical principles—justice, autonomy and privacy, doing good, promoting the good of the public—and caring, represent important values widely shared by people across cultures and can serve as core moral justifications for choices and preferences of intervention goals and strategies. Values associated with responsibility, science and rationality, participation, and market autonomy, also used as value-laden justifications in the frameworks presented in this book, can serve as a reflection of dominant social values and ideological commitments in Western cultures. Values such as national development or adherence to tradition may have special meanings in particular social contexts and thus may also serve as important justifications in particular contexts. These or other social values can serve as bases for expanded or alternative analytic dimensions. The following five questions, adapted from Vandeford, Smith, and Harris (1992), can help identify and prioritize values and justifications embedded in the intervention process in various social contexts: (a) What are the core social values and ideological commitments used to justify the intervention? (b) What ethical principles or justifications represent or underlie these core values? (c) What values are viewed as less important when deciding on the goals and strategies of the intervention and why? (d) Are alternative, even contested, value preferences represented in the analytic framework? (e) What "price" or what compromises are accepted as reasonable for achieving the intervention's goals? Responses to these questions can help identify what values should be included in the analytic framework or serve as criteria for moral decision making.

Contributions and Limitations

The application of value-centered analyses can contribute to theories *of* public health communication intervention phenomena. The analysis can examine the way the intervention's social context and values of dominant stakeholders influence the formation of specific objectives, preferences for particular strategies over others, and the desirability of certain outcomes. The specification of the justifications associated with each of the facets can enable us to identify what values are emphasized in the goals and strategies of the intervention or in its evaluation. This can allow us to make distinctions within and across interventions according to embedded values. The analytic framework, however, is limited by the way it focuses on the locus of the intervention and in the particular justifications it uses. The justifications as conceived in the analysis may not incorporate particular values cherished by populations that did not have much voice in the design or analysis of the intervention. The strength of the analytic framework lies in that it guides us to recognize that each facet of the intervention is justified by particular values. Specification of the justifications and their application to each intervention facet enables us to examine the extent to which different values may be emphasized within and across interventions. This can help make important distinctions between interventions and can indicate what values of what stakeholders tend to influence the design and implementation of each intervention. Another important feature of the analytic framework is that it can enable the identification of deemphasized values. The frameworks presented underscore several broad ethical concerns associated with intervening in the name of health. Having these ethical concerns included as a major facet or dimension in the frameworks greatly contributes to the analytic task. It forces us to examine—as with the justifications—what ethical concerns may be linked to each intervention component. The analysts and interventionists are thus compelled to identify justifications embedded in each aspect of the intervention. Also, we can expect them to recognize ethical concerns that may arise when they examine the goals of the intervention, its strategic approach and activities, and the assessment of its outcomes.[3]

Ethical dilemmas can serve to point out why it is important to identify what value-laden issues are embedded in the public health communication intervention phenomenon. First, we cannot take for granted that there are clear-cut answers to what is right and good in health promotion—as the tensions between competing values that produce the ethical dilemmas remind us. Second, we cannot make the assumption that potential effects of health interventions are ultimately beneficial. The public health communication intervention context is complex, involves multiple and diverse stakeholders with competing interests, and can lead to adverse, unintended, often invisible outcomes. We therefore need conceptual apparatus to consider what public health communication interventions might actually do, what they cannot do, what we should expect from interventions, and what should raise our concerns and alert us to consider alternative courses of action. Key to addressing these concerns are decisions based on a careful consideration of the embedded and often conflicting values. The identification and articulation of specific values conflicts that serve to create ethical dilemmas can contribute to public discourse and policy making, according to Harron et al. (1983):

> By outlining and describing the elements that go into making moral choices, especially a choice in the context of a moral dilemma, we are making explicit the ways people generally deliberate and make a decision. These elements are means of making one's position clear; they also increase the possibility for an open, democratic society, which is morally pluralistic, to debate and make informed public policy. (p. 4)

As outlined in the previous chapters, ethical dilemmas may be associated with having interventions enhance the power and control as well as the legitimacy of dominant stakeholders. Interventions may also result in the exploitation of certain stakeholders to achieve the goals of the sponsors of the intervention, which although they aim to promote the good of individuals or the public, may cause some unintended harm. Other potentially harmful outcomes may be inadvertently caused by the intervention that may stigmatize certain populations or blame them as the cause of problems that are not under their control. This would be particularly true regarding vulnerable or disadvantaged populations who have adopted what are considered risky practices. Last, interventions may cultivate cultural changes and reinforce or contribute to transformation of specific values or ideologies. Whereas these values may appear to be prohealth by promoting health as an important social value, they may in fact reinforce a new kind of moralism that is not compatible with values cherished by those who would like to minimize an emphasis on individualism and would prefer to support ideologies based on values of egalitarianism and compassion. Each of these dilemmas is based on shared agreement that the values they are associated with are important and represent core moral issues. The exposition of ethical dilemmas can thus help underscore social processes and conflicting social values directly or indirectly associated with the intervention phenomenon. The conceptualization of potential ethical dilemmas can serve to develop analytic approaches to examine moral implications in each intervention facet and the intervention as a whole.

Theories for public health communication interventions[4] can benefit from a value-centered approach by incorporating a broader ethical framework that focuses not only on ethical concerns associated with strategies but also on cultural or institutional aspects of society. From a normative perspective, a value-centered analytic approach that applies a moral framework can help articulate (a) the most pertinent ethical dilemmas, (b) the most highly cherished values, (c) the moral frameworks preferred by diverse stakeholders, and (d) the types of interventions that may serve various interests, beyond their formal goals and objectives. Using value-laden criteria, it can help evaluate the extent to which interventions meet implicit moral criteria and advance society according to a vision of a good society in their design and implementation. Furthermore, a value-centered analysis can proffer tools to examine the extent to which the values embedded in the intervention reflect core values associated with a good society and meet the requirements of moral decision making.

Minkler (1989) describes a normative stance increasingly adopted by many health promoters that offers an approach to answer these questions. It proposes that health promoters have a moral imperative to contribute to the advancement of health through social action. This calls for proactively moving forward what Minkler called the open society, a society that is democratic and offers equal opportunities to all of its members. The normative assumptions drawn from Minkler's list of imperatives suggest that (a) health promotion efforts or analyses should include the moral obligation to develop people's understanding of the causes of hazards, across various levels of intervention; (b) people should be able to participate in defining and solving their problems; (c) the public health communication intervention should address or at least acknowledge structural-level as well as individual-level factors; (d) discourse within and across stakeholders should be promoted, and the opportunity should be given for diverse opinions to be heard and explained; (e) people should be made aware of social and environmental conditions that foster health and reduce risk; and (f) because people live in social entities, the promotion of a healthy society entails collaboration, cooperation, and mutuality.

If these assertions are accepted as a basis for a normative perspective regarding the development or analysis of public health communication interventions, the six following questions adapted from Minkler (1989) can help operationalize the process. They can also serve to examine whether the analytic framework meets normative requirements by being able to assess each of the following: Does the intervention and its analysis (a) help to develop a critical understanding of the causes of hazards to health across different levels of problem definitions and solutions; (b) include mechanisms for meaningful involvement and participation of its target population and intervention personnel; (c) help inform and educate policymakers, the mass media, and other influential entities through effective advocacy on the importance of public policy and healthier environments for the promotion of health; (d) foster appreciation of both nonprofessional expertise and the importance of cross-sectorial and multicultural views; (e) create or enhance opportunities for discourse and participation of target populations; (f) promote a social environment that reinforces social support, mutual aid, community development or other democratic responses?

By implication, a normative stance regarding the proactive role of interventions in enhancing target populations' critical understanding of the causes of social problems needs to be articulated. Furthermore, a conscious adoption of this normative stance in the design and implementation of public health communication interventions implies that we need to consider the extent to which these interventions enhance or reduce people's opportunities to engage in open discourse about these problems and ways to address them. John Forester's (1989, 1993)[5] work in the area of planning also underscores a normative obligation of planners of social interventions and the importance of a critical analysis by bringing to our attention the notion of distortions that can take place in the planning process. Distortions, or misrepresentation of the social phenomenon, may occur during the process of planning and implementing interventions and reflect what Tesh (1988) had described as hidden arguments: the implicit claims embedded in health promotion endeavors. Forester's (1989, 1993) analytic approach for examining ethical implications of such distortions, as they relate to particular core social values, has been adapted in this book to the public health communication intervention context. It is particularly suited to the analysis of public health communication interventions because the main focus of this framework is the communicative aspect of the intervention. Forester's analytic approach has been used in part in the development of the ethical concerns outlined in previous chapters. It is further elaborated in this concluding chapter to illustrate a cogent approach that can be adapted for the purpose of developing frameworks for making value-laden distinctions and decisions.

DISTINCTIONS AND DISTORTIONS

Public health communication interventions are a communication phenomenon: Messages are purposefully developed, tested, and disseminated; communication channels are strategically employed; claims, arguments, and appeals are articulated; and networks and relationships are fostered and exploited. Forester (1989, 1993), in his adaptation of Habermas's work, presents an analytic approach that carries a normative commitment for those involved in the planning process that specifically addresses the communicative aspects of planned social interventions. Forester explains that planners, or in the public health communication intervention context, designers or practitioners, make normative claims that relate to Habermas's three processes of social reproduction. These are *cultural,* in which views are elaborated and shaped; *social integration,* in which norms, rules, and obligations are shaped or reinforced; and *socialization,* in which social identities and expressions of self are influenced. Forester adds the processes of *comprehension* or framing, in which certain definitions or understandings are prioritized and accepted.

Communicative action, Forester (1989, 1993) explains, can be conceptualized as making inseparable but distinct claims in four corresponding dimensions: (a) shaping listeners' sense of *truth*—this can affect target populations' beliefs and can result in cultural reproduction; (b) establishing legitimacy through acceptance of things as "common-sense" or "natural," through routines, standard practices, and the suppression of conflict (Deetz, 1994)—this can affect people's *consent,* and results in a particular form of social integration; (c) *framing* and prioritizing issues—this can affect people's comprehension or their perception of priorities; and (d) making particular claims that influence the way people construct their *identities*. The effects of these communicative processes, which can result in misconceptions of what is true and legitimate, who should have the authority to make decisions, what the causes and solutions are for certain social problems, or how people view themselves and others, may jeopardize the accomplishment of democratic ideals.[6] Claims and information presented in public health communication interventions may contain a multitude of distortions, akin to what Tesh (1988) described as hidden arguments, which may contribute to the processes that comprise what has been labeled social reproduction.

Forester (1989, 1993) explains that distortions can occur in the way claims are presented—whether intended or not. Certain data are given priority (e.g., morbidity associated with specific sociodemographics), certain claims are not questioned (e.g., that early detection of disease is important and certain medical procedures, such as screenings for the detection of disease, are cost-effective), whereas certain issues are ignored (e.g., political considerations). The ethical imperative of analysts, whether they are designers, evaluators, members of the intended population, or scholars is thus to identify distortions. Some distortions may be related to differences in technical capacities of people with different professional backgrounds (e.g., to interpret epidemiological findings) or cultural perspectives. Other distortions may be due to politics, ideologies, and factors related to power and control.

The production of distortions can be viewed as unethical because they can undermine the "possibility of critical self-reflection" and can promote "processes through which certain realities are privileged over others" (Mumby, 1997, p. 9).[7] As such, these distortions—even when they are not purposefully intended—may result in serving the interests of dominant social groups or reinforcing current structural arrangements. These may not necessarily benefit, and in fact may be detrimental to, some of the population the public health communication intervention aims to help.

As stated in the propositions in the first chapter, ways to define or frame a health-related issue as a problem are numerous. The way the problem is framed emphasizes a certain perspective. This may be at the expense of alternative perspectives, may deemphasize alternative priorities, and may affect the way people see themselves and others. The way interventionists frame the health problem and present it to the public or policymakers may therefore elicit certain types of distortions. Distortions may shape certain beliefs about what is good or right, what one should strive for, what one should expect, what one should need, or what is not needed, according to particular ideologies. For example, health campaigns that reproduce beliefs that people's nutritional needs can be met by unregulated marketplace processes may serve corporate interests. Similarly, an emphasis in intervention messages that collective action is not a public responsibility is likely to serve current dominant political groups and ideologies and reproduce a status-quo situation in which unorganized members of society have minimal power. Distortions can also, either purposefully or inadvertently, work to establish the legitimacy of certain groups to make decisions that affect the population as a whole. They may serve to frame and prioritize issues in ways that obscure the importance of other critical social issues. In the context of public health communication interventions, by stressing particular types of solutions, interventions may distort the significance of social factors, such as inequitable distribution of economic resources, corporate interests, and political power in people's health and well-being (Wallack, 1989). Distorted public health communication campaign messages may serve to affect people's identities so that they may see themselves as having certain roles or obligations. For example, they may see themselves as at risk or as irresponsible. As a result, distortions may serve to privilege certain ideological perspectives and institutional arrangements, to benefit certain constituencies (Lupton, 1993; Martin, 1994).[8]

Table 7.1 presents examples of how particular claims can contribute to processes that may be viewed as distortions in the context of public health communication interventions, which may lead to the social reproduction of particular beliefs. The examples are drawn from interventions for the prevention of heart disease and stroke.

Distortions in public health communication interventions may result from different causes and be linked to different normative implications. Forester (1993), in his adaptation of Herbert Simon's conceptualization of bounded rationality, explains that it is important to distinguish between different types of distortions. Some may be random, ad hoc, spontaneous, unpredicted, or unavoidable. Such distortions may result from inherent differences in training and expertise among stakeholders (Slovic, 1987)[9] and not from purposeful attempts at powerful persuasion. Although they may cause inadvertent harm through the distorted communicative process and may raise serious ethical concerns, these kinds of distortions would not be a result of a systematic cause

Table 7.1   Examples of Social Reproduction in the Context of Health Communication Interventions: Examples From Interventions for the Prevention of Heart Disease and Stroke

Reproduction Process	Pragmatic Claims	Potential Output
Cultural Reproduction	Reducing fat in one's diet or taking certain medications will lower one's blood cholesterol level.	*Social belief:* Biomedical models and health care professionals provide optimal solutions to health-related problems and disease prevention.
Social integration	One should not become a burden on one's family by having a disabling stroke or heart attack; one has the obligation to support one's family.	*Consent:* One should follow the recommended medical regimen; one should be employed and work and keep one's job to support one's family.
Comprehension	The issue of high blood pressure is an important national problem; inattendance to it can lead to disability in large segments of the population and loss of workdays, as well as human suffering. It can be a burden on the economy and adversely affect the well-being of individuals and families.	*Framing, prioritizing:* Prevention and treatment of high blood pressure should be put on the national agenda and addressed through social interventions sponsored by public funds. *Alternative framing* (typically less emphasized): Disparities in socioeconomic opportunities, reflected in a relative higher prevalence of high blood pressure in certain populations, are a serious social problem that should be addressed.
Socialization	The health communication intervention's purpose is to promote people's health and to help people be responsible and take care of themselves and significant others.	*Identity:* People who adopt the recommendations are responsible and good. People who do not adopt health recommendations may lack a sense of willpower or responsibility to their family and society.

SOURCE: Adapted from Forester (1993).

but rather, would depend on the circumstances of the situation. In contrast, other types of distortion reflect an ingrained systematic cause, such as the institutionalization of social roles, or they may be structural products of social relationships. These kinds of distortions would be systematic misinformation . . . rooted in the political-economic structures that define who initiates and who reacts; who invokes authority or expertise and who is mystified or defers; who appeals to trust and who chooses to trust or be skeptical; and who defines agendas of need and who is thus defined. (Forester, 1993, p. 35)

Such distortions could be anticipated and would not be considered unexpected, even if they are unintended.[10]

Making a distinction between different types of distortions allows an examination of the ethical implications of each type and specification of normative requirements for morally sound activities of interventionists or researchers. It also can present ways to address and remedy the situation or to learn to avoid potential distortions. A response to the first type of nonsystematic distortion may be to ask for further clarification or to look for ways to overcome communicative obstacles. Responses to distortions that occur from systematic causes would require a more concerted effort of addressing institutional and structural factors. Both types of distortions may in fact result from a sincere effort to help people. Even when well-intentioned, distinctions need to be made regarding the causes of the distortions and their moral impacts. Table 7.2 presents examples of ad hoc and systematic distortions and their potential effects in the context of public health communication interventions.[11]

Theory, and the distinctions it enables us to discern, can steer us to pay attention to different types of accomplishments as well as to distortions associated with the intervention process (Deetz, 1992). Analyses that allow us to recognize potential distortions and to make distinctions among the different types of intervention approaches can serve to identify when a problem that is inherently political has been framed as technical (Forester, 1993), or as medical in the health context, thus belittling its institutional or political ramifications. Similarly, making distinctions between levels of intervention and distortions associated with the ways problems are defined can serve to identify when a problem that is essentially structural is framed as a lack of individual motivation (Wallack, 1989). The analysis of distortions and the distinctions among them can serve to identify the social conditions that allow these processes to take place. Identifying the social processes that allow for distorted problem and solution definitions can enable these definitions to be contested and can thus facilitate alternative conceptualizations. The framework adapted by Forester (1993) and the distinctions he makes between types of distortions present a normative approach to the design and analysis of interventions. Interventionists and analysts need to examine the extent to which an interven-

Table 7.2   Communicative Distortions and Bounded Rationality in the Health Interventions Context

Circumstances of Distortion	Examples of Ad Hoc or Personal, Cognitive Factors	Examples of Systematic Structural or Routine Factors
Inevitable or involuntary	Not having optimal data on prevalence or etiology of certain health-related conditions Personal traits and capabilities of stakeholders in presenting and interpreting issues Perceptual-cognitive processes of target audience members (e.g., optimistic biases or people's beliefs that their chances of being at risk are lower than those of others)[a]	Limitations in understanding technical issues (e.g., difficulties in perceiving health risks that are estimated in small probabilities) that result from differences in occupational training, work, and expertise Differences in perceptions and conceptualizations of different stakeholders associated with different sociocultural groups
Unnecessary or avoidable	Manipulation of individuals' emotions Choosing what are seen as "obvious" problems Applying strategies that intervention planners are more comfortable with personally Not seeking additional training, technical assistance, or expertise in identifying alternative or underlying causes of the health-related problem or strategies to address them	Prominence of certain groups' or experts' definitions of problems and solutions Focusing on definitions that identify the locus of problems and solutions on the individual level and deemphasize other levels (e.g., ignoring restrictive workplace schedules, limited access to health-promoting resources) Rationalization of institutional power of medicine and its expertise as the dominant legitimate criteria for problem definition and evaluation Providing selective access to information, resources, expertise, and decision making to certain stakeholders Creation of needs and expectations and affecting self-identity by prioritizing health as a super value

SOURCE: Adapted from Forester (1989, p. 34).
a. See Weinstein (1989).

tion may serve to foster certain beliefs about what is true and legitimate, who has the authority to decide, what people should do, and how to understand particular social phenomena and to prioritize what should be attended to. The distinctions between distortions that are inevitable and those that are systematic and avoidable offer an approach to develop a value-laden, value-centered analysis that underscores the communicative aspects of the intervention and the moral obligation of the interventionists and analysts. A normative approach that focuses on the identification of potential distortions in the intervention phenomenon can move the analytic process "from the assessment of more narrow processes of experimentation and testing (social engineering) to the study of processes of argumentation and dialogue, political discourse and design criticism, mediated negotiations and democratization and organizing" (Forester, 1989, p. 157)—in other words, to a commitment to values associated with democratic ideals, with all their complexity and contradictions.

In an interview in 1993, Dan Beauchamp commented how values, ideology, and public health interventions are inextricably linked. His words reiterate the conceptualization of health promotion and disease prevention as an inherently communicative action and the challenge of making health promotion claims and strategies more explicit for moral and practical reasons:

> I don't think that people [health promotion practitioners] ignore [values], but they try to conceal what they are doing. You can't do public health . . . without, in some way or another telling people what to do, or at least being very direct about what you think society's expectations are, or what people should do. Not so much in a strict moral sense, but in a prudent sense to protect their own health. . . . It would be a lot better if we were very clear about the fact that health behavior is central to our way of talking to each other and structuring what I sometimes call the "common life."

The centrality of health in personal and public discourse and the clarity Dan Beauchamp calls for require that we acknowledge value commitments, value conflicts, and ethical dilemmas. The problem is that the moral imperatives of the professionals engaged in planning, implementing, and evaluating public health communication interventions, including analysts, social scientists, and policymakers, often tend to be diffuse. Scholars and practitioners may take on diverse roles and genuinely aim to "do good," yet many eschew any seemingly conflictual or moral or political dimensions of their work. Nonetheless, as stated in the propositions at the outset of this book, work in health promotion is value-laden. Ethical issues, which are not easily resolved, thus, become inescapable components of the intervention phenomenon and its assessment and need to be unveiled and challenged. This also allows the enterprise of health promotion to be intellectually stimulating.

NOTES

1. For a brief discussion of axiological issues in theory, see Littlejohn (1996, pp. 36-37).

2. Kurtines, Alvarez, and Azmitia (1990) review the role of values in science and argue that values "play a central role in *all* scientific discourse" and constitute "one type or category of metatheoretical assumptions" that are substantive presuppositions that underlie the scientific activity (p. 283).

3. The analytic process of exposition of values—both those emphasized and those deemphasized in the intervention—can make value conflicts more explicit. This explication can lead to making more apparent any ethical dilemmas inherent in the intervention phenomenon. The exposition of ethical dilemmas, in turn, can serve as another conceptual framework for sensitizing us to particular ethical concerns associated with the design and implementation of the intervention as illustrated in the sixth chapter. Dewy and Tufts (as quoted in Douard & Winslade, 1994) explain that value conflicts that help identify ethical dilemmas would ideally lead to the recognition that one needs to engage in making moral decisions:

> The struggle is not between a good which is clear and something else which attracts him but which he knows to be wrong. It is between values each of which is an undoubted good in its place but which now get in each others' way. He is forced to reflect in order to come to a decision. (p. 319)

4. The distinction and implications of theories for and of interventions is made by Salmon (1992) and described in the first chapter.

5. Forester's framework was similarly used in the previous chapter to identify certain ethical concerns.

6. As elaborated in Chapter 6.

7. Or as described by Mumby (1997) as the Critical Modernist Project.

8. See Bellah et al.'s (1991) discussion of the notion of a good society.

9. There is a large literature on risk perception that discusses cognitive processes that affect the way risk is perceived by nonexperts and experts. These differences may be perceived as unavoidable. However, researchers and advocates in this area also maintain that some of the distortions may be systematic or based on value differences (Slovic, 1987, 1993).

10. Windahl, Signitzer, and Olson (1992) discuss intended and unintended effects of interventions and distinguish between positive and negative and intended and unintended effects and present a matrix of four types. The authors characterize the "Negative Intended/Foreseen" outcomes as "The price we had to pay," indicating the role of value-laden priorities.

11. Identifying communicative distortions and devising analytic tools to make distinctions among them allows us to challenge the social phenomena that cause them or to develop means to address them. This can be a moral charge of the analyst and the normative mission of theory development: "The critical, ethical content of the theory focuses attention on the systematic and unnecessarily distorted nature of communicative interactions, on the promises, appeals, reports, and justifications that so shape the lives of citizens in our societies" (Forester, 1993, p. 139).

Resource A

Sample Work Sheets for
Analysis of Intervention Facets

Work Sheet A.1

Identifying Values or Justifications Embedded in the Way Problems and Solutions Are Defined

Analytic Facets	Specification, Definition	Main Level	Embedded Values: Official (stated)	Embedded Values: Implicit
Problem				
Justifications				
Solution				
Strategies				
Outcomes, Evaluation Criteria				
Ethical concerns				

Work Sheet A.2
Identifying Values and Ethical Concerns in Strategies

Strategies	Types of Activities	Emphasis in Intervention None Low Medium High	Embedded Values (Specify which dominate, which do not)	Ethical Concerns (Note value conflicts)
Engineering				
Enforcement				
Incentives				
Education				
Collaboration				
Facilitation				
Other				

Work Sheet A.3

Sample Worksheet for Comparing Intervention Emphasis Across Facets

Emphasis in the Intervention	Locus of Problem				Locus of Solution				Locus of Outcome			
	None	Low	Medium	High	None	Low	Medium	High	None	Low	Medium	High
Level												
Individual												
Family												
Organizational												
Community												
Marketplace												
Structural, institutional												
Cultural, Normative												
Justifications												
Doing good, care												
Doing no harm												
Autonomy (individual, community)												
Market autonomy												
Public good												
Justice, fairness												
Utility, efficiency												
Personal responsibility												
Science												
Self-actualization												
Other												
Ethical concerns												
Content												
Target												
Channel												
Control												

Resource B

Sample Work Sheets for Comparing
Health Communication Interventions

Work Sheet B.1

Sample Work Sheet for Comparing Health Communication Interventions According to
Their Emphasis or Deemphasis of Values: Locus of the Problem

Main Emphasis Found in Locus of the Problem	Intervention 1	Intervention 2	Intervention 3	Intervention 4	Intervention 5
Level of intervention					
Individual					
Family					
Organizational					
Community					
Marketplace					
Structural, institutional					
Cultural, normative					
Justifications, embedded values					
Doing good/care					
Doing no harm					
Autonomy (individual, community)					
Market autonomy					
Public good					
Justice, fairness					
Utility, efficiency					
Self-actualization					
Personal responsibility					
Science					
Other					
Ethical concerns					
Content					
Target					
Channel					
Control					
Unintended effects					

Work Sheet B.2

Sample Work Sheet for Comparing Health Communication Interventions According to the Emphasis or Deemphasis of Values: Locus of the Solution

Main Emphasis Found in Locus of the Solution	Intervention 1	Intervention 2	Intervention 3	Intervention 4	Intervention 5
Level of intervention					
Individual					
Family					
Organizational					
Community					
Marketplace					
Structural, institutional					
Cultural, normative					
Justifications, embedded values					
Doing good, care					
Doing no harm					
Autonomy (individual, community)					
Market autonomy					
Public good					
Justice, fairness					
Utility, efficiency					
Self-actualization					
Personal responsibility					
Science					
Other					
Ethical concerns					
Content					
Target					
Channel					
Control					
Unintended effects					

Work Sheet B.3

Sample Work Sheet for Comparing Health Communication Interventions According to the Emphasis or Deemphasis of Values: Strategies

Main Emphasis Found in Locus of the Problem	Intervention 1	Intervention 2	Intervention 3	Intervention 4	Intervention 5
Level of intervention					
Individual					
Family					
Organizational					
Community					
Marketplace					
Structural, institutional					
Cultural, normative					
Justifications, embedded values					
Doing good, care					
Doing no harm					
Autonomy (individual, community)					
Market autonomy					
Public good					
Justice, fairness					
Utility, efficiency					
Self-actualization					
Personal responsibility					
Science					
Other					
Ethical concerns					
Content					
Target					
Channel					
Control					
Unintended effects					

Work Sheet B.4

Sample Work Sheet for Comparing Health Communication Interventions According
to the Emphasis or Deemphasis of Values: Locus of the Outcomes

Main Emphasis Found in Locus of the Outcomes	Intervention 1	Intervention 2	Intervention 3	Intervention 4	Intervention 5
Level of intervention					
Individual					
Family					
Organizational					
Community					
Marketplace					
Structural, institutional					
Cultural, normative					
Justifications, embedded values					
Doing good, care					
Doing no harm					
Autonomy (individual, community)					
Market autonomy					
Public good					
Justice, fairness					
Utility, efficiency					
Self-actualization					
Personal responsibility					
Science					
Other					
Ethical concerns					
Content					
Target					
Channel					
Control					
Unintended effects					

Resource C

Analyses of Intervention Types

1. Comparison Between Different Interventions That Appear to Rely on the Same Value

2. Comparison Between Ideal and Actual Intervention Models

Analysis 1: Comparison Between Different Interventions That Appear to Rely on the Same Value

Table C.1   Description of the Analytic Process for the Comparison Between Different Interventions That Appear to Rely on the Same Value

Process	Examples of Specific Questions
1. Determine to which model each intervention corresponds.	What kind of model best represents what actually occurs in each intervention?
	What is the relationship between practitioners and target population members in each intervention?
	What kind of messages does each intervention emphasize?
	What values are dominant in each intervention
2. Identify additional embedded values.	What other dominant values are associated with each intervention?
	What values were not emphasized in the interventions?
3. Compare the interventions and identify similarities and differences.	In what ways are the interventions similar?
	What values were emphasized in one intervention but not in the others?
	What factors explain the similarities between the interventions?
	What factors explain the differences between the interventions?
4. Draw implications for design, evaluation, and ethical concerns.	What different design or strategic approaches may be used to achieve shared goals?
	What sociopolitical factors or institutional conditions may be necessary for the intervention to become more similar to the interventions that represent a more desired model?
	What sociopolitical factors or institutional conditions may impede the implementation of an intervention according to a desired model?

Work Sheet C.1

Sample Worksheet for Comparison Between Different Interventions That Appear to Rely on the Same Value

	Intervention 1	Intervention 2	Intervention 3	Intervention 4
Model type				
Dominant values: Explicit, formally stated Implicit				
Deemphasized values				
Relationships between practitioners and stakeholders				
Prominent messages and privileged stakeholders				
Emphasized, reproduced institutional practices and arrangements				

Analysis 2: Comparison Between Ideal and Actual Intervention Models

Table C.2   Description of the Analytic Process for the Comparison Between Ideal and Actual Intervention Models

Process	Examples of Specific Questions
1. Determine the ideal model.	What was the intended or ideal model?
	What type of model should the intervention actually belong to according to normative expectations (highly valued)?
	What is the desired and ideal relationship between practitioners and target stakeholders?
	What kinds of capacities or skills would the intervention's professionals need in order to accomplish the intervention goals in this model?
	What kind of capacities or skills would the intervention's populations need in order to accomplish the intervention goals in this model?
	What kinds of messages should the intervention emphasize that reflect and correspond to cherished social values and moral frameworks?
2. Determine the actual model.	What kind of model best represents what actually occurred in the intervention?
	What were the actual relationships between intervention practitioners and target population members?
	What were the actual capacities or skills the intervention professionals had?
	What actual capacities or skills did the intervention's targeted population acquire?
	What kinds of messages did the intervention actually emphasize?
3. Compare between the ideal and actual models.	In what ways does the actual model of the intervention correspond to the intended model?
	What factors caused the discordance between the ideal and actual?
	What values were prioritized and what were deemphasized?
	What factors contributed to correspondence between the ideal and actual?
4. Draw implications for evaluation and for planning future initiatives.	To which type of model did the intervention strive for in the long run?
	What goals or strategies needed to be modified or changed to move the intervention from one type of model to another?
	What training do the intervention practitioners need for the intervention to correspond to the ideal model?
	What resources may be necessary for the intervention to correspond to the ideal model?
	Is the ideal model compatible with dominant social values?
	Can the ideal model be implemented within current institutional arrangements of the intervention?

Work Sheet C.2

Sample Work Sheet for Comparison Between Ideal and Actual Intervention Models

	Actual Model	Ideal Model	Evaluation and Planning for the Future
Dominant values: Explicit, formally stated			
Implicit			
Deemphasized values			
Relationships between practitioners and stakeholders			
Prominent messages and privileged stakeholders			
Emphasized, reproduced institutional practices and arrangements			

References

Agich, G. J. (1982). The concept of responsibility in medicine. In G. J. Agich (Ed.), *Responsibility in health care* (pp. 53-73). Dordrecht, Holland: Reidel.

Ajzen, I., & Fishbein, M. (1980). *Understanding attitudes and predicting social behavior.* Englewood Cliffs, NJ: Prentice Hall.

Alexander, J. (1988). The ideological construction of risk: An analysis of corporate health promotion programs in the 1980s. *Social Sciences & Medicine, 26*(5), 559-567.

Allegrante, J. P., & Green, L. W. (1981). When health policy becomes victim blaming. *New England Journal of Medicine, 305,* 1528-1529.

Allegrante, J. P., & Sloan, R. P. (1986). Ethical dilemmas in workplace health promotion. *Preventive Medicine, 15,* 313-320.

Altman, K. E. (1990). Consuming ideology: The Better Homes in America Campaign. *Critical Studies in Mass Communication, 7,* 286-307.

Anderson, J. A. (1996). *Communication theory: Epistemological foundations.* New York: Guilford.

Andreasen, A. R. (1995). *Marketing social change: Changing behavior to promote health, social development, and the environment.* San Francisco: Jossey-Bass.

Arkin, E. B. (1990). Opportunities for improving the nation's health through collaboration with the mass media. *Public Health Reports, 105*(3), 219-223.

Atkin, C. K. (1989). Be smart. Don't start. In R. E. Rice & C. K. Atkin (Eds.), *Public communication campaigns* (2nd ed., pp. 224-226). Newbury Park, CA: Sage.

Atkin, C. K., & Wallack, L. (Eds.). (1990). *Mass communications and public health: Complexities and conflicts.* Newbury Park, CA: Sage.

Backer, T. E., Rogers, E. M., & Sopory, P. (1992). *Designing health communication campaigns: What works?* Newbury Park, CA: Sage.

Baier, A. C. (1993). What do women want in moral theory? In M. J. Larrabee (Ed.), *An ethic of care: Feminist and interdisciplinary perspectives* (pp. 19-32). New York: Routledge.

Ball, M. S., & Smith, G. W. (1992). *Analyzing visual data.* Newbury Park, CA: Sage.

Ball-Rokeach, S. J., Rokeach, M., & Grube, J. W. (1984). *The great American values test: Influencing behavior and belief through television.* New York: Free Press.

Balshem, M. (1991). Cancer, control, and causality: Talking about cancer in a working-class community. *American Ethnologist, 18*(1), 152-173.

Barr, J. K., Waring, J. M., & Warshaw, L. J. (1992). Knowledge and attitudes about AIDS among corporate and public service employees. *American Journal of Public Health, 82*(2), 225-228.

Barry, V. (1982). *Moral aspects of health care.* Belmont, CA: Wadsworth.

Barsky, A. J. (1988). *Worried sick: Our troubled quest for wellness.* Boston: Little Brown.

Baxter, J. D., & Gluckman, S. J. (1994). AIDS hot lines and information agencies: The consistency of their information. *Archives of Family Medicine, 3,* 429-436.

Beauchamp, D. E. (1987). Life-style, public health and paternalism. In S. Doxiadis (Ed.), *Ethical dilemmas in health promotion* (pp. 69-81). New York: John Wiley.

Beauchamp, D. E. (1988). *The health of the republic: Epidemics, medicine, and moralism as challenges to democracy.* Philadelphia, PA: Temple University Press.

Beauchamp, T. L. (1994). Ethical theory and bioethics. In T. L. Beauchamp & J. F. Childress (Eds.), *Principles of biomedical ethics* (4th ed., pp. 1-43). New York: Oxford University Press.

Beauchamp, T. L., & Childress, J. F. (1994). *Principles of biomedical ethics* (4th ed.). New York: Oxford University Press.

Becker, M. H. (1986). The tyranny of health. *Public Health Reviews, 14,* 15-25.

Becker, M. H. (1993). A medical sociologist looks at health promotion. *Journal of Health and Social Behavior, 34,* 1-6.

Bellah, R. N., Madsen, R., Sullivan, W. M., Swidler, A., & Tipton, S. M. (1985). *Habits of the heart: Individualism and commitment in American life.* Berkeley: University of California Press.

Bellah, R. N., Madsen, R., Sullivan, W. M., Swidler, A., & Tipton, S. M. (1991). *The good society.* New York: Knopf.

Berger, P. L., & Luckmann, T. (1967). *The social construction of reality: A treatise in the sociology of knowledge.* New York: Anchor, Doubleday.

Bernstein, E., Wallerstein, N., Braithwaite, R., Gutierrez, L., LaBonte, R., & Zimmerman, M. (1994). Empowerment forum: A dialogue between guest editorial board members. *Health Education Quarterly, 21*(3), 281-294.

Best, J. (1989a). Introduction: Typification and social problem construction. In J. Best (Ed.), *Images of issues: Typifying contemporary social problems* (pp. xv-xxii). New York: Aldine de Gruyter.

Best, J. (1989b). Extending the constructionist perspective: A conclusion and an introduction. In J. Best (Ed.), *Images of issues: Typifying contemporary social problems* (pp. 243-253). New York: Aldine de Gruyter.

Birth-control implant gains among poor under Medicaid. (1992, December 17). *The New York Times,* pp. B1, B20-B21.

Blakeslee, S. (1992, March 15). Faulty math heightens fears of breast cancer. *The New York Times,* Section 4, p. 1.

Blane, D. (1995). Editorial: Social determinants of health—Socioeconomic status, social class, and ethnicity. *American Journal of Public Health, 85*(7), 903-905.

Bloom, J. R., & Monterossa, S. (1981). Hypertension labeling and sense of well-being. *American Journal of Public Health, 71,* 1228-1232.

Bok, S. (1978). *Lying: Moral choice in public and private life.* New York: Harper & Row.

Borg, I., & Shye, S. (1995). *Facet theory: Form and content.* Thousand Oaks, CA: Sage.

Botvin, G., Goldberg, C. J., Botvin, E. M., & Dusenbury, L. (1993). Smoking behavior of adolescents exposed to cigarette advertising. *Public Health Reports, 108*(2), 217-224.

Bracht, N. (Ed.). (1990a). *Health promotion at the community level.* Newbury Park, CA: Sage.

Bracht, N. (1990b). Introduction. In N. Bracht (Ed.), *Health promotion at the community level* (pp. 19-25). Newbury Park, CA: Sage.

Bracht, N., & Gleason, J. (1990). Strategies and structures for citizen partnerships. In N. Bracht (Ed.), *Health promotion at the community level* (pp. 109-124). Newbury Park, CA: Sage.

Braithwaite, S. S. (1994). Distributive justice: Must we say yes when society says no? In J. F. Monagle & D. C. Thomasa (Eds.), *Health care ethics: Critical issues* (pp. 295-304). Gaithersburg, MD: Aspen.

Brickman, P., Rabinowitz, V. C., Karuza, J., Coates, D., Cohn, E., & Kidder, L. (1982). Models of helping and coping. *American Psychologist, 37*(4), 368-384.

Brown, E. R. (1983). Community organization influence on local public health care policy: A general research model and comparative case study. *Health Education Quarterly, 10,* 205-233.

Brown, E. R. (1991). Community action for health promotion: A strategy to empower individuals and communities. *International Journal of Health Services, 21*(3), 441-456.

Brown, J. (1985). An introduction to the uses of facet theory. In D. Cantor (Ed.), *Facet theory: Approaches to social research* (pp. 17-57). New York: Springer-Verlag.

Brown, J. D., Waszk, C. S., & Childers, K. W. (1989). Family planning, abortion and AIDS: Sexuality and communication campaigns. In C. T. Salmon (Ed.), *Information campaigns: Balancing social values and social change* (pp. 85-112). Newbury Park, CA: Sage.

Brown, W. J. (1991). An AIDS prevention campaign: Effects on attitudes, beliefs, and communication behavior. *American Behavioral Scientist, 34*(6), 666-678.

Brown, W. J., & Singhal, A. (1990). Ethical dilemmas of prosocial television. *Communication Quarterly, 38*(3), 268-280.

Brownson, R. C., Koffman, D. M., Novotny, T. E., Hughes, R. G., & Eriksen, M. P. (1995). Environmental and policy interventions to control tobacco use and prevent cardiovascular disease. *Health Education Quarterly, 22*(4), 478-489.

Bull, S. B., Pederson, L. L., & Ashley, M. J. (1994). Restrictions on smoking: Growth in population support between 1983 and 1991 in Ontario, Canada. *Journal of Public Health Policy, 15*(3), 310-328.

Burdine, J. N., McLeroy, K. B., & Gottlieb, N. H. (1987). Ethical dilemmas in health promotion: An introduction. *Health Education Quarterly, 14*(1), 7-9.

Burgoon, J. K., & Hale, J. L. (1984). The fundamental topoi of relational communication. *Communication Monographs, 51,* 193-214.

Burns, W. D. (1992). *Connections and connectedness: Ideas of the self and their relationship to achieving our "Common Health."* Text of remarks given at the New Jersey Collegiate Summer Institute for Health in Education and the New Jersey Peer Education Institute. Rutgers University, New Brunswick, New Jersey.

Callahan, D. (1984). Autonomy: A moral good, not a moral obsession. *Hastings Center Report* (Oct.), 40-42.

Callahan, D. (1990). *What kind of life: The limits of medical progress.* New York: Simon & Schuster.

Cambridge, V., McLaughlin, E., & Rota, J. (1995, May). *Entertainment-education and the ethics of social intervention.* Paper presented at the International Communication Association's Annual Conference, Albuquerque, New Mexico.

Campbell, A. V. (1990). Education or indoctrination? The issue of autonomy in health education. In S. Doxiadis (Ed.), *Ethics in health education* (pp. 15-27). New York: John Wiley.

Capek, S. (1992). Environmental justice, regulation, and the local community. *International Journal of Health Services, 22*(4), 729-746.

Carlaw, R. W., Mittelmark, M. B., Bracht, N., & Luepker, R. (1984). Organization for a community cardiovascular health program: Experiences from the Minnesota Heart Health Program. *Health Education Quarterly, 11,* 243-252.

Carter, W. B. (1990). Health behavior as a rational process: Theory of reasoned action and multiattribute utility theory. In K. Glanz, F. M. Lewis, & B. K. Rimer (Eds.), *Health behavior and health education: Theory, research and practice* (2nd ed., pp. 63-91). San Francisco: Jossey-Bass.

Casswell, S. (1994, Summer). Moderate drinking and population-based alcohol policy. *Contemporary Drug Problems,* 287-299.

Chanda, C., Baggaiey, R., Phiri, M., & Kelly, M. (1994). Does counseling help to empower women to negotiate for safer sex? *Abstract book: Tenth international conference on AIDS: The global challenges of AIDS* (p. 22). Yokohama, Japan.

Childress, J. F. (1982). *Who shall decide? Paternalism in health care.* New York: Oxford University Press.

Childress, J. F. (1990). The place of autonomy in bioethics. *The Hastings Center Report, 11*(5), 12-17.

Clark, C. F., & Knox, M. D. (1993). The effectiveness of condoms: An individual versus a societal perspective. *AIDS and Public Policy Journal, 6,* 193-194.

Clarke, A. (1994). What is a chronic disease? The effects of a re-definition in HIV and AIDS. *Social Science and Medicine, 39*(8), 591-597.

Clayton, R. B., Cattarello, A. M., & Johnstone, B. M. (1996). The effectiveness of drug abuse resistance education (Project DARE): 5-year follow-up results. *Preventive Medicine, 25*(3), 307-318.

Cole, E. B., & Coultrap-McQuin, S. (Eds.). (1992). *Explorations in feminist ethics: Theory and practice.* Bloomington: Indiana University Press.

Conrad, P., & Walsh, D. C. (1992). The new corporate health ethic: Lifestyle and the social control of work. *International Journal of Health Services, 22*(1), 89-192.

Coreil, J., & Levin, J. S. (1984). A critique of the lifestyle concept in public health education. *International Quarterly of Community Health Education, 5,* 103-114.

Crawford, R. (1977). You are dangerous to your health: The ideology and politics of victim blaming. *International Journal of Health Services, 7,* 663-680.

Crawford, R. (1979). Individual responsibility and health politics in the 1970's. In S. Reverby & D. Rosner (Eds.), *Health care in America: Essays in social history.* Philadelphia: Temple University Press.

Crawford, R. (1994). The boundaries of the self and the unhealthy other: Reflections on health, culture and AIDS. *Social Science and Medicine, 38*(10), 1347-1356.

Daniels, N. (1985). *Just health care.* New York: Cambridge University Press.

Davis, R. M. (1996). The effects of tobacco advertising: Brand loyalty, brand switching, or market expansion? *American Journal of Preventive Medicine, 12*(1), 2-3.

de Bruyn, M. (1992). Women and AIDS in developing countries. *Social Science and Medicine, 34*(3), 249-262.

Deetz, S. A. (1992). *Democracy in an age of corporate colonization: Developments in communication and the politics of everyday life.* Albany: State University of New York Press.

Deetz, S. A. (1994). Future of the discipline: The challenges, the research, and the social contribution. *Communication Yearbook 17* (pp. 565-600). Thousand Oaks, CA: Sage.

Dervin, B. (1980). Communication gaps and inequalities: Moving toward a reconceptualization. In B. Dervin & M. Voigt (Eds.), *Progress in Communication Science* (Vol. 2). Norwood, NJ: Ablex.

Des Jarlais, D. C. (1995). Harm reduction: A framework for incorporating science into drug policy. *American Journal of Public Health, 85*(1), 10-11.

Des Jarlais, D. C., & Friedman, S. R. (1988). The psychology of preventing AIDS among intravenous drug users: A social learning conceptualization. *American Psychologist, 43,* 865-870.

Des Jarlais, D. C., Padian, N. S., & Winkelstein, W. (1994). Targeted HIV-prevention programs. *New England Journal of Medicine, 331*(21), 1451-1453.

Devine, P. G., & Hirt, E. R. (1989). Message strategies for information campaigns: A social psychological analysis. In C. T. Salmon (Ed.), *Information campaigns: Balancing social values and social change* (pp. 229-258). Newbury Park: CA: Sage.

DiFranza, J. R., Norwood, B. D., Garner, D. W., & Tye, J. B. (1987). Legislative efforts to protect children from tobacco. *Journal of the American Medical Association, 257,* 3387-3389.

DiFranza, J. R., Richards, J. W., Paulman, P. M., Wolf-Gillespie, N., Fletcher, C., Jaffe, R. D., & Murray, D. (1991). RJR Nabisco's cartoon camel promotes Camel cigarette to children. *Journal of the American Medical Association, 266*(22), 3149-3153.

Donohew, R. L., Sypher, H. E., & Bukoski, W. J. (Eds.). (1991). *Persuasive communication and drug abuse prevention.* Hillsdale, NJ: Lawrence Erlbaum.

Douard, J. W., & Winslade, W. J. (1994). Tarasoff and the moral duty to protect the vulnerable. In J. F. Monagle & D. C. Thomasa (Eds.), *Health care ethics: Critical issues* (pp. 316-324). Gaithersburg, MD: Aspen.

Douglas, M., & Wildavsky, A. (1982). *Risk and culture: An essay on the selection of technical and environmental dangers.* Berkeley: University of California Press.

Doxiadis, S. (1987). Conclusions. In S. Doxiadis (Ed.), *Ethical dilemmas in health promotion* (pp. 225-229). New York: John Wiley.

Doxiadis, S. (Ed.). (1990). *Ethics in health education.* New York: John Wiley.

Duke, S. I., & Omi, J. (1991). Development of AIDS education and prevention materials for women by health department staff and community focus groups. *AIDS Education and Prevention, 3*(2), 90-99.

Dullea, G. (1989, December 3). What to eat? Confusion is the main course. *The New York Times,* p. 72.

Duncan, P., & Cribb, A. (1996). Helping people change—An ethical approach? *Health Education Research, 11*(3), 339-348.

Dusenbury, L., Diaz, T., Epstein, J. A., Botwin, G. J., & Caton, M. (1994). Attitudes toward AIDS and AIDS education among multi-ethnic parents of school-aged children in New York City. *AIDS Education and Prevention, 6*(3), 237-248.

Edwards, G., Anderson, P., Babor, T., Cassewell, S., et al. (1996). Alcohol policy and the public good: A good public debate. *Addiction, 91*(4), 477-481.

Eisen, A. (1995). Survey of neighborhood-based, comprehensive community empowerment initiatives. *Health Education Quarterly, 21*(2), 235-252.

Eisenberg, L. (1987). Value conflict in social policies for promoting health. In S. Doxiadis (Ed.), *Ethical dilemmas in health promotion* (pp. 99-116). New York: John Wiley.

Elder, J. P., Hovell, M. F., Lasater, T. M., Wells, B. L., & Carleton, R. A. (1985). Applications of behavior modification to community health education: The case of heart disease prevention. *Health Education Quarterly, 12*(2), 151-168.

Ellison, R. C., Capper, A. L., Goldberg, R. J., Witschi, J. C., & Stare, F. J. (1989). The environmental component: Changing school food service to promote cardiovascular health. *Health Education Quarterly, 16*(2), 285-297.

Ellsworth, E., & Whatley, M. H. (Eds.). (1990). *The ideology of images in educational media: Hidden curriculums in the classroom.* New York: Teachers College Press.

Emanuel, E. J., & Emanuel, L. L. (1992). Four models of the physician-patient relationship. *Journal of the American Medical Association, 267*(16), 2221-2226.

Engelhardt, H. T. (1986). *The foundations of bioethics.* New York: Oxford University Press.

Ennet, S. T., Tobler, N. S., Ringwalt, C. L., & Flewelling, R. L. (1994). How effective is drug abuse resistance education? A meta-analysis of Project DARE outcome evaluations. *American Journal of Public Health, 84,* 1394-1401.

Evans, R. I. (1988). Health promotion: Science or ideology? *Health Psychology, 7*(3), 203-219.

Faden, R. R. (1987). Ethical issues in government sponsored public health campaigns. *Health Education Quarterly, 14*(1), 227-237.

Faden, R. R., & Faden, A. I. (1978). The ethics of health education as public health policy. *Health Education Monographs, 6*(2), 180-197.

Faden, R. R., & Faden, A. I. (1982). The ethics of health education as public health policy. In B. P. Mathews (Ed.), *The practice of health education* (pp. 5-23). Oakland, CA: Society for Public Health Education (Reprinted from *Health Education Monographs, 6*(2), 180-197)

Fahlberg, L. L., Poulin, A. L., Girdano, D. A., & Dusek, D. (1991). Empowerment as an emerging approach in health education. *Journal of Health Education, 22*(3), 185-193.

Farley, C., Haddad, S., & Brown, B. (1996). The effects of a 4-year program promoting bicycle helmet use among children in Quebec. *American Journal of Public Health, 86*(1), 46-51.

Farquhar, J. W., Fortmann, S. P., Maccoby, N., Haskell, W. L., Williams, P. T., Flora, J. A., Taylor, C. B., Brown, B. W., Solomon, D. S., & Hully, S. B. (1985). The Stanford five-city project: Design and methods. *American Journal of Epidemiology, 122*(2), 323-334.

Farrant, W., & Russell, J. (1987). The politics of health information: "Beating Heart Disease": A case study of Health Education Council publications. *Bedford Way Paper No. 28.* London: Kegan Paul.

Fawcett, S. B., Paine-Andrews, A., Francisco, V. T., Schultz, J. A., Richter, K. P., Lewis, R. K., Harris, K. J., Williams, E. L., Berkley, J. Y., Lopez, C. M., & Fisher, J. L. (1996). Empowering community health initiatives through evaluation. In D. M. Fetterman, S. J. Kaftarian, & A. Wandersman (Eds.), *Empowerment evaluation: Knowledge tools for self-assessment and accountability* (pp. 161-187). Thousand Oaks, CA: Sage.

Feighery, E., Altman, D. G., & Shaffer, G. (1991). The effects of combining education and enforcement to reduce tobacco sales to minors. *Journal of the American Medical Association, 266*(22), 3168-3171.

Feingold, E. (1994). Editorial: Your privacy or your health. *The Nation's Health, 24*(6), 2.

Fetterman, D. M., Kaftarian, S. J., & Wandersman, A. (1996). *Empowerment evaluation: Knowledge tools for self-assessment and accountability.* Thousand Oaks, CA: Sage.

Fine, S. H. (1981). *The marketing of ideas and social issues.* New York: Praeger.

Finnegan, J. R., Murray, D. M., Kurth, C., & McCarthy, P. (1989). Measuring and tracking education program implementation: The Minnesota Heart Health Program experience. *Health Education Quarterly, 16*(1), 77-90.

Fisher, E. B. (1995). Editorial: The results of the COMMIT Trial. *American Journal of Public Health, 83,* 159-160.

Fisher, J. D., & Misovich, S. J. (1990). Evolution of college students' AIDS-related behavioral responses, attitudes, knowledge and fear. *AIDS Education and Prevention, 2*(4), 322-337.

Fitzgerald, F. T. (1994). The tyranny of health. *New England Journal of Medicine, 331*(3), 196-198.

Flay, B. R., & Burton, D. (1990). Effective mass communication strategies for health campaigns. In C. Atkin & L. Wallack (Eds.), *Mass communication and public health: Complexities and conflicts* (pp. 129-146). Newbury Park, CA: Sage.

Fleishman, J. L., & Payne, B. L. (1980). *Ethical dilemmas and the education of policymakers.* New York: Hastings Center.

Flora, J. A., Maccoby, N., & Farquhar, J. W. (1989). Communication campaigns to prevent cardiovascular disease: The Stanford community studies. In J. Wasserheit, S. Aral, & K. Holmes (Eds.), *Monograph on behavioral research for prevention and control of sexually transmitted disease* (pp. 1-25). Philadelphia: Annenberg School of Communication.

Flora, J., & Maibach, E. W. (1990). Cognitive responses to AIDS information: The effects of issue involvement and message appeal. *Communication Research, 17*(6), 759-774.

Foderaro, L. W. (1994, February 19). Battling demons and nicotine: Hospitals' smoking bans are new anxiety for mentally ill. *New York Times,* pp. 44, 48.

Forester, J. (1985). Practical rationality in plan making. In M. Breheny & A. Hooper (Eds.), *Rationality in planning: Critical essays on the role of rationality in urban and regional planning* (pp. 48-59). London: Pion.

Forester, J. (1989). *Planning in the face of power.* Berkeley: University of California Press.

Forester, J. (1993). *Critical theory, public policy, and planning practice: Toward a critical pragmatism.* Albany: State University of New York.

Forster, J. L., McBride, C., Jeffrey, R., Schmid, T. L., & Pirie, P. L. (1991). Support for restrictive tobacco policies among residents of selected Minnesota communities. *American Journal of Health Promotion, 6,* 99-104.

Foucault, M. (1975). *The birth of the clinic: An archaeology of medical perception.* New York: Vintage.

Foucault, M. (1977). *Discipline and punish.* New York: Pantheon.

Fox, M. L., Dwyer, D. J., & Ganster, D. (1993). Effects of stressful job demands and control on physiological and attitudinal outcomes in a hospital setting. *Academy of Management Journal, 36*(2), 289-318.

Fox, R. C. (1977). The medicalization and demedicalization of American society. In J. H. Knowles (Ed.), *Doing better and feeling worse: Health in the United States* (pp. 9-22). New York: Norton & Company.

Frank, E., Winkleby, M., Frotmann, S. P., & Farquhar, J. W. (1993). Cardiovascular disease risk factors: Improvements in knowledge and behavior in the 1980s. *American Journal of Public Health, 83*(4), 590-593.

Franzini, L. R., Sideman, L. M., Dexter, K. E., & Elder, J. P. (1990). Promoting AIDS risk reduction via behavioral training. *AIDS Education and Prevention, 2*(4), 313-321.

Freimuth, V. S. (1992). Theoretical foundations of AIDS media campaigns. In T. Edgar, M. Fitzpatrick, & V. S. Freimuth (Eds.), *AIDS: A communication perspective* (pp. 91-110). Hillsdale, NJ: Lawrence Erlbaum.

Freimuth, V. S., Hammond, S. L., & Stein, J. A. (1988). Health advertising: Prevention for profit. *American Journal of Public Health, 78*(5), 557-561.

Freimuth, V. S., & Mettger, W. (1990). Is there a hard-to-reach audience? *Public Health Reports, 105*(3), 232-238.

Freire, P. (1968a). *Education for critical consciousness*. New York: Seabury.

Freire, P. (1968b). *Pedagogy of the oppressed*. New York: Seabury.

Freudenberg, N. (1990). AIDS prevention in the United States: Lessons from the first decade. *International Journal of Health Services, 20*(4), 589-599.

Freudenberg, N., Eng., E., Flay, B., Parcel, G., Rogers, T., & Wallerstein, N. (1995). Strengthening individual and community capacity to prevent disease and promote health: In search of relevant theories and principles. *Health Education Quarterly, 22*(3), 290-306.

Garret, T. M., Baillie, H. W., & Garret, R. M. (1989). *Health care ethics: Principles and problems*. Englewood Cliffs, NJ: Prentice Hall.

Gaylin, W. (1993, September 15). The health plan misses the point. *The New York Times,* p. A27.

Giddens, A. (1979). *Central problems in social theory*. Berkeley: University of California Press.

Giddens, A. (1984). *The constitution of society*. Berkeley: University of California Press.

Giesbrecht, N., Conley, P., Denniston, R. W., Gliksman, L., Holder, H., Pederson, A., Room, R., & Shain, M. (Eds.). (1990). *Research, action, and the community: Experiences in the prevention of alcohol and other drug problems* (OSAP Prevention Monograph 4, DHHS Publication No. ADM 89-1651). Washington, DC: Alcohol, Drug Abuse, and Mental Health Administration.

Gillick, M. R. (1984, Fall). Health promotion, jogging, and the pursuit of the moral life. *Journal of Health Politics, Policy and Law, 9,* 369-387.

Gilligan, C. (1982). *In a different voice: Psychological theory and women's development*. Cambridge, MA: Harvard University Press.

Gillon, R. (1990). Health education: The ambiguity of the medical role. In S. Doxiadis (Ed.), *Ethics in health education* (pp. 29-41). New York: John Wiley.

Glantz, S. A. (1996). Editorial: Preventing tobacco use—The youth access trap. *American Journal of Public Health, 86*(2), 156-157.

Glanz, K., Lankenau, B., Forester, S., Temple, S., Mullis, R., & Schmid, T. (1995). Environmental and policy approaches to cardiovascular disease prevention through nutrition: Opportunities for state and local action. *Health Education Quarterly, 22*(4), 512-527.

Glanz, K., & Mullis, R. M. (1988). Environmental interventions to promote healthy eating: A review of models, programs, and evidence. *Health Education Quarterly, 15*(4), 395-415.

Gold, M., & Franks, P. (1990). The social origin of cardiovascular risk: An investigation in a rural community. *International Journal of Health Services, 20*(3), 405-416.

Goodman, L. E., & Goodman, M. J. (1986). Prevention: How misuse of a concept undercuts its worth. *Hastings Center Report, 16*(2), 26-38.

Gorman, D. M., & Speer, P. W. (1996). Preventing alcohol abuse and alcohol-related problems through community interventions: A review of evaluation studies. *Psychology and Health, 11,* 95-131.

Gostin, L. O., & Brandt, A. M. (1993). Criteria for evaluating a ban on the advertisement of cigarettes. *Journal of the American Medical Association, 269*(7), 904-909.

Goswami, D., & Melkote, S. (1997). Knowledge gap in AIDS communication: An Indian study. *Gazette, 59*(3), 205-221.

Grace, V. M. (1991). The marketing of empowerment and the construction of the health consumer: A critique of health promotion. *International Journal of Health Services, 21*(2), 329-343.

Green, L. W. (1989). Comment: Is institutionalization the proper goal of grantmaking? *American Journal of Health Promotion, 3,* 44.

Green, L. W., & Kreuter, M. W. (1991). *Health promotion planning: An educational and environmental approach* (2nd ed.). Mountain View, CA: Mayfield.

Green, L. W., & Raiburn, J. (1990). Contemporary developments in health promotion: Definitions and challenges. In N. Bracht (Ed.), *Health promotion at the community level* (pp. 29-44). Newbury Park, CA: Sage.

Grube, J. W., Mayton, D. M., II, & Ball-Rokeach, S. J. (1994). Inducing change in values, attitudes, and behaviors: Belief system theory and the method of value self-confrontation. *Journal of Social Issues, 50*(4), 153-173.

Grube, J. W., & Wallack, L. (1994). Television beer advertising and drinking knowledge, beliefs, and intentions among school children. *American Journal of Public Health, 84*(2), 254-259.

Gruning, J. E. (1989). Publics, audiences and market segments: Segmentation principles for campaigns. In C. T. Salmon (Ed.), *Information campaigns: Balancing social values and social change* (pp. 199-228). Newbury Park, CA: Sage.

Guba, E. G., & Lincoln, Y. S. (1981). *Effective evaluation.* San Francisco: Jossey-Bass.

Guba, E. G., & Lincoln, Y. S. (1989). *Fourth generation evaluation.* Newbury Park, CA: Sage.

Guttmacher, S., Teitelman, M., Chapin, G., Garbowski, G., & Schnall, P. (1981). Ethics and preventive medicine: The case of borderline hypertension. *Hastings Center Report, 11*(1), 12-14.

Guttman, N. (1994). *A value-centered analysis of health communication interventions: The relationship of goals and strategies to health promotion values.* Unpublished doctoral dissertation, Rutgers University, New Brunswick, New Jersey.

Guttman, N., Kegler, M., & McLeroy, K. R. (1996). Health promotion paradoxes, antinomies, and conundrums. *Health Education Research: Theory and Practice, 11*(1), 1996.

Guttman, N., & Zimmerman, D. R. (in press). Low-income mother's views on breastfeeding. *Social Science & Medicine.*

Habermas, J. (1979). *Communication and the evolution of society.* Boston: Beacon.

Hamlin, C. (1995). Could you starve to death in England in 1839? The Chadwick-Farr controversy and the loss of the "social" in public health. *American Journal of Public Health, 85*(6), 856-866.

Harmon, M. M. (1995). *Responsibility as paradox: A critique of rational discourse on government.* Thousand Oaks, CA: Sage.

Harron, F., Burnside, J., & Beauchamp, T. (1983). *Health and human values: A guide to making your own decisions.* New Haven, CT: Yale University Press.

Hatch, J., & Derthick, S. (1992). Empowering black churches for health promotion. *Health Values, 16*(5), 3-9.

Hennenberger, M. (1992, August 29). Two officials are resolute on AIDS but foes still hope for review of policy. *The New York Times,* p. 22.

Henry, R. C. (1996). An update on the community partnerships. In R. W. Richardson (Ed.), *Building partnerships: Educating health professionals for the communities they serve* (pp. 33-49). San Francisco: Jossey-Bass.

Herek, G. M., & Capitanio, J. P. (1993). Public reactions to AIDS in the United States: A second decade of stigma. *American Journal of Public Health, 83*(4), 574-577.

Hiller, M. D. (1987). Ethics and health education: Issues in theory and practice. In P. M. Lazes, L. H. Kaplan, & K. A. Gordon (Eds.), *The handbook of health education* (2nd ed., pp. 87-107). Rockville, MD: Aspen.

Hilton, M. E., & Kaskutas, L. (1991). Public support for warning labels on alcoholic beverage containers. *British Journal of Addiction, 86,* 1323-1333.

Hollander, R. B., & Hale, J. F. (1987). Worksite health promotion programs: Ethical issues. *American Journal of Health Promotion, 2*(2), 37-43.

Hornik, R. (1989). The knowledge-behavior gap in public information campaigns: A development communication view. In C. T. Salmon (Ed.), *Information campaigns: Balancing social values and social change* (pp. 113-138). Newbury Park, CA: Sage.

Hornik, R. (1990). Alternative models of behavior change. In J. Wasserheit, S. Aral, & K. Holmes (Eds.), *Monograph on behavioral research for prevention and control of sexually transmitted disease* (pp. 1-25). Philadelphia: Annenberg School of Communication.

Hornik, R. (1997). *Public health communication: Making sense of contradictory evidence.* Paper presented at the 47th Annual Conference of the International Communication Association, Montreal, Canada.

Hughes, P., & Brecht, G. (1975). *Vicious circles and infinity: A panoply of paradoxes.* Garden City, NY: Doubleday.

Illich, I. (1975). *Medical nemesis.* London: Calder & Boyars.

Israel, B. A., Checkoway, B., Schulz, A., & Zimmerman, M. (1994). Health education and community empowerment: Conceptualizing and measuring perceptions of individual, organizational, and community control. *Health Education Quarterly, 21*(2), 149-170.

Jaccard, J., Turrisi, R., & Wan, C. K. (1990). Implications of behavioral decision theory and social marketing for designing social action programs. In J. Edwards, R. S. Tindale, L. Heath, & E. J. Posavac (Eds.), *Social influence processes and prevention* (pp. 103-142). New York: Plenum.

Janes, C. R., & Corbet, K. K. (1996, November). *On believing eight impossible things before breakfast: Fallacies and foibles in community-based health promotion.* Paper presented at the Annual Meeting of the American Public Health Association, New York.

Jason, L. A., Ji, P. Y., Anes, M. D., & Birkhead, S. H. (1991). Active enforcement of cigarette control laws in the prevention of cigarette sales to minors. *Journal of the American Medical Association, 266*(22), 3159-3161.

Jeffery, R. W., Forster, J. L., Schmid, T. L., McBride, C. M., Rooney, B. L., & Pirie, P. L. (1990). Community attitudes toward public policies to control alcohol, tobacco, and high-fat food consumption. *American Journal of Preventive Medicine, 6*(1), 12-19.

Jitsukawa, M., & Djerassi, C. (1994). Birth control in Japan: Realities and prognosis. *Science, 265,* 1048-1051.

Johnson, E. (1991). Introduction. In Office for Substance Abuse Prevention (Ed.), *Turning awareness into action* (p. 4; DHHS publication No. ADM 91-1562). Rockville, MD: U.S. Department of Health and Human Services.

Jones-Webb, R., Greenfield, T. K., & Graves, K. (1994). The relationship between ethnicity, social class, alcohol use, and public opinion regarding alcohol control policies. *Contemporary Drug Use, 20*(4), 719-738.

Kahn, J. G. (1996). The cost-effectiveness of HIV prevention targeting: How much more bang for the buck? *American Journal of Public Health, 86,* 1709-1712.

Kahn, J. P. (1994). Sin taxes as a mechanism of health finance: Moral and policy considerations. In J. F. Humber & R. F. Almeder (Eds.), *Biomedical ethics review* (pp. 179-202). Totowa, NJ: Harmon.

Karasek, R., & Theorell, T. (1990). *Healthy work: Stress, productivity, and the reconstruction of working life.* New York: Basic Books.

Katcher, B. S. (1993). Benjamin Rush's educational campaign against hard drinking. *American Journal of Public Health, 83*(2), 273-281.

Keeney, R. L. (1994). Decisions about life-threatening risks. *New England Journal of Medicine, 331*(3), 193-196.

Kelman, H. C. (1969). Manipulation of human behavior: An ethical dilemma for the social scientists. In W. G. Bennis, K. D. Benne, & R. Chin (Eds.), *The planning of change.* New York: Holt Rinehart & Winston.

Kelman, S. (1975). The social nature of the definition problem in health. *International Journal of Health Services, 5,* 625-642.

King, A. C., Jeffery, R. W., Fridinger, F., Dunsenbury, L., Provence, S., Hedlund, S. A., & Spangeler, K. (1995). Environmental and policy approaches to cardiovascular disease prevention through physical activity: Issues and opportunities. *Health Education Quarterly, 22*(4), 499-511.

Kleining, J. (1990). The ethical challenge of AIDS to traditional liberal values. *AIDS and Public Policy Journal, 5*(1), 42-44.

Knowles, J. H. (1977). The responsibility of the individual. In J. H. Knowles (Ed.), *Doing better and feeling worse: Health in the United States.* New York: Norton.

Knox, E. G. (1987). Personal and public health care: Conflict, congruence or accommodation? In S. Doxiadis (Ed.), *Ethical dilemmas in health promotion* (pp. 59-81). New York: John Wiley.

Kolata, G. (1993, October 22). Panel tells cancer institute to stop giving advice on mammograms. *The New York Times,* p. A14.

Kolata, G. (1995, May 10). Amid inconclusive health studies, some experts advise less advice. *The New York Times,* p. C12.

Kolata, G. (1996, March 1). Vitamin to protect fetuses will be required in foods: First new fortification order since 1943. *The New York Times,* p. A10.

Kreps, G. L., & Maibach, B. (1991, May). *Communicating to prevent health risks.* Paper presented to the International Communication Association Annual Conference, Chicago.

Kreps, G. L., & Thornton, B. C. (1992). *Health communication: Theory and practice* (2nd ed.). Prospect Heights, IL: Waverland.

Kristiansen, C. M., & Zanna, M. P. (1994). The rhetorical use of values to justify social and intergroup attitudes. *Journal of Social Issues, 50*(4), 47-65.

Kurtines, W. M., Alvarez, M., & Azmitia, M. (1990). Science and morality: The role of values in science and the scientific study of moral phenomena. *Psychological Bulletin, 107*(3), 283-295.

LaBonte, R. (1994). Health promotion and empowerment: Reflections on professional practice. *Health Education Quarterly, 21,* 235-268.

Laczniak, G. R., Lusch, R. F., & Murphy, P. E. (1979, Spring). Social marketing: Its ethical dimensions. *Journal of Marketing, 43,* 29-36.

Lappe, F. M. (1989). *Rediscovering America's values.* New York: Ballentine.

Lau, R. R., Hartman, K. A., & Ware, J. E. (1986). Health as a value: Methodological and theoretical considerations. *Health Psychology, 5*(1), 25-43.

Lefebvre, R. C. (1990). Strategies to maintain and institutionalize successful programs: A marketing framework. In N. Bracht (Ed.), *Health promotion at the community level* (pp. 209-228). Newbury Park, CA: Sage.

Lefebvre, R. C., & Flora, J. A. (1992). Social marketing and public health interventions. In B. C. Thornton & G. L. Kreps (Eds.), *Perspectives on health communication.* Norwalk, CT: Appleton & Lange.

Lefebvre, R. C., & Flora, J. A. (1998). Social marketing and public health intervention. *Health Education Quarterly, 15*(3), 299-315.

Leichter, H. (1986). Saving lives and protecting liberty: A comparative study of the seat-belt debate. *Journal of Health Politics, Policy and Law, 11*(2), 323-344.

Leichter, H. M. (1991). *Free to be foolish: Politics and health promotion in the United States and Great Britain.* Princeton, NJ: Princeton University Press.

Levin, L. S. (1987). Every silver lining has a cloud: The limits of health promotion. *Social Policy, 18*(1), 57-60.

Levine, J. M. (1986). The politics of diet and heart disease. In H. M. Sapolsky (Ed.), *Consuming fears* (pp. 40-79). New York: Basic Books.

Levine, S., Feldman, J. J., & Elinson, J. (1983). Does medical care do any good? In D. Mechanic (Ed.), *Handbook of health, health care and the health professions.* New York: Free Press.

Leviton, L. C. (1989). Program theory and evaluation theory in community-based programs. *Evaluation Practice, 15*(1), 89-92.

Levy, A. S., & Stokes, R. C. (1987). Effects of a health promotion advertising campaign on sales of ready-to-eat cereals. *Public Health Reports, 102,* 398-403.

Lewin, T. (1992, December 4). Baltimore school clinics to offer birth control by surgical implant. *The New York Times,* p. 1.

Littlejohn, S. W. (1996). *Theories of human communication* (5th ed.). Belmont, CA: Wadsworth.

Loken, B., Swim, J., & Mittelmark, M. B. (1990). Heart health program: Applying social influence processes in a large-scale community health promotion program. In J. Edwards, R. S. Tindale, L. Heath, & E. J., Posavac (Eds.), *Social influence processes and prevention* (pp. 159-181). New York: Plenum.

Luepker, R. V., Murray, D. M., Jacobs, D. R., Mittelmark, M. B., Bracht, N., Carlow, R., Crow, R., Elmer, P., Finnegan, J., Folsom, A. R., Grimm, R., Hannan, P. J., Jeffrey, R., Lando, H., McGovern, P., Mullis, R., Perry, C., Pechacek, T., Pirie, P., Sparfka, M., Weisbrod, R., & Blackburn, H. (1994). Community education for cardiovascular disease prevention: Risk factor changes in the Minnesota Heart Health Program. *American Journal of Public Health, 84*(9), 1383-1393.

Lugo, N. R. (1996). Empowerment education: A case study of the Resource Sisters/Companeras Program. *Health Education Quarterly, 23*(3), 281-289.

Lupton, D. (1993). Risk as mortal danger: The social and political functions of risk discourse in public health. *International Journal of Health Services, 23*(3), 425-435.

Lupton, D. (1994). Toward the development of critical health communication praxis. *Health Communication, 6*(1), 55-67.

Lyman, C., & Engstrom, L. (1992). HIV and sexual health education for women. In R. P. Keeling (Ed.), *Effective AIDS education on campus* (pp. 23-37). San Francisco: Jossey-Bass.

MacDonald, L. A., Sackett, D. L., Haynes, R. B., & Taylor, D. W. (1984). Labeling in hypertension: A review of the behavioral and psychological consequences. *Journal of Chronic Disease, 37,* 933-942.

Mackey-Kallis, S., & Hahn, D. F. (1991). Questions of public will and private action: The power of the negative in the Regans' "Just Say No" morality campaign. *Communication Quarterly, 39*(1), 1-17.

Maibach, E., Flora, J. A., & Nass, C. (1991). Changes in self-efficacy and health behavior in response to a minimal contact community health campaign. *Health Communication, 3*(1), 1-5.

Maibach, E., & Hotgrave, D. R. (1995). Advances in public health communication. *American Review of Public Health, 16,* 19-38.

Maibach, E., & Parrot, R. L. (Eds.). (1995). *Designing health messages: Approaches from communication theory and public practice.* Thousand Oaks, CA: Sage.

Mandelblatt, J., Andrews, H., Kao, R., Wallace, R., & Kerner, J. (1996). The late-stage diagnosis of colorectal cancer: Demographic and socioeconomic factors. *American Journal of Public Health, 86,* 1794-1797.

Manning, R. (1992). *Speaking from the heart: A feminist perspective on ethics.* Lanham, MD: Rowan & Littlefield.

Manoff, R. K. (1985). *Social marketing: New imperative for public health.* New York: Praeger.

Manuel, C., Enel, P., Charrel, J., Reviron, D., Larher, M. P., Auquier, P., & San Marco, J. L. (1991). Ethics and AIDS: The protection of society versus the protection of individual rights. *AIDS and Public Policy Journal, 6*(1), 31-35.

Mappes, T. A., & Zembaty, J. S. (1991). *Biomedical ethics* (3rd ed.). New York: McGraw-Hill.

Marantz, P. R. (1990). Blaming the victim: The negative consequence of preventive medicine. *American Journal of Public Health, 80*(10), 1186-1187.

Marin, B. V., & Marin, G. (1990). Effects of acculturation on knowledge of AIDS and HIV among Hispanics. *Hispanic Journal of Behavioral Sciences, 12*(2), 110.

Marshall, J. R. (1995). Editorial: Improving Americans' diet—Setting public policy with limited knowledge. *American Journal of Public Health, 85*(12), 1609-1611.

Marshall, M., & Oleson, A. (1994). In the pink: MADD and public health policy in the 1990s. *Journal of Public Health Policy, 15*(1), 54-70.

Martin, E. (1994). *Flexible bodies: Tracking immunity in American culture from the days of polio to the age of AIDS.* Boston: Beacon.

Masergh, G., Rohrbach, L. A., Montgomery, S. B., Pentz, M. A., & Johnson, A. (1996). Process evaluation of commuity coalitions for alcohol and other drug abuse prevention: A case study comparison of research- and community-initiated models. *Journal of Community Psychology, 24,* 118-135.

Maslow, A. H. (1954). *Motivation and personality.* New York: Harper & Row.

Maulitz, R. C. (1988). Is this the way we want to die? In R. C. Maulitz (Ed.), *Unnatural causes: The three leading killer diseases in America* (pp. 3-10). New Brunswick, NJ: Rutgers University Press.

McAlister, A., Puska, P., Salonen, J. T., Tuomilehto, J., & Koskela, K. (1982). Theory and action for health promotion: Illustrations from the North Karelia Project. *American Journal of Public Health, 72,* 43-50.

McGuire, W. J. (1989). Theoretical foundations of campaigns. In R. E. Rice & C. K. Atkin (Eds.), *Public communication campaigns* (2nd ed., pp. 39-65). Newbury Park, CA: Sage.

McKinlay, J. B. (1975). A case for refocusing upstream: The political economy of illness. In A. J. Enelow & J. B. Henderson (Eds.), *Applying behavioral science to cardiovascular risk* (pp. 7-17). Washington, DC: American Heart Association.

McKnight, J. (1987, Winter). Regenerating community. *Social Policy,* 54-58.

McKnight, J. L. (1992). Redefining community. *Social Policy, 23*(2), 56-62.

McKnight, J., & Kretzmann, J. (1984). Community organizing in the 80s: Toward a post-Alinsky agenda. *Social Policy, 14,* 15-17.

McLachlan, H. V. (1995). Smokers, virgins, equity and health care costs. *Journal of Medical Ethics, 21,* 209-213.

McLeroy, K. R., Bibeau, D., Steckler, A., & Glanz, K. (1988). An ecological perspective on health promotion programs. *Health Education Quarterly, 15,* 351-377.

McLeroy, K. R., Gottlieb, N. H., & Burdine, J. N. (1987). The business of health promotion: Ethical issues and professional responsibilities. *Health Education Quarterly, 14*(1), 91-109.

Milio, N. (1981). *Promoting health through public policy.* Philadelphia: F. A. Davis.

Mill, J. S. (1978). *On liberty.* Indianapolis, IN: Hackett. (Original work published in 1863)

Miller, A. (1990, January 29). Oat-bran heartburn. *Newsweek,* 50-52.

Minkler, M. (1989). Health education, health promotion and the open society: An historical perspective. *Health Education Quarterly, 16*(1), 17-30.

Minkler, M. (1990). Improving health through community organization. In K. Glanz, F. M. Lewis, & B. K. Rimer (Eds.), *Health behavior and health education: Theory, research and practice* (pp. 257-287). San Francisco: Jossey-Bass.

Mish, F. C., et al. (Eds.). (1994). *Merriam-Webster's Collegiate Dictionary* (10th ed.). Springfield, MA: Merriam-Webster.

Moore, T. J. (1989). *Heart failure: A critical inquiry into American medicine and the revolution in heart care.* New York: Simon & Schuster.

More obese adults despite awareness of the risk. (1994, July 17). *The New York Times,* pp. 1, 18.

Morgan, M. G., & Lave, L. (1990). Ethical considerations in risk communication practice and research. *Risk Analysis, 3,* 355-358.

Morgan, R. F. (Ed.). (1983). *The iatrogenics handbook.* Toronto: IPI.

Mumby, D. K. (1988). *Communication and power in organizations: Discourse, ideology, and domination.* Norwood, NJ: Ablex.

Mumby, D. K. (1997). Modernism, postmodernism, and communication studies: A rereading of an ongoing debate. *Communication Theory, 7*(1), 1-28.

Nagel, S. S. (1983). Ethical dilemmas in policy evaluation. In W. N. Dunn (Ed.), *Values, ethics, and the practice of policy analysis* (pp. 65-85). Lexington, MA: Lexington Books.

National Cholesterol Education Program. (1990, November). *Report of the Expert Panel on Population Strategies for Blood Cholesterol Reduction* (NIH Publication No. 90-3046). Washington, DC: Government Printing Office.

Niebuhr, H. R. (1978). *The responsible self.* New York: Harper & Row.

Noddings, N. (1984). *Caring: A feminine approach to ethics and moral education.* Berkeley: University of California Press.

Noddings, N. (1990). Ethics from the standpoint of women. In M. Pearsall (Ed.), *Women and values: Readings in recent feminist philosophy* (2nd ed., pp. 379-390). Belmont, CA: Wadsworth.

Northouse, P. G., & Northouse, L. L. (1992). *Health communication: Strategies for health professionals* (2nd ed.). Norwalk, CT: Appleton & Lange.

Nyamathie, A., Flaskerud, J., Bennet, C., Leake, B., & Lewis, C. (1994). Evaluation of two AIDS education programs for impoverished women. *AIDS Education and Prevention, 6*(4), 296-309.

Odets, W. (1994). AIDS education and harm reduction for gay men: Psychological approaches for the 21st century. *AIDS and Public Policy, 9,* 1-5.

Office for Substance Abuse Prevention. (1991). *Turning awareness into action: What your community can do about drug use in America* (DHHS publication No. ADM 91-1562). Rockville, MD: U.S. Department of Health and Human Services.

Olien, C. N., Donohue, G. A., & Tichenor, P. J. (1983). Structure, communication and social power: Evolution of the knowledge gap hypothesis. In E. Wartella, D. C. Whitney, & S. Windahl (Eds.), *Mass communication review yearbook* (Vol. 4). Beverly Hills, CA: Sage.

Orr, S. T., Celmentano, D. D., Santelli, J., & Burwell, L. (1994). Depressive symptoms and risk factors for HIV acquisition among black women attending urban health centers in Baltimore. *AIDS Education and Prevention, 6*(3), 230-236.

Ostaria, T., & Sullivan, G. (1991). The impact of religion and cultural values on AIDS education programs in Malaysia and the Philippines. *AIDS Education and Prevention, 3*(2), 133-146.

Packer, C., & Kauffman, S. (1990). Reregulation of commercial television: Implications for coverage of AIDS. *AIDS and Public Policy, 5*(2), 82-87.

Paisley, W. (1989). Public communication campaigns: The American experience. In R. E. Rice & C. K. Atkin (Eds.), *Public communication campaigns* (2nd ed., pp. 15-38). Newbury Park, CA: Sage.

Parrot, R. L., Kahl, M. L., & Maibach, E. W. (1995). Policy and administrative practices at a crossroads. In E. Maibach & R. L. Parrot (Eds.), *Designing health messages: Approaches from communication theory and public practice* (pp. 270-283). Thousand Oaks, CA: Sage.

Parsons, T. (1958). Definitions of health and illness in the light of American values and social structure. In E. G. Jaco (Ed.), *Patients, physicians and illness.* Glencoe, IL: Free Press.

Payer, L. (1993). Hyping cholesterol and blood pressure: Risk factors aren't diseases. *Consumers' Research, 76*(3), 10-15.

Pellegrino, E. D. (1985). The virtuous physician and the ethics of medicine. In E. E. Shelp (Ed.), *Virtue and medicine: Exploration in the character of medicine* (Philosophy and Medicine Series, No. 17, pp. 243-255). Dordrecht, Holland: Reidel.

Pellegrino, E. D. (1993). The metamorphosis of medical ethics: A 30-year retrospective. *Journal of the American Medical Association, 269*(9), 1158-1162.

Perry, C. L., Baranowski, T., & Parcel, G. S. (1990). How individuals, environments, and health behavior interact: Social learning theory. In K. Glanz, F. M. Lewis, & B. K. Rimer (Eds.),

Health behavior and health education: Theory, research and practice (pp. 161-186). San Francisco: Jossey-Bass

Perry, C. L., Williams, C. L., Veblen-Motenson, S., Toomey, T. L., Komro, K. A., Asntine, P. S., McGovern, P. G., Finnegan, J. R., Forster, J. L., Wagenaar, A. C., & Wolfson, M. (1996). Project Northland: Outcomes of a communitywide alcohol use prevention program during early adolescence. *American Journal of Public Health, 86*(7), 956-965.

Peterson, D. E., Zeger, S. L., Reimington, P. L., & Anderson, H. A. (1992). The effect of state cigarette tax increase on cigarette sales, 1955-1988. *American Journal of Public Health, 82*(1), 94-96.

Pierce, J. P., & Giplin, E. A. (1995). A historical analysis of tobacco marketing and the uptake of smoking by youth in the United States: 1890-1977. *Health Psychology, 14,* 500-508.

Pinet, G. (1987). Health legislation, prevention and ethics. In S. Doxiadis (Ed.), *Ethical dilemmas in health promotion* (pp. 83-97). New York: John Wiley.

Piotrow, P. T., Kincaid, D. L., Rimon, J. G., & Rinehart, W. (1997). *Health communication: Lessons from family planning and reproductive health.* Westport, CT: Praeger.

Pollay, R. W. (1989). Campaigns, change and culture: On the polluting potential of persuasion. In C. T. Salmon (Ed.), *Information campaigns: Balancing social values and social change* (pp. 185-196). Newbury Park, CA: Sage.

Price, R. H. (1990). Whither participation and empowerment? *American Journal of Community Psychology, 18*(1), 163-167.

Priester, R. (1992a). A values framework for health system reform. *Health Affairs, 11*(1), 84-107.

Priester, R. (1992b). *Taking values seriously: A values framework for the U.S. health care system.* Minneapolis: The Center for Biomedical Ethics, University of Minnesota.

Proctor, R. (1995). *Cancer wars: How politics shape what we know and don't know about cancer.* New York: Basic Books.

Puska, P., Nissinen, A., & Tuomilehto, I. (1985). The community-based strategy to prevent coronary health disease: Conclusions from the ten years of the North Karelia Project. *Annual Review of Public Health, 6,* 147-193.

Rakow, L. F. (1989). Information and power: Toward a critical theory of information campaigns. In C. T. Salmon (Ed.), *Information campaigns: Balancing social values and social change* (pp. 164-184). Newbury Park, CA: Sage.

Rappaport, J. (1981). In praise of paradox: A social policy of empowerment over prevention. *American Journal of Community Psychology, 9*(1), 1-25.

Ratzan, S. R. (1994). Editor's introduction: Communication—The key to a healthier tomorrow. *American Behavioral Scientist, 38*(2), 202-207.

Ratzan, S. R., Payne, G., & Massett, H. A. (1994). Effective health message design. *American Behavioral Scientist, 38*(2), 294-309.

Rawls, J. (1971). *A theory of justice.* Cambridge, MA: Harvard University Press.

Rayner, S. (1992). Cultural theory of risk analysis. In S. Krimsky & D. Golding (Eds.), *Social theories of risk* (pp. 83-115). Westport, CT: Praeger-Greenwood.

Rayner, S., & Cantor, R. (1987). How fair is safe enough? The cultural approach to social technology choice. *Risk Analysis, 7,* 3-9.

Regier, D. A., Hirschfeld, M. A., Goodwin, F. K., Burke, J. D., Lazar, J. B., & Judd, L. L. (1988). The NIMH Depression Awareness, Recognition, and Treatment Program: Structure, aims, and scientific basis. *American Journal of Psychiatry, 145,* 1351-1357.

Reinarman, C. (1988). The social construction of an alcohol problem: The case of Mothers Against Drunk Drivers and social control in the 1980s. *Theory and Society, 17*(1), 91-120.

Repetti, R. L. (1993). Short-term effects of occupational stressors on daily mood and health complaints. *Health Psychology, 12*(2), 125-131.

Rhode, D. L. (1993-1994). Adolescent pregnancy and public policy. *Political Science Quarterly, 108*(4), 635-669.

Rice, R. E., & Atkin, C. K. (Eds.). (1989). *Public communication campaigns* (2nd ed.). Newbury Park, CA: Sage.

Riis, P. (1990). Ethics, health education, and nutrition. In S. Doxiadis (Ed.), *Ethics in health education* (pp. 181-190). New York: John Wiley.

Robertson, A., & Minkler, M. (1994). New health promotion movement: A critical examination. *Health Education Quarterly, 21*(3), 295-312.

Roccella, E. J., & Ward, G. (1984). The national high blood pressure education program: A description of its utility as a generic program model. *Health Education Quarterly, 11*(3), 225-242.

Rogers, E. M. (1994). The field of health communication today. *American Behavioral Scientist, 38*(2), 208-214.

Rogers, E. M. (1996). The field of health communication today: An up-to-date report. *Journal of Health Communication: International Perspectives, 1*(1), 15-23.

Rogers, E. M., & Antola, L. (1985). Telenovelas in Latin America: A success story. *Journal of Communication, 35*, 24-35.

Rogers, E. M., & Storey, J. D. (1987). Communication campaigns. In C. R. Berger & S. H. Chaffee (Eds.), *Handbook of communication science* (pp. 817-846). Newbury Park, CA: Sage.

Rogers, E. M., Vaughan, P., & Shefner-Rogers, C. L. (1995, May). *Evaluating the effects of an entertainment-education radio soap opera in Tanzania: A field experiment with multi-method measurement.* Paper presented at the International Communication Association's Annual Meeting, Albuquerque, New Mexico.

Rokeach, M. (1973). *The nature of human values.* New York: Free Press.

Rokeach, M. (1979). Value theory and communication research: Review and commentary. In D. Nimmo (Ed.), *Communication yearbook 3* (pp. 7-28). New Brunswick, NJ: Transaction.

Roman, P. M., & Blum, T. C. (1987). Ethics in worksite health programming: Who is served? *Health Education Quarterly, 14*(1), 57-70.

Rose, G. (1981). Strategy of prevention: Lessons from cardiovascular disease. *British Medical Journal, 282*, 1847-1851.

Rose, G. (1985). Sick individuals and sick populations. *International Journal of Epidemiology, 14*(1), 32-38.

Rosenstock, I. M. (1990). The past, present and future of health education. In K. Glanz, F. M. Lewis, & B. K. Rimer (Eds.), *Health behavior and health education: Theory, research and practice* (pp. 405-420). San Francisco: Jossey-Bass

Rosenstock, I. M., Stretcher, V. J., & Becker, M. H. (1988). Social learning theory and the health belief model. *Health Education Quarterly, 15*(2), 175-193.

Ross, C. (1995, May 6). Japanese patients do not have to be told of cancer. *The Lancet, 345*, 1166.

Rossi, H., & Freeman, H. E. (1985). *Evaluation: A systematic approach* (3rd ed.). Beverly Hills, CA: Sage.

Rothman, J. (1979). Three models of community organization practice, their mixing and phasing. In F. M. Cox, J. L. Erlich, J. Rothman, & J. E. Tropman (Eds.), *Strategies of community organization* (pp. 25-45). Itasca, IL: Peacock.

Rothman, J., & Tropman, J. E. (1987). Models of community organization practice and macro practice perspectives: Their mixing and phasing. In F. M. Cox, J. L. Erlich, J. Rothman, & J. E. Tropman (Eds.), *Strategies of community organization: Macro practice* (pp. 3-26). Itasca, IL: Peacock.

Rowland, J., Rivara, F., Salzberg, B., Sodenberg, R., Maier, R., & Koepsell, T. (1996). Motorcycle helmet use and injury outcome and hospitalization costs from crashes in Washington State. *American Journal of Public Health, 86*(1), 41-45.

Rudd, R. E., & Comings, J. P. (1994). Learner developed materials: An empowerment product. *Health Education Quarterly, 21*(3), 313-327.

Russell, L. B. (1986). *Is prevention better than cure?* Washington, DC: Brookings Institution.

Russell, L. B. (1987). *Evaluating preventive care: Report on a workshop.* Washington, DC: Brookings Institution.

Ryan, W. (1976). *Blaming the victim.* New York: Random House.

Salmon, C. T. (1989). Campaigns for social "improvement": An overview of values, rationales and impacts. In C. T. Salmon (Ed.), *Information campaigns: Balancing social values and social change* (pp. 19-53). Newbury Park, CA: Sage.

Salmon, C. T. (1992). Bridging theory "of" and theory "for" communication campaigns: An essay on ideology and public policy. In S. A. Deetz (Ed.), *Communication yearbook 15* (pp. 346-358). Newbury Park, CA: Sage.

Salmon, C. T., & Kroger, F. (1992). A systems approach to AIDS communication: The example of the National AIDS Information and Education Program. In T. Edgar, M. Fitzpatrick, & V. S. Freimuth (Eds.), *AIDS: A communication perspective* (pp. 131-146). Hillsdale, NJ: Lawrence Erlbaum.

Salmon, C. T., Wooten, K., Gentry, E., Cole, G., & Kroger, F. (1996). AIDS knowledge gaps in the first decade of the epidemic and implications for future information efforts. *Journal of Health Communication, 1,* 141-145.

Schechter, C., Vanchieri, C. F., & Crofton, C. (1990). Evaluating women's attitudes and perceptions in developing mammography promotion messages. *Public Health Reports, 105*(3), 253-260.

Scheper-Hughes, N. (1993). AIDS, public health and human rights in Cuba. *The Lancet, 342,* 965-967.

Scherer, C. W., & Juanillo, N. K. (1992). Bridging theory and praxis: Reexamining public health communication. In S. A. Deetz (Ed.), *Communication yearbook 15* (pp. 312-345). Newbury Park, CA: Sage.

Schiller, H. (1989). *Culture Inc.: The corporate takeover of public expression.* Oxford, UK: Oxford University Press.

Schmid, T. L., Jeffrey, R. W., Forester, J. L., Rooney, B., Klepp, K. I., & McBride, C. (1990). Public impressions of policy initiatives regulating alcohol use in Minnesota: A multi-community survey. *Journal of Studies on Alcohol, 51,* 438-442.

Schmid, T. L., Pratt, M., & Howze, E. (1995). Policy as intervention: Environmental and policy approaches to the prevention of cardiovascular disease. *American Journal of Public Health, 85*(9), 1207-1211.

Schmitt, E. (1996, March 1). House approves biggest change in farm policy since new deal: Legislation phases out subsidies over 7 years. *The New York Times,* p. A1.

Schoepf, B. G. (1992). AIDS, sex and condoms: African healers and the reinvention of tradition in Zaire. *Medical Anthropology, 14*(2-4), 225-242.

Schwartz, R., Goodman, R., & Steckler, A. (1995). Policy advocacy interventions for health promotion and education: Advancing the state of practice. *Health Education Quarterly, 22*(4), 421-426.

Schwartz, S. H. (1992). Universals in the content and structure of values: Theoretical advances and empirical tests in 20 countries. In M. Zanna (Ed.), *Advances in experimental social psychology* (Vol. 25, pp. 1-65). Orlando, FL: Academic Press.

Schwartz, S. H. (1994). Are there universal aspects in the structure and content of human values? *Journal of Social Issues, 50*(4), 19-45.

Scott, S. J., & Mercer, M. A. (1994). Understanding cultural obstacles to HIV/AIDS prevention in Africa. *AIDS Education and Prevention, 6*(1), 81-89.

Scriven, M. S. (1983). Evaluation ideologies. In A. S. Bryk (Ed.), *Stakeholder-based evaluation* (pp. 229-260). San Francisco: Jossey-Bass.

Seedhouse, D. (1988). *Ethics: The heart of healthcare.* New York: John Wiley.

Seidman, E., & Rappaport, J. (1986a). Framing the issues. In E. Seidman & J. Rappaport (Eds.), *Redefining social problems* (pp. 1-8). New York: Plenum.

Seidman, E., & Rappaport, J. (1986b). Justice, values, and social science: Unexamined premises. In E. Seidman & J. Rappaport (Eds.), *Redefining social problems* (pp. 235-258). New York: Plenum.

Shadish, W. R., Cook, T. D., & Leviton, L. C. (1991). *Foundations of program evaluation: Theories of practice.* Newbury Park, CA: Sage.

Shaw, D. (1996). *The pleasure police: How bluenose busybodies and lily-livered alarmists are taking all the fun out of life.* New York: Doubleday.

Shickle, D., & Chadwick, R. (1994). The ethics of screening: Is "screeningitis" an incurable disease? *Journal of Medical Ethics, 20,* 12-18.

Shoemaker, P. J. (1989). Introduction. In P. J. Shoemaker (Ed.), *Communication campaigns about drugs: Government, media, and the public* (pp. 1-5). Hillsdale, NJ: Lawrence Erlbaum.

Shye, S., Elizur, D., & Hoffman, M. (1994). *Introduction to facet theory: Content design and intrinsic data analysis in behavioral research.* Thousand Oaks, CA: Sage.

Simon, H. (1976). From substance to procedural rationality. In F. Hahn & M. Hollis (Eds.), *Philosophy and economic theory* (pp. 65-86). Oxford, UK: Oxford University Press.

Simon, H. B., & Kirschenbaum, H. (Eds.). (1973). *Readings in value clarification.* Minneapolis, MN: Winston.

Singhal, A., & Rogers, E. M. (1989). Prosocial television for development in India. In R. Rice & C. Atkins (Eds.), *Public communication campaigns* (pp. 331-350). Newbury Park, CA: Sage.

Slovic, P. (1987). Perception of risk. *Science, 236,* 280-285.

Slovic, P. (1993). Perceived risk, trust, and democracy. *Risk Analysis, 13*(6), 675-682.

Smith, M. (1977). *A practical guide to value clarification.* La Jolla, CA: University Associates.

Solomon, D. S. (1989). Social marketing perspective on communication campaigns. In R. E. Rice & C. K. Atkin (Eds.), *Public communication campaigns* (2nd ed., pp. 87-104). Newbury Park, CA: Sage.

Spector, M., & Kitsuse, J. I. (1977). *Constructing social problems.* Menlo Park, CA: Cummings.

Springarn, N. D. (1976). *Heartbeat: The politics of health research.* Washington, DC: Robert B. Luce.

Stack, C. B. (1993). The culture of gender: Women and men of color. In M. J. Larrabee (Ed.), *An ethic of care: Feminist and interdisciplinary perspectives* (pp. 108-111). New York: Routledge.

Stanton, B., Kim, N., Galbraith, J., & Parrot, M. (1996). Design issues addressed in published evaluations of adolescent HIV-risk reduction interventions: A review. *Journal of Adolescent Health, 18,* 387-396.

Stein, Z. (1994). What was new at Yokohama—Women's voices at the 1994 International HIV/AIDS Conference. *American Journal of Public Health, 84*(12), 1887-1888.

Strasser, T., Jeanneret, O., & Raymond, L. (1987). Ethical aspects of prevention trials. In S. Doxiadis (Ed.), *Ethical dilemmas in health promotion* (pp. 183-193). New York: John Wiley.

Suchman, E. A. (1967). *Evaluation research: Principles and practice in public service and social action programs.* New York: Russell Sage.

Susser, M. (1974). Ethical components in the definition of health. *International Journal of Health Services, 4,* 539-548.

Susser, M. (1995). Editorial: The tribulation of trials—Interventions in communities. *American Journal of Public Health, 85,* 156-158.

Sutcliffe, J., & Duin, N. (1992). *A history of medicine.* New York: Barnes & Noble.

Sweanor, D., Ballin, S., Corcoran, R. D., Davis, A., Deasy, K., Ferrence, R., Lahey, R., Lucido, S., Nethery, W. J., & Wasserman, J. (1992). Report of the Tobacco Policy Research Study Group on tobacco pricing and taxation in the United States. *Tobacco Control, 1* (Suppl.), S31-S36.

Syme, G. J., & Eaton, E. (1989). Public involvement as a negotiation process. *Journal of Social Issues, 45*(1), 87-107.

Taylor, P. (1990). Testimony on alcohol advertising. *Journal of Public Health Policy, 11*(3), 370-381.

Tesh, S. N. (1988). *Hidden arguments: Political ideology and disease prevention policy.* New Brunswick, NJ: Rutgers University Press.

Thomas, S. B. (1990). Community health advocacy for racial and ethnic minorities in the United States: Issues and challenges for health education. *Health Education Quarterly, 17*(1), 13-19.

Thomas, S. B., & Quinn, S. C. (1991). The Tuskegee syphilis study, 1932 to 1972: Implications for HIV education and AIDS risk education program in the black community. *American Journal of Public Health, 81*(11), 1498-1505.

Thompson, B., & Kinne, S. (1990). Social change theory: Applications to community health. In N. Bracht (Ed.), *Health promotion at the community level* (pp. 45-65). Newbury Park, CA: Sage.

Thompson, T. L., & Cusella, L. P. (1991). Communication and drug abuse prevention: Information, incentives, and metaphors. *Health Communication, 3*(4), 251-262.

Thornton, B. C., & Kreps, G. L. (1993). *Perspectives on health communication.* Prospect Heights, IL: Waverland.

Trostle, J. A. (1988). Medical compliance as an ideology. *Social Science and Medicine, 22*(12), 1299-1308.

Turshen, M. (1989). *The politics of public health.* New Brunswick, NJ: Rutgers University Press.

U.S. Department of Health and Human Services. (1988). *The Surgeon General's report on nutrition and health* (DHHS Publication No. PHS 88-50210). Washington, DC: Government Printing Office.

U.S. Department of Health and Human Services. (1989). *Promoting health/preventing disease: Year 2000 objectives for the nation* (draft for public review and comment). Washington, DC: Government Printing Office.

U.S. Department of Health and Human Services. (1990). *Healthy people 2000: National health promotion and disease objectives* (DHHS Publication No. PHS 91-50213). Washington, DC: Government Printing Office.

U.S. Department of Health and Human Services. (1991). *Depression: Define it, defeat it* (campaign packet, DHHS Publication No. ADM 91-1874). Washington, DC: Government Printing Office.

U.S. Department of Health and Human Services, Public Health Service, Centers for Disease Control and Prevention. (1994). *America responds to AIDS marketing initiative.* Washington, DC: Author.

Vandeford, M. L., Smith, D. H., & Harris, W. S. (1992). Value identification in narrative discourse: Evaluation of an HIV education demonstration project. Unpublished manuscript.

Veatch, R. M. (1980). Voluntary risks to health: The ethical issues. *Journal of the American Medical Association, 243*(1), 50-55.

Veatch, R. M. (1982). Health promotion: Ethical considerations. In R. B. Taylor, J. R. Ureda, & J. W. Denham (Eds.), *Health promotion: Principles and clinical applications.* Norwalk, CT: Appleton-Century-Crofts.

Veatch, R. M. (1985). Value systems: Their roles in shaping policy decisions. In Z. Bankowski & J. H. Bryant (Eds.), *Health policy, ethics and human values* (pp. 84-86). Geneva: CIOMS.

Viswanath, K., Finnegan, J. R., Hannan, P. J., & Luepker, R. V. (1991). Health and knowledge gaps. *American Journal of Behavioral Scientist, 34*(6), 712-726.

Vlahov, D., & Brookmeyer, R. S. (1994). Editorial: The evaluation of needle exchange programs. *American Journal of Public Health, 84*(12), 1889-1891.

Waitzkin, H. (1989). A critical theory of medical discourse: Ideology, social control, and the processing of social context in medical encounters. *Journal of Health and Social Behavior, 30,* 220-239.

Waitzkin, H. (1991). *The politics of medical encounters: How patients and doctors deal with social problems.* New Haven, CT: Yale University Press.

Wallace-Brodeur, P. H. (1990). Community values in Vermont health planning. *Hastings Center Report, 20*(5), 18-19.

Wallack, L. M. (1989). Mass communication and health promotion: A critical perspective. In R. E. Rice & C. K. Atkin (Eds.), *Public communication campaigns* (2nd ed., pp. 353-367). Newbury Park, CA: Sage.

Wallack, L. M. (1990). Improving health promotion: Media advocacy and social marketing approaches. In C. Atkin & L. Wallack (Eds.), *Mass communication and public health: Complexities and conflicts* (pp.147-163). Newbury Park, CA: Sage.

Wallack, L. M., Dorfman, L., Jernigan, D., & Themba, M. (1993). *Media advocacy and public health: Power for prevention.* Newbury Park, CA: Sage.

Wallerstein, N. (1992). Powerless, empowerment, and health: Implications for health promotion programs. *American Journal of Health Promotion, 6,* 197-205.

Wallerstein, N., & Bernstein, E. (1988). Empowerment education: Freire's ideas adapted to health education. *Health Education Quarterly, 14*(4), 379-394.

Wallerstein, N., & Bernstein, E. (1995). Introduction to community empowerment, participatory education, and health. *Health Education Quarterly, 21*(2), 141-148.

Wang, C. (1992). Culture, meaning and disability: Injury prevention campaigns and the production of stigma. *Social Science and Medicine, 35*(9), 1093-1102.

Warner, K. E. (1986). Smoking and health implications of a change in federal cigarette excise tax. *Journal of the American Medical Association, 255*(8), 1028-1032.

Wartella, E., & Middlestadt, S. (1991). The evolution of models of mass communication and persuasion. *Health Communication, 3*(4), 205-215.

Warwick, D. P., & Kelman, H. C. (1973). Ethical issues in social intervention. In G. Zaltman (Ed.), *Processes and phenomena of social change* (pp. 377-417). New York: John Wiley.

Watzlawick, P., Beavin, J., & Jackson, D. (1967). *Pragmatics of human communication: A study of interactional patterns, pathologies, and paradoxes.* New York: Norton.

Weinstein, N. D. (1989). Perceptions of personal susceptibility to harm. In V. M. Mays, G. W. Albee, & F. Schneider (Eds.), *Psychological approaches to the primary prevention of acquired immune deficiency syndrome* (pp. 142-167). Newbury Park, CA: Sage.

Weisman, S. R. (1992, March 19). Japan keeps ban on birth control pill. *The New York Times,* p. A3.

Weiss, C. H. (1983). The stakeholder approach to evaluation: Origins and promise. In A. S. Bryk (Ed.), *Stakeholder-based evaluation* (pp. 3-14). San Francisco: Jossey-Bass.

Weiss, R. S., & Rein, M. (1983). The evaluation of broad-aim programs: Experimental design, its difficulties and alternative. In A. S. Bryk (Ed.), *Stakeholder-based evaluation.* San Francisco: Jossey-Bass.

Weston, E., Ray, K., Landers, C., Vaccaro, D., Futterman, R., Haley, N. J., & Orlandi, M. A. (1992). Mobilization and educational strategies in a model community cholesterol education program. *Health Values, 16*(4), 8-21.

White, M. S., & Maloney, S. K. (1990). Promoting healthy diets and active lives to hard-to-reach groups: Market research study. *Public Health Reports, 105*(3), 224-231.

Whitehead, M. (1992). The concepts and principles of equity and health. *International Journal of Health Services, 22*(3), 429-445.

Whitelaw, S., & Whitelaw, A. (1996). What do we expect from ethics in health promotion and where does Foucault fit in? *Health Education Research, 11*(3), 349-354.

Wikler, D. (1978). Persuasion and coercion for health: Ethical issues in government efforts to change life-style. *Millbank Memorial Fund Quartile/Health and Society, 56*(3), 303-338.

Wikler, D. (1987). Who should be blamed for being sick? *Health Education Quarterly, 14*(1), 11-25.

Williams, D. (1990). Socioeconomic differences in health. *Social Psychology Quarterly, 53*(2), 81-99.

Wilson, M. G., & Olds, R. S. (1991). Application of the marketing mix to health promotion marketing. *Journal of Health Education, 22*(4), 254-259.

Windhal, S., Signitzer, B., & Olson, J. T. (1992). *Using communication theory: An introduction to planned communication.* Newbury Park, CA: Sage.

Winett, R. A., King, A., & Altman, D. G. (1989). *Health psychology and public health: An integrative approach.* New York: Pergamon.

Wingood, G. M., & DiClemente, R. J. (1997). The effects of an abusive primary partner on the condom use and sexual negotiation practices of African American women. *American Journal of Public Health, 87,* 1016-1018.

Winkleby, M. A. (1994). The future of community-based cardiovascular disease intervention studies. *American Journal of Public Health, 84*(9), 1369-1372.

Winkleby, M. A., Taylor, B., Jatulis, D., & Fortmann, S. P. (1996). The long-term effects of a cardiovascular disease prevention trial: The Stanford five-city project. *American Journal of Public Health, 86,* 1773-1779.

Witte, K. (1994). The manipulative nature of health communication research: Ethical issues and guidelines. *American Behavioral Scientist, 38*(2), 285-293.

Woods, D. R., Davis, D., & Wesover, B. J. (1991). "America responds to AIDS": Its content, development process, and outcome. *Public Health Reports, 106*(6), 616-662.

Yows, S. R., Salmon, C. T., Hawkings, R. P., & Love, R. R. (1991). Motivational and structural factors in predicting different kinds of cancer knowledge. *American Behavioral Scientist, 34*(6), 727-741.

Zaltman, G., & Duncan, R. (1977). *Strategies for planned change.* New York: John Wiley.

Ziff, M. A., Conrad, P., & Lachman, M. E. (1995). The relative effects of perceived personal control and responsibility on health and health-related behaviors in young and middle-aged adults. *Health Education Quarterly, 22*(1), 127-142.

Zola, I. K. (1972). Medicine as an institution of social control. *Sociological Review, 20,* 487-504.

Zola, I. K. (1975). In the name of health and illness: On some socio-political consequences of medical influence. *Social Science and Medicine, 9,* 83-87.

Zook, E. G., & Spielvogel, C. (1992, May). *The management and making of illness: Toward a broader legitimation of health communication.* Paper presented at the 1992 International Communication Association's Annual Convention, Miami.

Author Index

Subject Index

About the Author

Nurit Guttman is Lecturer in the Department of Communication at Tel Aviv University and is on the faculty of the Department of Family Medicine at the University of Medicine and Dentistry of New Jersey-Robert Wood Johnson Medical School. She received her BA from the Hebrew University, her master's degree in communication from the Annenberg School of Communication at the University of Pennsylvania, and her PhD from the School of Communication, Information and Library Studies at Rutgers University. She has done postdoctoral work as a Primary Care Heath Services Research Fellow at the University of Medicine and Dentistry of New Jersey-Robert Wood Johnson Medical School. Her current research projects include developing methodologies for involving the public in policy decisions regarding health care rationing and in the development of health promotion messages and programs. She works with the Israel Ministry of Health and the Israel cancer Society on smoking-prevention issues, and she has served as a consultant on projects evaluating AIDS and substance abuse prevention interventions and on the enhancement of a population approach in medical education.

6 0 50